MAXIMUM PREJUDICE:

A Love Story

Robert Workman

Direct Media Marketing, Inc.

Copyright © 2024
Direct Media Marketing, Inc.

by Robert Workman

All rights reserved.

No part of this book may be reproduced in any form or by any electronic or mechanical means, including information storage and retrieval systems, without written permission from the author, except for the use of brief quotations in a published book review.

This is a work of fiction. Unless otherwise indicated, all names, characters, businesses, places, events and incidents in this book are either the product of the author's imagination or used in a fictitious manner. Any resemblance to actual persons, living or dead, or actual events is purely coincidental.

Cover illustration produced with the help of OpenArt.

* * *

"Now," she said with a stern look in her eye, *"are you going to marry me or what?"*

There are a lot of ways to answer a question like that. But when the woman who asks it is charged with battle lust - and holds a smoking automatic shotgun in each hand - you've got to figure that "No" is not a wise response.

"You're out of ammo, right?"

* * *

MAXIMUM PREJUDICE:
A Love Story

1

The gnarled fingers of the driver's hands crushed a pair of folded Franklins into his palm. My spiff of C-notes bought his disappearance with no recollection of my ride. I stepped out of his cab a couple of blocks from Georgetown University's running track; night had fallen, and families shared dinner behind the warm yellow glow of lights in the windows of the red bricks and black shutters of their Williamsburg homes.

My black ballistic climbing shoes splashed through street puddles and front yard marshes that formed from the day's intermittent rainfall. A minute later I slipped among the shadows at the toney home of the Director of the Office of Terrorist Financing and Financial Crimes, Percival Hunter.

I don't play by sporting rules. I don't play to win. I don't play at all. There are no rules for what I do. Most of the time, somebody's life rides on the outcome. My only rule is, whatever it takes to get the job done.

For this job I contracted a lady I met through industry contacts. Her background was as interesting as her skills were unique - and beyond valuable. Margo could write her ticket, and she did. We never met in person, and this wasn't a cheap date.

Margo leveraged her M.I.T. education with years of experience at a couple of confidential business enterprises that took government contract work. She went independent and became my Go To source for impossible missions. She wasn't a computer whiz or an Internet guru; Margo was the Leonardo da Vinci of technology.

Margo could bend the Internet. She was particularly gifted as a hacker of government top-level security. If she set her mind to it, she could sway the statewide vote for a national election in a state with a small population, by herself.

I approached through the next door neighbor's tiny front yard. My pocket-sized black Bluetooth speaker fit inside the ivy that pooled around a tree on their lawn.

Night vision cameras patrolled the property. A small narrow corner was obscured by trees and privacy fence junctions that created a slim eternal dark spot. My black night-raid gear made everything including my face invisible in the shadows.

But all that cloak and dagger work was moot because of the marvelous Margo. She filtered the video feed of every security camera for the outside and the inside of the Director's house. At the time of my one-man incursion, she placed a cycler on them, so every camera replayed a loop of the previous hour of video that night.

After its half-minute delay, my Bluetooth recording blared the cacophony of a bloodcurdling catfight. Behind that distraction I slid over the eight-foot cedar fence into the wedge-shaped backyard.

Gathering storm clouds defeated the contrast between light and dark and hid me in obscurity. Under a moonless night perfect for nocturnal animals of prey, I slipped through the darkness to a hot tub atop a redwood deck. A hinged section lifted and revealed a bomb shelter's hatch.

It took 15 seconds to break the school-gym combination padlock. I descended and gagged for breath when I reached the bottom. The Director's tunnel to his living room needed infrastructure improvement.

Now I knew what it smelled like to be trapped in a mausoleum. *When was the last time someone was down here?* Cobwebs stuck to my fingers, hands and clothes when I swept them aside. Mice, vermin - I flicked on my flashlight, swept away more cobwebs and made my way up the dark, dusty steps.

The thick, heavy door at the top moved with a steady push, like a steel vault. I pressed it forward. The living room fireplace swiveled open:

smooth, quiet. In the last couple of inches, it cried out with a loud screech.

Directly across from me, an ATF agent backed into the living room from the kitchen. He spread his elbows wide apart and pushed himself in reverse through a pair of saloon half-doors. Each of his hands held a plate of steaming food above a big revolver that hung in his brown leather hip holster.

When he heard the hidden door's pained outcry, he jerked his head around toward the fireplace. His gun hand dropped his plate; knife and fork clattered on top of the terrazzo tile floor. He reached for his pistol, but by then I was behind him. I yanked it from its holster and pistol-whipped him, slumped him over in a chair on the side.

A voice from the kitchen called over the barroom doors. "Hey, Sam, you left your beer in here."

Sam dreamed of counting T-Bills and couldn't reply. The voice came again, with a slight laugh.

"Sam - who was your servant last year?" The Director, the one and only Percy Hunter, stepped through the saloon doors with a plate of food and a pair of beers in his hands.

Percy liked to see himself in TV interviews and in the papers. I gave him a new view. The moment he pushed through the split doors he saw his true blue bodyguard slumped out cold in his chair. His mouth gaped in astonishment. He farted.

I took him from behind. Twenty seconds later he lay on the floor, the unconscious victim of my sleeper hold.

When he woke up, he laid face down on his lavish bed with his face planted into a pillow. He was blindfolded, gagged and bound butt naked to its four massive corner posts. He turned his face to the side and tried to speak through his red ball gag. When he felt the long cold barrel of Sam's .357 revolver up his ass, he screamed.

I'm not going to use my own gun for that.

Director Percy Hunter wasn't happy. He twisted and writhed but couldn't see me. And such language.

"Shut up," I said. "This is your fault, Percival. You've pussyfooted around because you think you're untouchable hot shit. You weaponized your department against one of our best families and put two of your own in traction. This is getting done, now."

"You're lucky it's me. A couple of guys want to keelhaul you for what you're trying to do to their family. You're going to sign three papers."

He thrashed and struggled against his bonds. Even through the S&M gag, I heard him swear he'd have my hide.

"Stow it, Percy. You may be the heap Big Chief downtown, but right now you're just 200 pounds of flab with a gun up your ass. And I'm just two clicks from blowing your guts, hide and feathers out the top of your head. The long way."

When I lashed him down with oversized zip ties, I made sure his right hand was mobile enough to grasp a pen and make his signature. I slid the pen between his fingers and thumb. A wide, coffee table book served as a portable desk surface beneath the documents.

I snatched his right hand in a vice grip and held it toward the signature lines. He struggled and strained at the massive plastic bindings that cut thin purple lines into his wrists and ankles. The gag proved more than adequate to stifle his screams. He shook the bed with so much violence a picture frame fell from the wall and crashed to the floor.

I half-cocked the hammer of the gun in his butt. "That's one."

He stopped, scribbled his name. I checked it; completely illegible.

"What the Hell's this, Percy!" I clicked the hammer back once more into its firing position. "That's two."

He screamed, then tried to tell me something through his gag. He waved his left hand, spread its fingers and made a fist with it. Then he moved it in a signature position, as if signing.

"Oh, Hell," I said. I slid the pen out of his right hand and walked around to the other side of the bed. "OK, southpaw. Sign."

He scribbled his name on all three documents.

My examination of the signatures assured me they were legible. They weren't perfect, but they were legit. I squeezed the trigger and dropped the magnum's hammer with two heavy clicks.

"I'm going to leave your new butt plug in place. Sam may want it back."

I leaned close to his ear and whispered with force. "Pray that these are the last words you'll ever hear from me. In five minutes, three law firms will have these papers on record. Make any effort whatsoever to rescind ... well, don't. If anything happens that prevents these getting officially enrolled tomorrow, I'll be - peeved."

I folded the papers and slid them into a pocket.

"I'm playing nice on our first date tonight, Percy. You don't want to see me - peeved."

As I made my exit, I snapped a couple of compromising photos with my phone. "Have fun explaining your new boy toy. Think about how much TMZ will pay to get their hands on these glamor shots. The video is entertaining, too." I warned, "Be nice."

I left the same way I entered, without him or his comical sidekick ever seeing what hit them. And no record of anything ever taking place on any security cameras.

2

The next afternoon, I pushed through the doors of the U.S. Treasury Building and stepped outside. A focused laser beam of afternoon daylight was surrounded by intense glare. My eyes slammed shut in response, then squinted back open.

The setting sun burned a tight bright hole through a sky of black thunderheads and hit my eyes from its low angle. Dark drizzle fell from troubled clouds and foreboded anything but a sunny outcome.

I didn't care. Case closed. I'd catch the train home.

The Treasury Department. The Office of Terrorist Financing and Financial Crimes. Percival Hunter. Myself. Four parties that were glad to be through with each other. Done and done.

The Washington Hotel across 15th Street was my home for that week. Each day, I commuted on foot while I hand-walked legal papers through formal enrollment with the T-men. The conclusive events of last night, plus the enrollment of my three signed documents that I recorded that afternoon, cauterized a week of runarounds in the halls of bureaucracy.

It was done - a case that took too long and caused too much trouble. And paid too much money.

I didn't want to take this case to begin with, even for the ridiculous fee it paid. Jobs against the government – I hated them. And this became a typical government job. Every time I approached the finish line, the race got extended by bureaucracy and ran ahead of me so I couldn't catch it.

The weather was giving me internal feelings of physical angst, but I still relaxed with emotional relief. My exit from 1500 Pennsylvania Avenue was a departure I was happy to make. It meant I finished pounding the government-issue desks of career pencil pushers.

The Ionic colonnade of the Greek revival Treasury building provided cover from the onset of rain. I hunched my shoulders against the spray that blew within the columns, thumbed the wheel of my ancient Zippo. Its flame ignited and torched up a Red. A long, slow puff of post-goal satisfaction flowed out of my lips and up through my nostrils.

I gazed beyond the bronze statue centered on the walkway, reflected on the shortcuts I was forced to make. Then I cut some more, left pieces of myself in places they didn't belong. I even gave up-close and personal lessons in respecting their elders to some overzealous rookies.

The Treasury kids were OK. They were loyal agents, thrown in my path as deterrents by their odious superiors. I felt bad when I put them on the injured reserve list. But this case involved something more than the massive fortunes involved, and the T-men made vital mistakes.

* * *

It began years ago as a simple across-the-fence rhubarb. Then, attorneys stretched their paychecks when they escalated matters to the federal level. The results would keep or kill the legacy and fortune of a six-generation American family for its future progeny. But the family's high-priced attorneys kept challenging and appealing while they kept losing ground.

So, I was brought in – just in time. My client's family owned the vast property for well over a century. But the US of A suddenly decided it wanted half of the total estate back. It tried to claim eminent domain.

The Treasury Department stated it was for what they termed, "climate change initiatives." Some unelected elitist globalists wanted to convert 40,000 acres of American beauty, pristine ranchland and farmland into windmills and solar farms.

The family would have lost its land and heritage. The nation would have lost 50 square miles that provided sustainable food production for people nationwide.

I studied a similar case of the Bureau of Land Management versus the Bundy Ranch in Nevada. In that standoff, hundreds of armed volunteers drove their trucks from across the nation and assembled. They cocked their lever actions, overpowered and turned back armed federal government forces at gunpoint.

It was a case-in-point of Thomas Jefferson's reason for our second amendment, as defense against government tyranny. To cap it off, a U.S. District Judge in Las Vegas dismissed all of the government's criminal charges against the Bundys, "with prejudice."

That incident took years to clear up and required an organized volunteer citizen's militia. The benevolent dynasty that was my client didn't have years. Percy & Co. pushed to ram this through. And they didn't have a militia. They had me; and they paid me as much as they would pay a militia - because I guarantee results.

The overpriced and corrupt law firm had stalled the case for two years. I wrapped things up in a week, and that was a week longer than I wanted to stay inside the beltway.

The ones who caused the trouble were a cluster of elitist slimeballs in their unassailable ivory towers. Unfortunately, the cowards threw their loyal knights in my way as diversionary pawns. I removed their pieces from the board.

I finally said to Hell with all that. I decided to employ the tactic that never fails. I live by two mottos: "Talk to The Boss" and, "Whatever it takes to get the job done." So, a few nights before Halloween, I dressed in my formal black night raid attire and paid my back door trick or treat call on the home of Mr. Percival Hunter.

Results guaranteed; results delivered. I could have caught a cab for the train home out of Washington Union Station to Penn Station in New York. But I was hungry and didn't want to wait that long to eat.

A few yards ahead of me, a boy and girl opened and examined rolls of quarters at the feet of Albert Gallatin's bronze. They sorted them by year and mintmark to reorganize them into more valuable rolls of matching numbers. I smiled. I used to do the exact same thing at the exact same place.

The gentle drizzle soon gave way to scattered thick raindrops. When fat blotches splattered on the concrete, the kids scraped their quarters off the fountain ledge in front of the building. They scampered under some nearby trees and planned their next move.

I felt inside the pockets of my overcoat, already dampened by the cold afternoon drizzle. It would have fared better hanging on its hook back home in the Lower East Side. Cloud sweat from above spread small dark dots into large blotches. Its doeskin tan leather darkened into a deep brown.

Along with my sunglasses, I grabbed my lighter and a deck of Marlboro Reds. I snapped the aviators over my ears and poked the cigarette between my lips.

A light fog was deepening into a danger that could choke the navigational powers of planes, boats, cars on bridges. Somehow at their depressed altitude, the clouds still produced an awkward glare that made me avert my eyes behind my Ray-Bans.

I stared across the granite steps and turned down 15th Street. As soon as my shoes hit the steps, it hit me. I felt it the moment I stepped outside, but I hoped it would pass.

When heavy storms approached and the barometer dropped like a hammer, it created immense pressure inside my head. My internal trauma mounted until the clouds opened and the downpours hit. The buildup could last for hours, but when a storm finally broke, my relief was instantaneous.

Now, outside after a day full of breathing artificial air in hallways and fluorescent lit offices, I felt the approach of a tempest. My job at hand may have been complete, but this always served as a sign that something bigger was waiting ahead.

Already my hands were sweaty and wet. Heavy rain clouds stuck in a holding pattern over D.C. trapped the city beneath a dark gray front that should have cut loose days ago. The nation's capital's weather guys said a thermal inversion created the chilly October air and expected the heavens to explode.

I wished they would. The pressure inside me tried to drive its way out of my body through my head.

My eardrums pulsed; I tensed. It felt like an earthquake rumbled inside my body. My eyeballs felt stressed with light-sensitive vision.

Everyone else seemed fine. I leaned against a column and watched people going about their lives, unaffected by misting rain that belied the storm ahead.

I told myself I'd be OK when I knocked myself out on the train ride home. My Rx for these maladies was a 10 milligram Valium with 4 Advil pills chased by a bourbon and branch water on the rocks. This self-prescribed medicinal cocktail was a sure thing that opened the door for sleep to slink in and cloak the pain. But right then, I was really hungry.

A couple of blocks in another direction, the sign for a pizza shop blazed through the street's impending gloom. I paused to light up a smoke. I turned up the street toward the pizza shop.

3

Heavy water drops from above picked up their pace from a casual trot to a canter. A sudden blast of chilly air whipped past and cut an invisible channel through the humid heat of the street. Papers and trash blew before its gusts, as if driven by an oversized leaf blower.

The storm broke open with a thunderclap that resonated in my chest. I ducked beneath a nearby hotel's front entrance awning, but not before two fat raindrops doused the cigarette in my lips. The downpour created rivulets of rainwater that poured off the canopy and splashed around my ankles.

With my back turned against the deluge and my coat collar popped, I examined the soggy remains of the Marlboro that drooped in my fingers. I lifted a dry one from its pack. Three others lingered behind.

The uniformed doorman shot me a bemused look. "Any port in a storm, huh?"

I gave him a nod of thanks for the cover, offered him a Red from my crumpled pack. I lit his, then fired up my own replacement.

My head and body relaxed with relief the moment the sky opened and the rain hammered down. I exhaled, drew in a long deep breath. It felt as if I walked out of a room dense with smoke into an open mountain vista of fresh, clean air.

Thankfully, this episode of internal trauma was a short one. It made me wonder what could lie ahead.

I savored the absence of pressure in my brain as I breathed out a puff of smoke - when something else grabbed my attention.

Across the street in a parking lot between some brick buildings, a solitary little boy played a bounce-back game with his glove and baseball. In a pair of cuffed jeans, black Chuck Taylor Converse high-tops and a baseball jersey and cap, he caught his ball and paused. He looked up at the warring skies and frowned.

Something about his gear caught my attention; I peered closer through the downpour. He wore a white Washington Senators jersey with red number 9, blue ball cap with red piping and a pretzel **W** for the old American League team. When he removed his cap, his thick and wavy brown hair escaped. He faced skyward and licked at raindrops that grew fatter and came down faster, with increasing fury.

Then he kept playing.

The Senators left D.C. after 1969. Only an old-school die-hard fan would have a jersey and cap like that, and this kid was two generations too young. I inhaled a drag of smoke, decided I liked his dad.

His baseball caught a bad angle on one of the bricks in the wall and shot out toward the street. The boy's quickest shortstop moves failed, and the white horsehide with red laces bounced across the blacktop.

It popped up a rooster tail as it scampered across the street toward me and parked itself at my feet. I looked down at the first baseball that touched me in years.

Across the blacktop, the boy peered at me through the cloudburst with piercing, hopeful blue eyes. I caught a quick drag and looked down at the ball again. A thought came to me: *The last train from Union Station to Penn Station doesn't leave until 8:30 tonight.*

For a moment, through the magic of baseball, I forgot about Percival Hunter, the job, the money. I forgot about everything. I picked up the soggy horsehide.

Already ruined, it wasn't going to hurt it to get any wetter. I walked out into the street from under the canopy and winged it to the kid; he hauled it in and smiled. Then he pitched it back.

I almost fumbled my cigarette when I made the unexpected catch. The ball was also marked with the pretzel **W** for Washington. The kid was a real fan.

I was soaked the instant I stepped into the street, so I continued across to the kid's parking lot. *It isn't going to hurt me to get wet, too.* The boy stood still. He inspected me to see if this stranger was indeed as crazy as himself.

I tossed him the ball. He pitched it back. I looked across through the downpour at the doorman beneath his canopy. His expression of wonderment told me we were lunatics. Then he laughed and shot us two thumbs up.

Maybe he was right. Maybe I was crazy. Maybe this boy was, too. Maybe he reminded me of me.

We tossed a few more times and I called to him through the commotion of rain that pounded the pavement around us, "What's your name?"

"My name's Nick," he said. "What's yours, mister?"

"Same thing."

"You live around here?"

I hauled in a deep breath as I caught his soggy pitch, said, "I'm catching a train home, to New York."

From beneath the rain that dripped from the bill of his ball cap, he said only, "Oh." Then after a pause, "Well, I better get going. My mom's going to kill me for getting soaked."

"Which way you headed?" I asked.

The kid pointed up the street, a 90-degree angle from my path. "Just a couple blocks," he said. "I'm OK." I indicated the direction I was headed with my thumb and turned to leave. "Thanks, mister!"

I waved. I turned up my collars and clutched the lapels of my coat together. It didn't help much against the torrential rain. I splashed my way down the sidewalk toward the pizza shop.

4

The fogged glass doors of the Bolide Pizza Boutique swung open before me as I shoved through to get out of the storm. The first thing that hit me was the frigid, dry air conditioning.

I was soaked to my skin. The blast of arid frigid air inside the shop threatened to launch me into hypothermia. Water ran off the bottom of my overcoat and pooled on the floor.

The solid white tiles of the little mom and pop shop glared with bright light against the darkened skies outside the windows. I felt my pupils screw down as narrow as pinheads.

The bruiser behind the counter stopped what he was doing and studied my waterlogged condition. I stood alone, brushed off a shiver amidst the shop's empty tables and chairs.

"I was playing catch," I said, as if it made sense.

The roll of his eyes and nod of his head showed that I convinced the second person in fifteen minutes that I was crazy.

I couldn't help but scrutinize the astonished face of the heavyweight wrestler behind the counter. I stood 6' 4" and looked up at least four inches at his battered nose. His shaved head needed hair. Cuts and scars mapped earlier routes taken through an unmistakable career in professional combat marked by folding aluminum chairs and sundry devices.

With thick deliberation and a voice worthy of a basso profundo role in the Cacophony Chorale for Rock Crushers he asked, "Know what you want?"

I want to never tangle with you. I studied their overhead menu. Some of its symbols were – Hell, they looked weird – and they weren't familiar.

I felt distracted. "What I want right now," I said, "is to relieve an urgent need to use your men's room." I turned and quickly stepped down the short corridor to the door in the back.

"Hey! Hey!" he called. "It's being used!"

But I already crossed the few steps to the door and twisted its knob.

The guy up front yelled, "Hey, buddy! Come back here!"

His thick voice shouted, but my hearing shut down the instant I opened the bathroom door.

If a bomb detonated in front of me, it couldn't have blown my senses apart with greater disorientation. My vision became hyper-focused and intense, while my hearing shut down in a deep dive to a depressed sluggishness.

Before me, through the door she forgot to lock, a lady knelt on the white tile floor. I use the term, "lady" to be polite. She was so ugly, if you tied a pork chop around her neck dogs wouldn't go near.

She wrestled with a half-clothed little boy. The kid struggled; he tried to call out but couldn't through the sock in his mouth. Literally. A sock. Stuffed in the mouth of this kindergarten Asian boy.

I don't know how long I stood in shock; time was nonexistent as I stared.

More signs registered their vivid images through my stupefaction. Shocks of cut black hair splashed across the white tiles. A little girl's rumpled dress tossed next to a pair of tiny black strap shoes.

Then the woman came up at me from the floor and got in my face. She screamed, "Get out of here!" She shoved me as hard as she could and slammed the door.

For a woman, she sure had a deep voice, and that was one hell of a strong shove.

That was no little boy in there, and that bitch was about to meet Mister Nasty. I braced my back against the opposite wall and kicked the bathroom door off its hinges. It smashed flat on the floor before me. The little kid backed into a corner, wide-eyed and petrified.

But not the delicate princess. She rushed me like an MMA prizefighter. She shoulder-slammed me back against the wall, then pummeled my midsection with hammering fists. This was one helluva woman.

She became one hell of an uglier woman. I clapped my palms on both her ears and exploded her eardrums, then drove my thumbs through her eye sockets.

She crashed to the ground and gurgled her brain's blood in her throat. When I grabbed her head and yanked it up, her wig came off in my hands. I dropped the head of one hell of an ugly woman, but when it slapped on the floor, it identified as one hell of an uglier man.

I held the wig in my hand and looked over at the little kid. He cowered in the corner by the toilet. A horrifying image looked back at me in the bathroom mirror.

The picture I saw in the looking glass wasn't pretty. A scowling big guy stood over a twisted, unconscious woman in a dress. What looked like her scalp dangled from his hand, as she lay face down in a pool of her own blood on the floor.

I whipped the wig behind me out of the kid's sight. I tried to assure him - *her* - that everything was OK. She trembled with fear. Her hyperventilation choked down breaths of air in gulps so big she couldn't cry.

She looked up at me and her eyes showed the first glimmer of softening with relieved acceptance. As she began to relax, so did I. *Her entire body still trembled. It was my turn to catch my breath.*

What little wind I regained got crushed out of me when I was body-slammed from behind.

5

The guy from up front was built like The Rock's big brother and punched like Tyson. His meaty paws pounded my chin from both sides with a left hook, a right hook, a left hook, a right hook. Then he worked my midsection.

Where the hell did these guys come from? Was this joint a halfway house for ex-fighters?

I grabbed his head and chin as hard as I could. With everything I had, I wrenched it to break his neck. I might as well have tried to break the neck of a marble statue.

This was going to be a long afternoon.

I worked out daily and weighed 240 pounds. This guy lifted me like a flyweight and slammed my head against the wall. Twice. Then my head smashed up through the acoustic ceiling tiles. Twice.

He yanked me back to earth, then threw me down the short hallway into the dining area like a load of laundry. I did a quick reverse kip-up from the floor and faced him. On my left were three hot coffee pots. I grabbed one and tossed it at his face.

The beast had to weigh at least 350 and dodged it with the quickness of a gymnast. Long day, indeed.

When he rushed me, his massive frame filled the short corridor. I grabbed a pizza tray and hammered his head with it. That was as effective as stopping a battleship with a baseball bat.

Kiosks and tables flew across the room when he came at me again and flung them out of the way with his meat hook hands. He threw chairs at me across the room like they were beach balls. Nothing was going to stop this juggernaut from crushing me like a bug.

He grabbed at me and one of his mitts snatched my right arm. On any other day he would have stamped his fingerprints into my flesh, but the sleeve of my leather coat was soaked from the rain. My arm twisted and slid free from his grip.

Confusion and rage contorted his face; he lurched and crushed me in a bear hug. Wet clothes weren't going to help this time. Neither were my smashes to his face. I packed a mean punch and hammered the head of this monster with both fists, to no avail.

In a flash, I recognized my brother's touch. Michael became an angel about ten years ago and being named after the Archangel, I figured him for a natural to be drafted into Heaven's army of angels. No, I don't talk to my deceased brother. No, he doesn't talk to me. But I know his touch if you know what I mean, and I think you do.

I called out, "Michael, this isn't funny! Give me a break!" I have learned in recent years that this kind of thing never hurts.

Garganto growled, "My name ain't, Michael!"

I looked down at the scars on his bald pate as he ratcheted up his Grizzly grip; my spine cracked about five places. He sought a place to smash me over his shoulder in a Supplex onto the white floor of the shop. I reached out and grabbed for something, anything I could use against this beast.

My fingers hooked around a red metal fire extinguisher that hung on a white wall. I latched onto it with all the strength my fingers had. When the monster wrenched me, I wrenched it and broke it free of its mount.

I slammed it into his forehead. He stopped moving. I smashed it into his head again. His grip loosened. I spun it in my hands to use its cylinder end and hit him again between his eyes. His legs faltered.

As soon as I ripped myself clear, I swept his legs from beneath him. When he crashed to the floor, I smashed the cylinder into his head again. He laid there and looked up at me with death and destruction in his eyes, too hurt to move. He reached across the floor for me again.

I sprang over him and thrust the black rubber hose of the fire extinguisher down his throat. I mashed the trigger. He thrashed and convulsed on the floor, but after half a minute of the oral enema, he laid still.

I gathered myself, leaned against a wall. It took a minute to catch my wind. I bent over and rested my hands on my knees while I gasped for breath. I looked up. A poster ad on a wall promoted a new snack and showed a little Asian girl who enjoyed it with a big smile. *Cute kid. Little girls are cute. Hell, we're all cute when we're young ...*

The kid!

Before I approached her again, I turned down the short corridor and called, "Hey, kid. It's OK out here. You're safe, now."

My results reflected my level of experience with children. Nothing. I scaled back and found my most kid-reassuring voice. "Hey, kid. The bad guys are both gone. It's just you and me, and I'm the good guy. You're safe. I'm calling the police."

It took a few minutes of coaxing, but I got back to the lavatory. I picked up the flattened door and leaned it closed. The little girl got dressed into her original clothes.

Shanghai Pat had abducted the little Asian girl. He was in that pizza joint bathroom transforming her into a little Asian boy so she could be smuggled out. God only knows where her destination was going to be.

This was child trafficking in our nation's capital, only a couple of blocks from the power epicenter of the world. I didn't know kids. I didn't know anyone who had kids. But it made me sick to think about it.

The dead drag queen was in on it. Dead meathead up front was also in on it. That means the owner of the joint was in on it. God only knows how many people it involved.

I telephoned the Metro Police Department and reported the incident. When the white squad cars arrived, the little girl hugged my side hard and wouldn't let go for anyone. She still shivered with fear.

Her trembling body resonated through her intense grip around my hips; I felt her horror. It took a lot of coaxing by me and calming reassurance by the CPS social worker to get her to release her grip and go with them.

A Lieutenant of the Metro Police Department approached me to ask questions. I read his name on the brass bar opposite his MPD Lieutenant badge, pinned to his bulletproof body gear. Diliberto.

A couple of inches shy of six feet, he carried the overweight of a guy who stayed on the force after he could have retired. His face was round and, in other circumstances, probably pleasant. The six dollar chop job of thinning hair on his head and the wear on his heels was evidence that cops in D.C. are underappreciated and underpaid.

As he listened and jotted his notes, I narrated the events of the day.

The pizza shop owner arrived from the emergency call about his store. When he pulled up, the stereo blared in his BMW sedan. He got out in his trendy tennis suit and gold chain and swaggered to the police. He got cuffed and hauled in, too.

One coffee pot remained somehow untouched. I poured myself a black cup of java, on the house. I was still hungry. And I had a train to catch.

6

The next morning, I endured the forces of gravity during the 21-floor elevator ride up through the fog and mist to my Lower East Side office suite. The momentum of the lift triggered throbbing soreness in my ribs from yesterday's pounding. My jaws felt like raw steaks that I could have used to cover my eyes. I wore salt and pepper stubble and shades.

My office's frosted glass doors pushed open before the scabbed knuckles of my bruised mitts. A sarcastic voice greeted me. "Well, welcome back mister celebrity."

My guy Friday was partial to melodrama. He was also the most intuitive guy I ever met. Plus, he thrived on being a tech genius.

"Name the other celebrity whose jaws and guts feel like hammered mush," I replied.

A walking contradiction, James Murgatroyd Fontenot was a serendipitous discovery I snapped up to run the operations of my unorthodox business. He kept his finger on the pulse of the tech world by the hour. And he displayed an uncanny sixth sense to prepare for my immediate future needs.

Yet he dressed as though he lived and worked in a 1940s Midwest bank. I wanted very much to call him, Jeeves.

For that reason, the office was a juxtaposition of high technology and antique furniture. Gleaming laser TVs were powered by the newest, fastest computers. We ran a 5G Internet connection with a Gig of download speed. And Art Deco furnishings were complemented with British Bombay tables and classic Baccarat crystal.

"Well, they may not have seen you in Seattle or Honolulu yet, but everyone on the eastern seaboard knows about, 'Saint Nick'."

"What the hell are you talking about?" I hadn't had my coffee yet.

The nature of our work required James' network operations command of 15 oversized laser projection monitors. They stretched across one wall of the office in a configuration of three vertical rows of five 60" horizontal screens.

James was the kind of guy who could not contain the smiles or laughs that often burst from his well-fed features. He tried to look nonchalant as he punched a button on his handheld remote control.

A screen popped on that showed CNN:
"And in exciting action in our nation's capital last night, one man single-handedly broke up an underground pedophile ring ... "

He clicked on another monitor for ABC News:
"Yesterday afternoon, only blocks away from the White House, a man walked out of the storm, into a pizza parlor ... "

Another monitor for CBS came alive and reported:
"The nation has a new hero, ladies and gentlemen. Last night near the U.S. Treasury and White House in our nation's capital, one man .... "

Another screen buzzed with footage of the aftermath inside the pizza shop:
"This is Ken Kenny *reporting live* on Fox News from downtown Washington, D.C. at the scene where one man went Rambo and single-handedly took down ... "

One screen after another crackled with commands from James' remote. Each showed a network or cable channel that reported my late afternoon tea party from the day before.

James muted the screens. He said, "I would tell you that our phone is ringing off the hook. But the hook broke. The phone gave up and died. I'm glad you decided to come in ... " He paused for effect, pulled out his gold pocket watch with its chain. He popped it open and declared,
"... before eleven o'clock!"

"Bite me." I grabbed our vintage percolator coffee pot.

He knew my routine. Every morning, I began with a brisk walk to Jack's Gym for my workout. Then to the back corner booth of my neighborhood diner for eggs, bacon, sausage, pancakes and a pot of black coffee. I usually tackled the world's problems in my office by the crack of noon.

I said, "Back off, Murgatroyd. Don't try to lay no boogie-woogie on the king of rock and roll. I got back on the last train and haven't worked out or eaten."

He said, "I'll call Mr. DeMille and tell him you're ready for your close-up." He punched the universal ON button of his remote control. The energy and atmospheric ions of the office turned into the crackling electronics section of a big box store. All 15 screens blazed with video imagery.

I poured myself a tank of coffee in my pistol grip mug. When things were calm, I enjoyed the aroma of a strong black cup of Yuban, letting its vapors waft down inside as an alert from the Arabica Heralds to the eager sensory organs below of its impending arrival. My lower lip cracked when I smiled and said, "I needed this mother's milk ... "

The next sight I saw made the oversized coffee mug slip from my fingers. It crashed on the floor and broke apart into pieces. Hot coffee and ceramic shrapnel exploded in all directions.

I didn't feel a thing. My hand felt around behind me and located the counter. I sat back, stunned.

James set the remote control on the countertop. He spoke in a quiet, over-controlled voice: "Hey, Nick ... You OK there, pal?"

I picked up the remote, pointed it at one of the monitors, the one for WTTG in D.C.

It was a picture of the kid, my baseball buddy from the afternoon before. He smiled beneath his **W** baseball cap. The message on the bottom of the screen said, "Nick White – Missing."

I shut down the entire wall of other monitors and punched up the local TV station's volume: "Not far away, little Nick White went missing yesterday afternoon," said the news anchor. "He was last seen by his mother, Mrs. Preston T. White and servants, about 2:00 p.m. when he went out to play baseball, but never returned home."

7

The grade school Senators fan appeared to me in my mind like a hologram. He was dripping wet; he smiled, about to turn up the street and head home. "*My mom's going to kill me for getting soaked.*"

"My mom" was The Mrs. Preston T. White.

Ten years before, the marriage of young, beautiful Electra McDonald to older, Texas oil man Preston T. White made world headlines. It consummated the economic union of her daddy's vast South Texas cattle ranches and Preston's North Texas Barnett Shale oil and gas.

Preston T. White was a living legend. When he was a young Turk, he traveled to New Orleans on a train with only a C-note in his pocket.

He gambled it in their casinos over the course of a week and came away with winnings in the high six figures. He parlayed that into enough cash to acquire ownership of the biggest oil fields in east Texas.

In the beginning, Preston ran his operations from the gulf coast city of Corpus Christi. Several state universities enjoyed substantial contributions from the revenues of his east Texas oil fields and Barnett fracking operations.

He also donated heavily in time, energy and money to countless successful political campaigns.
Preston was the largest shareholder in the ruling party of the Lone Star State. For many years, this directed the economy of the nation and cemented the power base of Mr. White inside the Washington, D.C. beltway.

Preston dropped dead the year before on the steps outside the Supreme Court Building. He stood and spoke with his attorneys and was hit with a sudden heart attack. The irony is they just won a decision that involved fracking in New York that he'd been fighting in federal courts for years.

For the second time in two days, I stood frozen, dumbstruck. I rebooted the other monitors and watched one network after another broadcast its version of the story.

My body was rooted to the floor, motionless, while my mind raced. I finally managed to get some quiet words out to James. "That kid. We played catch."

James asked, "The son of Preston T. White? You played, catch?"

"Yeah. It was raining. His name's Nick."

I should have put things together when I sensed the prevailing weather conditions in D.C. The moment I stepped out of the Treasury building my internal pressure hit me like a freight train. I thought my destruction of the child traffickers answered the call.

But as I stood before the dazzling TV monitors, it hit me again - that feeling that something big was coming. It could only be another angelic assignment to serve as proxy. I passed off the earlier symptoms to that afternoon's pizza shop sparring sessions and thought it was over.

But here it was again, and worse. That cramped stress in the back of my neck, the sensitivity to light, the pressure in my eyes and ears - foretold an angelic assignment I would be called to answer. It was an unpleasant signal that unpleasant things were about to start happening.

Over time I learned that the only things could make it ease off were a small, quiet, dark room, and hours of solitude; or my prescription of Valium and ibuprofens with a shot of whiskey. Whichever was handier.

James observed me and muttered, "Uh-oh." He crossed over to our medicine chest in the kitchen.

James Murgatroyd Fontenot came from Algiers on the West Bank of New Orleans, the home of gumbo, *etouffe* and the nation's oldest apothecary. Not satisfied with a typical white box hung on a wall behind a hinged mirror, he made our medicine cabinet out of a vast oak industrial workshop pigeonhole cabinet. Each one of its 50 square oak drawers was labeled: from aspirin to acetaminophen to hydrocodone to diazepam to alligator claws and St. John the Conqueror root.

When he returned, his open palm offered a little blue pill with a "V" cut out of the middle. It nestled among four football-shaped ibuprofens. His other hand held a fresh cup of black coffee.

I didn't notice him. According to a clinical study conducted at MIT, we process and recognize an image in .0013 second. Thirteen microseconds. 769 images per second. My mind was overloaded with 46,153 images per minute electronically mainlined into my brain from the wall full of video screens. I massaged my scalp against the headache from Hell.

Finally, I shook free from my transfixed stare at the screens; I washed down the pills with his coffee and chicory and - "Murgatroyd! What the Hell's in this coffee?"

He shrugged.

Then, "It's good," I said. "Get my same adjoining rooms back again at the Hotel Washington. One in my name, one in - "

"Your other name," he said. "Same as last time. They'll still know you. Done. Go. I'll hold down the fort."

"Do me a favor and let my sister know?"

"She and Cody will be fine." He motioned me out the door. "Go."

An hour later I boarded the Amtrak Silver Star from New York Penn Station back to Union Station in D.C. I let Murgatroyd's concoction do its work and sank back into my seat. What was I getting myself into this time?

*   *   *

My Sunday school teachers cautioned me, "Vengeance is mine, sayeth the Lord."

But I knew something they didn't. God's a busy guy; so, He sub-contracts. That's where I come in.

Don't get me wrong – I'm not crazy. I don't claim to talk to God. I mean, come on, who talks to God, really?

But I do receive His messages. They aren't subtle. And when something gets to the point where He puts my chess piece into play on the board of Fate, it means He's really pissed. He grants His forgiveness, but when it comes to me, it means He wants consequences – with Maximum Prejudice.

In certain supremely evil cases, God assigns His vengeance to be delivered by proxy. That's where I pick up a Command Contract to serve as a pro bono avenging angel, incarnate. So, I walk alone. And work alone. And someday, I'd die alone. After I finish.

But I was about to get started again with something, and I didn't know what it was.

At the Washington Hotel, I checked into the two different rooms under two different names. I made this standard operating procedure ever since I almost bought it in the Shepeard Hotel in Cairo a decade back.

I stored some clothes and shoes in the room registered to my real name. Then I moved into the room that was registered under my alias. That would be Larry Talbot.

8

It happened one morning about five years ago. The printer didn't.

I grumbled with angst about squandering time and energy on mundane office tasks. The front doors opened, and James Murgatroyd Fontenot fumbled his way into my life.

Somewhere along the way, I mastered a leadership style that developed a loyal, hard-working staff. Until they departed due to emotional stress overloads. Various psychological conditions were cited; the most recent being hysterical amnesia. Net result: alone again in 3,000 square feet of top floor office space.

The building's windows were still black from the city's outside darkness before sunrise. My tech fail *du jour* was my wrestling match with the printer when James wandered through the wrong door.

The Superego Software offices he sought were one floor below. They wanted him to run hard at their video games, trying to break them before their release.

When he picked up on my situation and frustration, James offered to help. I studied him for a moment. He might have ended up in the wrong place, but he would have been wronger if he walked into the right place.

The tech guys downstairs rode the elevator up every day, unshaven and unkempt in whatever scroungy wrinkled rags they picked up off their floor. The guy who stood in front of me wore black slacks, a navy cashmere blazer with Brooks Brothers natural shoulders, a gray embroidered vest, and a black tie in a Windsor knot. A bamboo handled umbrella hung from the crook of his left elbow. I would have interviewed him as a butler.

He parked his slender cordovan leather attaché case and assessed the situation. He said, "Go ahead and make your coffee. I'll look at it."

Another of life's details I loathed, making coffee. Loved to drink it, hated to make it. I fussed my way through the process, watched the first glimmers of morning light break across the East

River through the windows. The proverb about a watched pot never boiling proved its meaning.

Sunlight peeked in through the windows. I poured roiling black java into two thick white coffee cups, didn't spill a drop all the way back.

James stood at the office door, briefcase in hand. He scrolled on his phone screen. He looked up when I came forward with the coffee.

"Oh, hi. No, thanks. It's fixed. It's doing some test printing for you now. I'm calling Superego."

"At least accept a cup of coffee as thanks," I countered. "They won't get in downstairs for hours. The sun just came up. They're mostly a noon to midnight crew."

As we shared a couple of cups of black caffeine, I showed him how the games I played for real were much more exciting than the ones Superego designed for fantasy.

Military experience with and against Afghanistan's warlords instilled in me a quick eye for expertise and loyalty. So, I offered him 25% of the million-dollar contract I signed the day before, the contract I was trying to print. James ran the office that day.

*   *   *

This afternoon, he sent me packing back to Washington. Every fighter pilot needs ground control. Though I rode the rails on the Silver Star from New York back to D.C., I was flying by the seat of my pants.

There was nothing to worry about behind me in New York when James backed me up. He'd contact my sister at my place and let her know I'd be gone again. And he'd make sure Cody got dinner and exercise.

24 hours after my game of parking lot catch with the kid, I picked up the trail. I started on the same northern steps of the U.S. Treasury building, retraced my cross-town trek the day before. This time, I paid more attention to the people than their surroundings, faceless blurs through windows and behind colorless headlights of rain-soaked traffic in the nation's capital.

Yesterday's downpour dwindled to today's steady drizzle. With it came the end of summer's warm blasts and the advent of cooler trick-or-treat weather. My collar popped up; my Senators ball cap covered my head. I walked down the steps toward 15th Street.

Within my bomber jacket hung my double-barrel .45s automatic pistol in its leather shoulder sling. Its lethal backup companions were stored elsewhere. On my left hand, I wore the baseball glove from my adolescence. My right hand tossed a horsehide into it that remembered better days. I used to bounce it off building walls when I played pitch-back.

The short trek from the Treasury Building to yesterday's apartment house canopy was uneventful. That changed when I talked to the doorman. I took it as a good sign that he was the same guy from the previous afternoon.

I walked up and waited a beat until he recognized me. I said, "Remember me?" He didn't.

I pulled out the same deck of Marlboro Reds I carried from the day before, now down to two sticks, offered him one. He laughed and said, "Yesterday - with the kid."

Then he caught himself. "Hey! The FBI was asking me about you! But they don't know who you are ... 'Cause I don't know who you are."

"I'm about to make it easy for them," I said. "I'm headed their way. You remember, don't you? The kid went back up that way toward his home, and I headed the other way down there?"

"Yeah, yeah! Hey - That's right! You're the guy that kicked ass in that pizza joint down there! I seen it on the news. I didn't tell them that," he said, smiling with confidence. "'Cause I didn't know it yet."

"Listen, do you know anything about that kid Nick that might help?"

"Ah," he said with a grimace. "FBI got all I know. Wasn't much. I seen the kid once in a while; never talked. He played ball against the wall of that place." He reassured me, "And I didn't know you was the pizza place guy."

A baseball bouncing off an outside wall tended to have an effect on the temperament on the people inside. I remembered the antipathies leveled at me from people inside the buildings where I played the same game, myself.

"Anybody ever come outside? Get on him about the noise it makes?"

He dropped his head in thought. A gust almost ripped his doorman's hat off his head; he caught it just in time. As he resituated it on his head he said, "I don't think so. I only seen him weekdays. That place is an art gallery. Mostly open weekends."

I thanked him and crossed the street amid sprinkles. I walked to the spot where we played catch, looked up at the sky.

The steady drizzle assured me this game was rained out. Or not. My baseball launched forward, bounced against the wall, and came back to me with a splash on the asphalt. I caught it, tossed it back again.

Prison camp catch became an exercise in mindless repetition. I fell into its rhythm.

Above the sounds of the rainstorm, I heard a voice in the perfect alto tone I liked in a woman. "What are you doing?" she asked. Before me stood the most perfect figure of a female I ever saw.

9

She stood every inch of six feet in short-heeled boots, a voluptuous raven-haired Amazon whose vivid green eyes glared at me from beneath glossy bangs. "You don't have anything better to do? In the rain? A grown man?"

I dropped the ball into my glove and approached her with a smile. "Well, I am grown, and I am a man - and I can think of several things I'd rather be doing right now."

Her slap came at me like lightning. I caught her wrist, held it a moment, then released it with a grin she didn't appreciate.

She stood strong in her ankle-length black leather overcoat. She eyed me with surprise, which changed to exasperation when I released my grip. I was always a sucker for a woman in a French braid, especially with bangs. Her jet-black hair, swept up just that way, glistened from the effects of the misting rain.

I spoke with as much honesty as I could register. "Look. I was here yesterday - played a dumb game of catch in the rain with this little kid."

"So, you're the one!" she said. "The FBI's looking for you!" She backed away.

"So, I've heard," I said. "Look, what's your name? My name's Nick. I'm retracing my steps to the kid's home to see if I can help get him back. Really."

She took another step back and gave me a more thorough once-over. "Your name is Nick," she said with suspicion. "The same as his." I marveled at my mind's eye of an 11 on a scale of 10. She stood tall and she stood proud. Then she said, "I own this gallery."

My visual once-over found a body that swept up from her heels in curves that redefined geometry. Her expressive use of those enchanting facial features could be destructive. A man could fall into them and lose himself in a nebula of sensuous mist.

My eyes read her eyes as they read mine.

"No," she said.

"That was fast. Care to elaborate?"

She tilted her head back so she could look down her nose at me.

"No," she repeated. "I will not have dinner with you. I will not laugh at your boyish charm. I will not date you. I will not sleep with you."

"OK ... Now that we've been there, done that and our future is *Shinda*, can you tell me anything you might know about little Nick White?"

She covered her eyes with one hand and looked up at the drops that fell from a mottled gray sky, plump with clouds. The drizzle grew and was headed into another downpour. She blinked and looked back at me. "Victoria," she said. "Do we need to continue this out here?"

"Well, since dinner, dating and sex are off the table, can I slide a cup of hot coffee in there somewhere?" I motioned with my head across the street in the direction of a cafe with umbrellaed sidewalk tables.

She smirked and walked with me stride for stride as we splashed across the wet, black asphalt between passing cars. When we reached the door, she bolted ahead so she could hold it open for me. I pawed her behind her shoulders and shoved her inside.

"Let's sit at the bar," she said.

Warmth from the steaming cups of coffee comforted our hands after the chilling rain. Her demeanor also thawed. Every head in the place: man, woman and child – turned and looked at us, meaning her.

She cut a tall and titillating figure. Her stunning features were pure Hollywood silver screen, while I looked like a palooka who fit the description of the other guy in, "you should see the other guy."

Victoria didn't know anything about little Nick. He never bounced against her wall on weekends.

She dealt in high-end collector art, but the Whites preferred their paintings and sculptures in a western vein. Her Victoria Taylor gallery expressionistic paintings and sculptures were not about to find their way into any White *haciendas.*

When we finished, she paid. "My honors," she said.

I asked for her card. We exchanged.

She rolled my .45 cartridge between her thumb and index finger and examined the engraving on the polished brass: Nick Wolfe - *El Peligro* – phone/text. She commented, "Really?" Then, on the street outside the cafe, "Maybe ... lunch."

I continued up the street toward the home of Nick White.

10

That afternoon, the sun cheated us out of an hour of daylight. *El Sol* left work early and let darkness clock in behind the thunderheads. I followed the streetlights through the gloom in the direction little Nick walked yesterday afternoon.

I turned a corner and came out from under the cover of some trees. My path led me toward a dazzling sight a couple of blocks ahead. Apollo 13 could have used it as a navigational point to track its way back to earth from space.

I've seen hotels smaller than little Nick White's house. The Greek revival source of the nova was emblazoned in the early night by its tungsten-halogen exterior lights. The mansion camouflaged itself in plain view. Its architectural design blended with the government buildings and shrines in the nation's capital in a style guaranteed to make Charles L'Enfant happy.

The location was formerly known as Pershing Park, at the intersection of Pennsylvania Avenue and 15th Street. The property was a National Park dedicated to General of the Army, Blackjack

General Pershing. Now, it was home to Preston T. White's family.

It was Preston's way of thumbing his nose at government bureaucrats.

To compensate for the property, he bought 20 acres near the southwest corner of West Point Academy and donated it to them. There, he personally financed the operations of relocating and rebuilding Pershing Park, bigger and better than it was before.

The White Mansion and its grounds occupied an entire trapezoidal city block of prime Washington, D.C. real estate. It rose five stories as a metaphorical ivory tower of power across the street from 1600 Pennsylvania Avenue.

The President and First Lady of the United States in the White House became next-door neighbors. They were, of course, on the other side of the tracks from Preston T. White *et al* who occupied the larger, White Mansion. The private residence was rumored to have over 60,000 square feet of floor space.

A living testament to the power of Preston T. White is how he engineered the acquisition of Pershing Park from the National Park Service to build his home. While the property was closed during the pandemic for reconstruction, Preston opened his checkbook and ushered in his own era of reconstruction.

Preston was a riverboat gambler, and this may have been the cleverest deal he ever pulled off. The official documents for the deal were classified as matters of national security, sealed in the National Archives.

He tried to usurp the address of 1500 Pennsylvania Avenue, but the U.S. Treasury claimed squatter's rights. Even Preston couldn't buy off the richest national treasury in the world. And he wasn't crazy about the official address: Reservation No. 617, City Square 226, Commerce Building Plaza and Pershing Square. So, he had to accept the negotiated address of "Pennsylvania Avenue and 15th Street, NW."

I dodged raindrops as I walked down the darkened street and sidewalk. Then I dropped down into stealth mode. For a case of this prominence the kidnapping team of the FBI would be on-site in a squad of six: four agents stationed outside, one on each corner of the property, and at least two inside with family and phones. Plus, their standard inconspicuous street van command center.

I learned a long time ago; it's better to beg forgiveness than to ask permission. It was imperative to avoid any preliminary introduction to the FBI.

I knew exactly what would happen. I would voluntarily approach one of their fine, friendly agents. I'd identify myself as likely the last person to see the kid.

Then I would be thrown down, cuffed, dragged off for questioning. A day or two would be wasted when I could have been working to get the kid back. All so the federal boys could chalk up a couple more pages of paperwork reports to score Brownie points with their mid-level managers.

I don't play.

I made a call on my untraceable secure satellite phone.

"Margo, you're awesome with T-men; are you as good with the FBI?"

Crickets: chirp; chirp.

"Don't be insulted. I'll wire your funds, but I need your wizardry right now. As they say in Texas, R-A-T-N-A, rat nah."

Does everybody have "Rush" charges? A job that involved Margo with no notice tripled her fee, and then only if you were a preferred client. My CPA wasn't going to like that at all, especially with no case revenue to back it up.

Margo's fingers tapped her keyboards as I described the White manse, the address, streets, the FBI set up and the location of their van.

She spoke in a charming Irish brogue: "Oh, that'll be Alton and Eddy. They always get the D.C. Metro van at night. No problem. Give me a couple of minutes. Why the surreptitious cover tonight? Aren't you dropping in to help?"

"A hunch," I said. "I'm not invited to the party."

"OK ... expensive hunch. I've got everything covered on the inside men at the skunkworks for an hour. OK ... hold on ... mansion and van ... both. Done. I should charge extra for the van monitors."

I whispered, "You'd have to help me pull a heist to pay you. You're a doll, Margo. But the main thing I need is the four G-men on the four corners of the house. Can you divert them for me to get to the front door?"

"No," she said.

What am I paying her triple for?

"But the van can. Here's what we do. You order five pizzas delivered to the van, locally. I'm sending each house guard a separate notice. They're getting called in to pick up their nice hot *Mystic Pizza* at the van. Each agent gets a unique message at the same time. That'll cover you for a couple minutes."

I said, "Erin, Go Bragh, baby."

"Just pay up. Tonight. I don't do this for my health, you know."

A few minutes later the van received its pizza delivery, and I stood before the massive hand-carved doors to the estate. Despite the Greek Revival architecture, the 12-foot front doors could have hung on the Texas Hall of State. Each door appeared as an imposing Western-themed monolith of Bois d'Arc.

The left side featured Texas Longhorn cattle that grazed on south Texas plains, carved in bas relief on the door's face. The right-side carvings showed oil rigs and derricks in the north end of the state.

This Big Bend Mount Olympus featured Doric peristyle colonnades spread along the mansion's wrap-around piazza on two levels. These columns and treatments were repeated on the third and fourth floors, as well. The fifth-floor penthouses displayed rows of dormers on all four sides.

I've always hated mansions with their pretentious contrived doorbells and almost knocked instead of ringing. This one caught me by surprise. It was a doorbell. Ding dong. Like the one at your aunt Mary's house.

The moment I pushed the button, I felt a concentrated hard pressure thrust into my lower spine. A gun. A smooth male voice spoke from behind me. "OK, smart guy, raise your hands."

He frisked me and yanked my .45s out of its shoulder rig. The voice said, "Yeah! What do we have here! I hope you've got a good lawyer, pal. I wondered what was going on when I saw three agents race-walk to the van at the same time."

"Are you going to take my ball and glove, too?" I asked. He took them, too. Then he found my cross-draw hammerless .38 snub-nosed revolver, followed by my derringer. "What the hell is this?" he asked.

I kept my gaze straight ahead, spoke back over my shoulder and cut him off. "Lighten up, pal. At point-blank range, if you pull that trigger, you're going to shoot through this door and blast whoever answers on the other side."

The grand doors parted and revealed a fresh-faced twenty-something guy. He stood before us, impeccably dressed in a black dinner tuxedo and gray striped ascot tie.

The guy behind me shoved me through the doors into the mansion's foyer. We dripped rainwater on the white marble floor of a vestibule the size of some homes. I half-turned for a look at my captor. There was nobody there.

I looked down and saw a Lilliputian. In his black elevator shoes, he stood about 5'4", in a gray suit with a white shirt and gray tie.

He still held his gun on me, reached up and pickpocketed my wallet from my jacket pocket.

The diminutive agent studied my licenses and permits, then started reading my rights. The young tux looked on, wide-eyed with awe. I said, "If I knew we were formal tonight, I would have dressed more appropriately."

The sharp sound of a woman's high heels click-clacked across the hard marble floor from a distance. With a smooth, confident voice that carried a subtle Texas accent, I heard her ask, "Horace? Is everything all right?"

I still faced front, said to my captor, "You're reading my rights? What's the charge?"

Federal agent Oompa Loompa fumbled with my three handguns at a safe distance. "How about these for starters? In Washington, D.C.?"

Showing caution, I moved my left hand upward toward my left collar. "I can show you those papers," I said, "They're in my other pocket."

He held his gun on me. The FBI's lead banty rooster strutted back toward me. He moved my hand away, reached up inside my jacket's other breast pocket. I turned my head away from his ugly mug, into an unforgettable view of Mrs. Preston T. White.

11

It was the day and the night for me to be shocked by stunning beauty. The woman who approached our minor melee emerged from a sitting room scaled for zeppelins. It didn't matter how big the room was that she entered, she could have stopped time in Grand Central Station.

Electra White drew near with innate poise. Her ingratiating charm highlighted the stunning cover girl in her little black dress. I picked up a familiar scent as she came near. It drifted into me for a brief pass and flirted with my senses.

It crept with stealth through the wall of my rational judgment and pussyfooted on its path inside me. Its invisible vapors stretched its claws on its favorite pillow before it curled up to rest on my memory's bed. I loved it. I hated it. *Coco by Chanel.*

The mysterious Oriental fragrance unlocked a long-sealed door to something lovely and luscious that I buried a long time ago. For a few moments, my emotions reminisced. But not my eyes.

Electra's thick auburn hair looked like it was taken from a magazine's back cover ad. It framed an oval face that was highlighted by her flashing dark brown eyes. A timeless Texas shag caressed shoulders shaped by athletic experience, above curves that gave any roller coaster envy of the wild ride they foretold.

Two guys approached from another room. They wore the same company issue as special agent Bonaparte: black shoes, gray slacks, white button-down shirts and gray ties.

"What's all this, Johnson?" asked the senior of the pair.

"Caught this guy at the front door, Brunneman. He's carrying this piece in his shoulder holster, plus these other two." My captor displayed my artillery in his outstretched hands as if they were the Crown Jewels.

The third agent remained off to one side, his hand within reach of his .38 Special. He was a respectable looking guy, the kind who spent several days a week in the gym. He unloaded my pistols from agent Johnson as the Lilliputian examined the contents of my wallet and papers.

Brunneman didn't look happy. "Oh?" he asked. "And how did he get to the front door with four of you on duty outside?"

My favorite FBI agent replied with a murmuring voice. "We ... got called to the van; for pizza," he said.

"What?" asked Brunneman. "I don't think I heard that right, Johnson."

I cut in. "It's my fault, agent Brunneman. I'm the guy you're looking for. At least for now. I played catch with little Nick yesterday afternoon in a parking lot a couple of blocks from here."

The agents' and Electra White's eyebrows raised. "After that, I went home to New York. I saw he was missing on the morning news. I hopped a train back to see if I could help."

"You couldn't have called?" he asked.

I looked around at the three G-Men. "I'm a face to face kind of guy. I jumped on that train and got back here as soon as I could."

Agent Johnson stuffed my wallet back into my pocket with disdain. I returned the expression. He said, "We're the FBI. We handle kidnappings. Your PI license is only good in New York. You've got nothing here."

Electra White grew tired of listening in the background. She spoke to the young guy in the tux: "Horace?"

Horace shrugged and looked at me.

"We apprehended this stranger at your front door, Mrs. White," said agent Brunneman. "Don't worry, we'll take him in for questioning."

She said, "Thank you, agent, but he did walk up to my door and ring my front doorbell. You didn't intercept him *en route*?"

"No ma'am," said agent Brunneman. "It won't happen again. We just got wires crossed and ..."

"Is he under arrest?"

Agents Brunneman and Johnson traded stares. "We don't know yet, ma'am," said Brunneman.

Johnson spoke without withholding his regret. "His documents check out."

She looked at me and said, "Did I hear this man say he's here to be of help? I believe I should be a good host and welcome him into my home. He did come down from New York City to my home and rang my bell."

I smiled at her. She returned the gesture. *I was starting to like this town.*

I took my glove, ball and "documents" back from agent Johnson. There was no chance they would return my guns until we parted ways. He said, "You can't do investigative work here."

Electra lifted my arm and slid hers beneath it. She guided us so I could escort her into the sitting hangar from whence she came. As we neared, a tall statesmanlike gentleman rose from his chair and approached us. He sat near an elegant woman, but with her chair around a corner and side table, I didn't have much chance to make her out.

Electra's discreet scent stirred things inside me that I locked away years ago.

She steered me to the high archway that set off the formal sitting coliseum. The ectomorph with graying temples stopped our progress when he planted himself in front of us.

Electra's Texas accent became more pronounced when she said, "Look what I found on our doorstep, John. And it isn't Halloween yet."

He gave away 40 pounds to me, but we stood eye to eye. I smelled a politician, in his traditional dark gray suit, black wingtip shoes, white shirt and solid blue tie, behind a clinical case of halitosis. My olfactory appraisal was proven correct when he scanned my full-length frame with one of those obsequious, phony politician smiles.

He did not offer his handshake and said, "I haven't had the pleasure. Are those little Nick White's ball and glove you hold in your hands?" He indicated the soggy things that dripped between my fingers.

"I believe that makes you the bag man here to deliver a ransom note. Or did I hear that you're some sort of private eye, here to offer your slimy services to Mrs. White?"

In a flash, I recognized him. Just as quickly, I wanted to slug him and wipe that politician's smiling assassin look off his face. But I didn't. He may have been just one of 27 U.S. Congressmen from the Big Apple, but he was the Speaker of the House, third in line for the most powerful position on earth.

I tossed my soggy baseball into my rain-soaked mitt and said, "These are mine. I played a game of catch with him near here yesterday. I might be the most recent person to see him. I'm here to help."

"We are all here to be of support to Mrs. White. I think the Federal Bureau of Investigation has things well in hand, Mr. ....?"

"Sure, they do," I said. "Your FBI's maximum security allowed me to play trick or treat early -

right up to the front doorbell without a costume. Tell me this ..." I looked at the three stooges, then at the Speaker of the House. "Got any clues? How about a ransom note?"

Speaker John Evans cut his eyes to agents Brunneman and Johnson.

"We don't discuss ongoing investigations," said Brunneman.

"With all due respect, Mr. Speaker, it's been over 24 hours. I'll take that as a 'no'."

Electra White touched my arm. "You seem to be very capable, Mr. .... "

Her scent. Teresa.

I snapped a couple of my calling cards out of my spare magazine and handed them out. "This is the kind of work I do," I said.

Electra turned my engraved cartridge over in her hands and said, "You see, Jack - I think we should hear out everyone. It's my son who's missing.

Mister Wolfe didn't have to come back here from New York City. What if he can help?"

"What was it that compelled you to play catch with my son, Mister Wolfe? Is that his baseball cap you're wearing?"

I removed my cap and examined it. I said, "No ma'am, I happen to wear the same one, early 60s Washington Senators. My dad saw their games. I don't know - it was pouring, but he kept playing bounce back by himself in the rain." Then, "He reminded me of me."

The scaled-down agent from the street corner rolled his eyes. He muttered, "Gimme a break."

Agent Brunneman said, "And that's the last you saw of him?"

"We were headed in different directions. I was going to walk him home. He said it was only a couple of blocks and he was OK. He walked this way. The doorman across the street from that art gallery parking lot will confirm it. I walked the other way to a pizza place, then caught a train to New York."

"Wait a minute!" exclaimed Horace. "You're him!"

12

Electra, agent Brunneman and Speaker Evans exchanged surprised looks.

"He's the guy! The guy on the news!" Horace exclaimed. "He's the one who took down that pedophile ring at the pizza place downtown!"

At that comment, I noticed the elegant lady in the sitting room. She leaned forward in her chair and turned in our direction. She raised a pair of white mother of pearl opera glasses to gain a closer look.

Across the zeppelin hangar, I couldn't make out much about her, except her hair. It was beyond blonde; it was gold, a true hue of golden blonde hair if ever there was one, worn up in a halo braid.

Electra put her hand to her cheek. She proclaimed in a voice reserved for southern college sororities, "Oh, My!"

"Oh, great!" said Brunneman with distaste. "Just what we need. A vigilante at a kidnapping case."

Speaker Evans tried to pull a Slick Willie politician's move. He put his arm around my shoulder to usher me to the door. "I think we better let the experts take care of this matter."

I didn't budge. My unexpected inertia jerked his momentum to a surprised standstill. I said, "You think this is a kidnapping case? Mister Speaker, you just told me you don't even have a ransom note."

"Jack," said Electra. "It's my son who's missing. It sounds like Mr. Wolfe has been closer to the case in the last 24 hours than the FBI."

She turned to me. "Would you find my Nick, please? I'll …"

A faint murmur came from the sitting room; Speaker Evans turned away and glided back in that direction.

I looked into Electra's welcoming brown eyes and tried not to remember what it felt like to fall into those deep spaces of a woman's soul. I said, "I'll bring him back, ma'am."

A few moments later Speaker Evans returned. "I'd like you to come to my office tomorrow morning. There may be some way that I can help you help Mrs. White in her hour of need. Nine o'clock?"

"Fine, sir," I said. "But I need to get moving on this right away."

Speaker Evans looked over at agents Johnson, Brunneman, and the capable inside FBI guy. Their eight eyes were not happy. He said, "I'm sure we can work together to bring this horrible affair to a quick and satisfactory end. See me in the morning." He smiled that patronizing smile that made me want to answer back with a left hook.

Agent Johnson kept the rounds from my .45's magazines along with the five cartridges from the .38 and handed the pistols back. He emptied my derringer's contents into a wastebasket and the kitchen sink and placed it in my hand.

I re-holstered and turned to Electra before I headed out. "You know there's just one thing I don't get."

She said, "What's that, Mister Wolfe?"

"If a kid has all this - I mean, you could play a baseball game inside your living room - I'm sure he has the best available resources to play ball. Why play pitch-back by himself against a brick wall in a parking lot - in the rain?"

Electra drew close. She drew a slow, deep breath. Her eyes looked up at me and she said, "Today is Nick's birthday. Ever since his father left us, he's gone through different moods. He has coaches; he has trainers; he has tutors; but sometimes he just likes to," she paused to find a word. "Escape."

Reminds me of me.

I turned to Speaker Evans. "Nine o'clock." I walked out as Horace held the front door open for me to rediscover the rain outside.

My rooms at the Hotel Washington were just around the corner. I could have walked there, but I didn't. Instead, I swung a couple of blocks east to the Victoria Taylor gallery. I hoped my one onion-paper-thin lead stayed late doing onion-paper-thin paperwork.

I had just begun working on the case, but the people I encountered weighed on my mind. They weren't my usual cast of suspects: a simple doorman, a stunning art gallery owner, an FBI kidnapping case crew, a tall Texas drink of top-shelf bourbon, the Speaker of the House of Representatives, and an enigma with golden blonde hair. I reloaded my guns.

My head and shoulders caught raindrops that dripped from overhead canopies until I reached Victoria's front entrance. Victoria was there, and so were a lot of other people and their valet-parked cars - doing everything but paperwork.

13

A stunning work of art dressed in a French maid outfit with fishnet hose and six-inch heels greeted me at the gallery's front door. She held open a register book for me to sign. I was walking straight into an artist's release party.

Another attendant with a 35" inseam in similar sexy black and white offered me *hors d'oeuvres* on a silver tray. I didn't notice whatever they were.

As I walked in, a jazz trio in one corner played a relaxing urban tempo. A moment later another French maid passed a tray of white wine glasses under my nose. I passed on both. What I wanted was Miller High Life and some chips.

I didn't care for the high-end existential art that covered the walls and stood atop pedestals. The work I was interested in was the focus of attention in the middle of the gallery's open floor space.

Victoria commanded the attention of everyone on the gallery as she wrapped up her glamorous introduction of the featured artist. He was a tall skinny guy with purple hair, dressed in cowboy boots, slacks, a 50s retro jacket, and a bolo tie.

The preponderance of artworks on display, his, were the ones I hated the most. Victoria concluded to polite applause, then handed her microphone to him. His high-pitched voice scratched into play about the arduous nature of his work.

Victoria's voluptuous body sashayed through the crowd in my direction while she chatted with a guest. When she bumped into me her eyes flew open. "Nick!" She caught herself and said, "Taking up an interest in non-Western art?"

The statuesque art form that stood before me could only have been created by the hand of God. Victoria's stunning womanhood would merit display in any art gallery on earth.

"Something like that," I countered. "You busy all night?"

There had been a wardrobe change between coffee and champagne. Victoria's long, curvy body was caressed by a full-length beaded and sequined affair in form-fitting indigo.

The snugly fitted dress strained against a tigress trapped inside the confines of its fabric and seams. This wild animal wanted to escape and run free. Her jet-black hair framed her sculpted face and vivid green eyes.

She bit her lower lip. "Well," she teased with an impish smile, "Not all night."

I called to the nearest French maid, "Champagne!"

A time-killing tour of the gallery kept me busy while Victoria hobnobbed and ran her business. Art. Not my kind of art. These were high-dollar pieces created for display in sterile over-engineered homes with no other forms of creature comfort to enjoy.

A centerpiece, displayed on its solitary pedestal, was a large blue velvet bulldog. It surveyed the crowd, wearing a spiked diamond collar. Fifty grand.

The gallery was a bigger joint than it looked from the outside. I'm sure I didn't see everything on display but what I did see paled in comparison to the owner.

Eventually, the crowd dwindled to a couple of people in conversation. A smiling French maid in a cute blonde bob and schoolgirl makeup approached. "Hello," she said. Then she presented a tray of *hors d'oeuvres*. "My name's Candy. Would you like some?"

I was beginning to like this town.

"I'm hanging around to see - "

"Me," came the firm interjection. Victoria stood directly behind the girl. She stood with arms akimbo and an expression that temporarily misplaced its hostess charm.

The blushing server said, "Excuse me," and slipped away.

"You are dangerous, aren't you?" came Victoria's rhetorical question. "What am I going to do with you?"

"I don't know. As I recall, dinner, dating, and sex are out of the question."

Victoria drew close. "As well as that boyish charm."

"I thought you could help me understand this little area around here. I walked every inch of the way up to the White Mansion and back. I didn't see anywhere between your parking lot and there that sets up to hijack a little kid."

"Every storefront isn't a pizza parlor, Mister private investigator," said Victoria. She wasn't in the mood to work. Tonight, she was in playtime mode. "And they don't all deliver; I can tell you that."

I'm so stupid sometimes! "That's how they did it!" My exclamation rattled the night's last pair of freeloaders. The couple registered their looks of disdain and downed their *gratis* glasses of house white wine.

I turned to Victoria. "He was targeted! They shanghaied him right off the street using a van or something. I need to get with every one of these buildings and storefronts. Security cameras."

Victoria enjoyed her glass of bubbly. "Now that we solved that case, I'm hungry. I'll renegotiate the ban on dinners."

I was deep into thought about getting all the available video footage. *Wouldn't the FBI have pursued that? They didn't mention it, but I didn't blame them for not offering their kidnapping case tactics to a stranger.*

"Hello?" Victoria reached up and tapped my forehead.

Still, couldn't hurt to make some inquiries in the morning ... but the Speaker ... Damn - I was going to need a leg man ...

Victoria gently waved one hand in front of my face and walked toward her front door. *Great legs.* "Earth to Mr. Wolfe - Earth to Mr. Wolfe - I'm hungry!"

I asked, "You know some of the people running businesses around here, don't you?"

"Everyone inside the beltway knows Victoria Taylor."

I said, "Let's get some late-night nosh."

A few minutes later we arrived at the Hotel Washington.

Victoria tried to steer us into their frou-frou boutique downstairs. Again, I resisted her maneuvers.

The front desk clerk eyed us. He picked up the phone and punched out a call. We contended for the lead in our dance across the lobby to the elevator. I escorted her inside and pushed the top-level button marked *POV*.

"Oh, but *Cherry* is so --- cherry!" she protested.

"So are the people I saw in there," I said. "A bunch of cherry sours." I met her eyes with mine. "I'd rather admire our national treasures."

Her mouth met mine in a sudden kiss, but one that wasn't sprung. Lip touched lip and our kiss nestled into place. She felt me out as a willing accomplice before she began serious work. Her mouth parted and let loose passion that didn't belong cooped up in any art gallery but wanted to run loose in the jungle.

She grabbed my jacket collars and body slammed me into the corner of the elevator. I slid my hands down the back of her dress, embraced her lush body through her sequins and beads. And sequins and beads. And sequins and beads.

I pulled her to me; she pulled back and reached for the STOP button. She mashed it and pressed back into me. The alarm screamed its warning that the elevator was stuck.

She spoke to it with a pout. "Killjoy." She pushed the button again and released us. Victoria stepped out of the elevator and surveyed the rooftop bar's view – a 360-degree view of Washington D.C. at night. Each national shrine presented its picture of America, represented by Greek revival architecture, bathed in white light against darkness that blanketed the rest of the city. Little Nick's home stood out the most.

Damn these distractions — but Victoria was my only lead. As flimsy as that was, the rest of her was as solid as Mount Rushmore.

"Isn't there somewhere else we can go?" she asked.

"I know the best Servi Bar in town."

14

We stepped out of the elevator on the fifth floor, then headed down the hallway of numbered room doors toward mine.

As we turned the corner toward my suite, a lone man passed us in the opposite direction. I wouldn't have noticed, but he was so inconspicuous I couldn't help but pick up on him. His measured stride was smooth, silent, the locomotion of someone who wanted to slide by unnoticed.

In a moment's blur, I saw that his hair was dark and short over taught tan skin. Dark slacks, brown blazer, blue turtleneck. And shades. Inside the hallway of a hotel on a rainy autumn night, he wore black cyclops visor sunglasses.

He turned the corner and vanished; we entered my room. I had other things on my mind.

This side of the suite provided two queen beds and a Servi Bar stocked with pony bottles of Miller High Life. Victoria parked herself on the bed nearest the door; "Is this one mine?"

I indicated the different pillowcase designs on each bed. "Do you prefer Colonel Teddy of the Rough Riders or Harry S. Truman of Nagasaki?"

"I'll go with the Big Stick over the A-Bomb."

"Let's Indian leg wrestle for it."

She laughed. "I grew up with three brothers bigger than you."

"I hope you didn't bring them."

She asked, "You said you specifically requested these two rooms together? Why?"

"Elvis."

She kicked her heels off, one at a time. Each shoe hit the carpet with a soft, inviting thump.

"Pray tell?" She stretched her long legs, extended her toes and cracked their knuckles. She laid back on the bed and stretched her arms to her sides. Her dark form made a voluptuous silhouette on top of the white bedding.

"When he flew to D.C. to meet President Nixon back in '70. He took out these two rooms, for security reasons. I do the same wherever I go. Fifty million Elvis fans can't be wrong."

Victoria sat up and pulled me to her. She pressed her lips against mine and pulled us both down onto the bed. "Nick," she sighed. "I need a man who can love me the way that I am."

I whispered, "Darling, you came to the right place."

The thumb and forefinger of my right hand guided her dress' zipper straight down her spine in a long, slow pulling motion. We laid back on top of the bed. Her body searched for and found another body that searched for someone like her.

She whispered, "I thought we were going to have dinner?"

"Twenty four hour room service," I said.

I wanted to take my time. I wanted this night to stay here and never dawn so none of tomorrow's harsh realities could come into play. Victoria was a woman who wanted to be experienced, enjoyed.

Smooth, firm muscles beneath her sequins answered the questions posed by my fingertips. She wanted to share that gratification of two people lost. Two people who were finding each other with hands and bodies that searched and intertwined in the dark.

My hands worked beneath the elegant armor of her beaded and sequined dress. My fingers slowed and savored their sensitivity training. They caressed the thin layer of softness above vigorous muscles and undulating peaks and valleys. I conducted a one-man treasure hunt – and hit the mother lode.

Somewhere, far away, footfalls in the hallway sounded. But they were too distant to capture my attention.

Then the banging on the door said this was real; no matter how wonderful our escape had been it was forcibly interrupted. I looked up; Victoria looked up at me. "Nick?"

I cautioned silence with a finger to my lips and moved to the desk chair. I reached for my jacket and chambered my .45s.

Then, outside the door: more footfalls, more commotion. Voices. Then a lot of voices, people talked, murmured, asked questions.

I slid into my pants and shirt. When I stepped toward the room's door, I grabbed my .45s. A wineglass against the door only served to amplify the murmurs.

Down the hallway, someone exclaimed with pride, "This is the room, officer!"

I cracked the door open and looked into the hallway. A motley group of people jammed together around the entrance to my diversionary room next door. MPD police, hotel staff, guests on the floor in PJs and bathrobes crowded the open doorway.

I looked back into my room. Victoria sat up in bed with a luscious body that showed every sign of arousal. The night's deep blue illumination through the windows were hands of light and shadow that caressed the lines of body: legs that stretched past the end of the bed, hips that narrowed into her slender waist, breasts and shoulders that would make cover models envious. Her enticing shadows beckoned me without words.

I gave her a silent sign and laid the pistol on the sofa. The hotel's courtesy white slippers caught my eyes in the night's dim light. I slid them on, pulled the door closed behind me.

As I stepped into the hall I heard, "I'm the one who phoned the front desk, officer!" This was proclaimed by a short, mousey man with a wreath of white hair around the base of Mount Baldy.

"I heard the commotion in the room!"

Two uniformed MPD officers cleared the hall of guests and onlookers. They removed most of the hotel staff, curiosity seekers themselves. The police looked confused when I identified myself as the man to whom the room was registered. I recognized the voice behind me. "Then maybe you can explain this?" it asked.

I turned and looked into the familiar round features and overworked eyes of Lieutenant Diliberto from the pizza shop the night before. When he saw me, his head dropped as he said with dismay, "Oh, Jeeeez."

Sprawled across the white sheets of the king-size bed, lay the naked body of an attractive woman in her thirties. A deep purple bruise darkened around her neck. Her wide-open eyes stared in death at a killer she would never identify.

Near the door, her partner slumped forward in a chair with his head bowed down. I studied his body: naked and kneeling by a desk-side chair. The red scarf wrapped around his neck was tied to a closet doorknob and dangled down at his side.

Lieutenant Diliberto jotted my name into his note pad, flipped it shut, slid it into his pocket. He glanced at the guy's body and said, "OK. Tonight, you're coming downtown."

I said, "I wasn't here. I'm in the room next door. I've got nothing to do with this."

"Nothing to do with it?" he chided. "Do you know these people?" I shook my head, no.

"Then do you mind telling me how there are two dead people, naked people, two dead naked people in your room registered under your name?"

I said, "No idea, officer. I was out tonight and just got in my room next door a few minutes ago."

Victoria came through the door. Her fingers clutched the hotel's white cotton terry robe above its belt. She arrived at my side, looked up at me and asked, "What is it, darling?"

Before I could prevent it, her eyes swept the room. She absorbed the whole scene in one horrifying glance: the garroted woman on the bed, naked and dead, her partner slumped forward on the floor with the red scarf around his neck, naked and dead, the cops, the medical examiner, the crime lab boys. It was too much for her.

Lieutenant Diliberto asked, "So why would you book two rooms in this hotel, this one in your name and one under an alias, next door?"

"I'm paranoid," I replied. "And I liked the Servi bar better next door. Honest. It has Miller High Life."

"About that — Larry Talbot?" he asked.

"I know," I said. "It's a full moon, Lieutenant."

Diliberto was not amused. He observed the shocked looks that stressed Victoria's lovely features, then said, "Ma'am, I'm sorry you had to see this. Can you shed any light on what happened here?"

She turned away from the murder scene. "No. We've been together, out, since about eight. We just got in the room next door. A few minutes ago."

"You've been together all night?" he asked.

I cut in. "No, Lieutenant Diliberto. I met Victoria at her art gallery right after I visited the White Mansion with Electra White and Speaker of the House John Evans. I have a meeting with Speaker Evans in his office tomorrow morning at nine. I can get Mrs. White or the Speaker on the horn to vouch for my time and whereabouts."

I don't know what it is about me and the police. I love cops. Blue blood flows through my veins. I think most of them are the bravest people on earth.

On Thanksgiving and Christmas days, I take cookies, donuts and coffee to our local precinct HQ, fire station and ER. On these major holidays everybody else feasts, relaxes, and quarterbacks football while those emergency teams are on duty keeping people safe. I would carry their shields into battle for them.

But we get along like lions and cheetahs; the same kingdom, phylum, class, order, family – fine, as long as we keep our distance from each other.

Lieutenant Diliberto scowled. He looked at Victoria, tapped his pad with his pencil. "This true?"

It was hard to tell whether Victoria shrugged or shivered. "Wwe've been together since about eight."

He looked up at me. "Mrs. Preston T. White ... and Speaker Evans?" he asked.

"There was another gal there," I said. "Didn't get her name."

He turned to the medical examiner. "Hey, Ed. Time of death?"

Ed attended the dead guy slumped in the chair. "About an hour, hour and a half," came the informed reply.

"The desk clerk can vouch for our arrival time," I said. "We were out together a couple of hours ago and just got into my room next door half an hour ago."

"OK," said Sal Diliberto. He turned to me, jotted something on his note pad. "Give me your contact information again." Then, to Victoria, "I'll need yours, too, ma'am."

She walked out in her bare feet to get her clutch. I gave him my .45 ACP calling card. He turned it around in his fingers and examined it. "Yeah," he said. "I'm going to need a lot of contact information from you."

As he began to issue the standard police command in this kind of case, I nodded and finished it for him, "And don't leave town."

15

That ended the night for Victoria. Those passionate embers were doused by the violence, the double deaths, the nearness of the room right next door. They were going to need to smolder awhile before they would re-ignite.

An hour later in the hotel foyer, I took her arm before we walked outside. "Victoria," I said. "I need to ask you something."

The tourmaline in her eyes glistened with her tears. "What, Nick?" she asked. "Do you want to take me to a children's matinee so we can witness a mass shooting?"

My head dropped and the corners of my mouth tightened into a grimace.

"I'm sorry," she said. "I'm in shock. My life is an art gallery, Nick. With pleasant, creative, artistic people. Harmless people. I need to go back there."

"I know you do, but I need to ask for your help," I said. "A little boy's life is at stake."

"This trail is growing cold fast, and I've got people bigger than I understand pulling me in all directions. Tomorrow morning I've got to see the Speaker of the House. I don't have the time; little Nick White doesn't have the time. But when the Speaker of the House wants you to meet him in his office, you kind of have to go."

"Why would he want to see you?"

"He says he can connect me with some people who can help get little Nick back. It can't hurt to get in at that high level. But I've got to get on this trail at ground zero, like yesterday. That's why I need your help."

"Doesn't the FBI handle kidnappings?" she asked.

I reminded her, "Don't forget. Your life is an art gallery."

I drew her to me in a soft embrace. "It's easy. You know people with places between your gallery and the White Mansion. They have security cameras. Just ask if we can review their videos. That's all."

"Won't the FBI have done that?"

I said, "Again; your life is an art gallery."

Victoria bowed her head in consideration, shook it and her dark mane of hair. She wiped her misty green eyes and looked at me. "We're not open tomorrow," she said softly. "I'll see some of my friends in the morning."

"You're wonderful," I said. "I'll come by tomorrow afternoon. Call to tell me anything. Any little thing at all can be important. Even a subtle nuance of a look that somebody shows when you ask them a question."

"Just call me, Mata Hari," she said with a grim smile and rode away in a cab.

* * *

I found my way down to the emergency exit area beneath the Beaux-Arts building. The discreet exit used by celebrities and power figures was situated near a service elevator. I arrived as the bodies were loaded out to ambulances on their way to their cold stainless-steel trays inside the city morgue. Officer Sal Diliberto wrapped up the crime scene.

Diliberto turned and faced me when I walked up. "Now what?" he asked. "You gonna level with me? I know you didn't knock these two off."

My look of startled relief begged its question.

"The guy at the registration desk. Charley Imhoff," he said.

"They were people he knew. I've heard of this stuff. Room stowaways. They get off in somebody else's hotel room, so they find one that's gonna be unoccupied for a few hours and sneak in. It's always an inside job. They got tipped off to available rooms from Imhoff. Sick stuff."

He snapped back to the present and gave me a hard look. "So, they used your room, with the single king-size because you checked in and left right after. That doesn't let you off the hook. It was your room. In your name. Who'd want to come after you to kill you?"

"Lieutenant, if I knew I'd tell you. I don't want them running around loose to take shots at me. I have no idea why."

He frowned.

I said, "Lieutenant, I'm on your side. I'm down here from New York because I'm helping Mrs. White get her boy back."

"The FBI ...!" he began.

I cut him off. "We've already met," I said. "At the White Mansion, tonight. They have my contact info, too. Their HQ is just down the street if you want to ..."

With controlled exasperation, the little round lieutenant flipped his notebook shut and stuffed it into his pocket. He spoke calmly when he began and controlled his demeanor as long as he could.

"This is off the record, Wolfe. I don't know what's going on here. I don't know what levels you operate at. But I'm running the show on that scene at the pizza joint and at this double homicide. And you're smack in the middle of both. I don't know how; I don't know why. I'm keeping my eyes on you, mister."

I smiled. "That's comforting, Lieutenant - I didn't know you cared."

The police officer looked up to address my eyes, leaned in close to my face and stared straight into them. His voice trembled with restraint:

"I don't want any New York p.i. gumming up my work. I don't want any phone calls from the Speaker of the House, or the FBI, or the Chief of Police or God Himself telling me how to handle my case. Or I'll drag you in for questioning for a month! In the drunk tank! Got that?"

"I don't need their help, lieutenant. Hell, they're the ones holding me up. I'll tell you what I've got when I get something. I'd like to call you for the same?"

"We'll see," he said. "So, what do you want? Why'd you come down here to see all this?"

"To share my information with you," I said, and turned to go back up to my room.

16

I stopped for a quick visit with the replacement night clerk at the front desk. In the nation's capital it is not uncommon to have clothes picked up in the room, cleaned, pressed, and returned within three hours. They must have had business coaching from Margo. After midnight it cost triple the rush rates.

It isn't every day you meet the person second in line for succession to the Presidency at his office in the U.S. Capitol. I wanted to clean up and be on time.

Room service was prompt at the dark hour of six, along with delivery of my only suit, an 80s navy blue double-breasted job with pinstripes. I shaved, dressed, and devoured my usual big breakfast.

At 7:00 a.m. I stepped out from the hotel and into an armored Cadillac Escalade. Murgatroyd had a hunch. Foreign city, nation's capital, the pedophile fracas, the high society level of the Speaker and the Whites, me …

These 40,000 pound affairs were chauffeured by former KGB agents who doubled as bodyguards. The driver was a clean-headed guy with fair skin and dark blue eyes. I verified his name: Andriy Boyko. "Good morning, Andriy. Ukraine?"

He turned with a look of pleasant surprise. "Moldova," he said. "We go to Capitol building, yes?"

"You got it, Kemosabe," I said. He pulled out and turned onto 14th Street.

"Kemosabe?" he asked. "I am hearing Americans saying this sometimes. What is this meaning? Who is Kemosabe?"

"The Lone Ranger, Andriy. Silver bullets. Tonto. Silver. Scout." Andriy looked confused. "It means, 'my friend'," I said.

He smiled and laughed. "Comrade Kemosabe! You are being in luck! Andriy driving so early this morning. When your friend orders my armored vehicle - Andriy is ready!"

"A bit of overkill to drive a dozen blocks down Pennsylvania Avenue, don't you think, Andriy?"

"Total protection, sir. No overkill for that. Andriy is being ready any of the time."

"That service doesn't come cheap," I said.

"Total protection, sir. No price for that."

"You're right," I said. I sank back into the leather interior and enjoyed the smoothness of riding in twenty tons of steel security. "It's such a short trip, not much opportunity to test your Escalade's constitution. But it rides great."

I thought out loud, "I need to get some coffee somewhere."

Andriy Boyko half turned. "This is America! Coffee everywhere!" he said with a laugh.

He looked at me in his rear-view mirror and said, "We have famous Moldavian philosopher, Dimitrie Cantemir. He said," he paused and concentrated to get the words right.

"It is like your Kemosabe. Cantemir, he said, 'Friendship is the soul's voluntary imprisonment in a stranger's body'."

I said, "We have a famous philosopher too, Andriy."

"Yes. I am knowing this."

I said, "Groucho Marx. The Marx Brothers: Night at the Opera? Day at the Races? Duck Soup?"

Andriy furrowed his brow, confused. "Not Karl Marx brothers! I am hating the Karl Marx!"

I laughed. "No, Andriy. Far from it. You'd like Groucho. He said, 'I refuse to join any club that would have me as a member'."

Andriy worked through a Russian translation in his mind. His lips silently mouthed the words. Then he processed it again. A grin spread across his features, then his face broke open with laughter.

Out of nowhere, a white light flashed into my eyes from all sides and blinded me. An explosion's shockwave slammed my ears; I was deafened by its impact. I felt the blast crush me down into the car seat.

Before I could think, 40,000 pounds of armored Escalade launched straight up off the ground. It rebounded off another vehicle, bounced into a building wall, flipped, and violently slammed to the pavement.

The big black Caddy crashed and skidded to a stop. upside down and on its roof. Both doors on the passenger side were blocked, smashed up against the building wall that stopped us. I was conscious, aware that I was nearly dead, and more fully aware of life than ever.

Everything I saw was vividly defined - *the little white Mazda Miata we crushed as we crashed down, that dirty white toy poodle on the blue leash* - everything before my eyes appeared in ultra-vivid high definition, and extreme slow motion.

My ears screamed with ringing so high pitched I wondered if I could hear a dog-whistle. A grueling minute later, I tried to move. I found myself suspended upside down. My head and chin were bent into my chest, my legs dangled above me.

I could only manage short breaths, and my guts killed me.

I struggled to get out of the four-point safety strap. My ears didn't ring; they screamed. My headache was aided and abetted by the blood rush from my body's inversion. I looked through blurred vision out the driver's side windows.

He stood at a distance in a small crowd. They all looked down at me. Some used their phones and shot videos. *I must be delirious.*

Brown blazer, blue turtleneck. Black cyclops shades. *Do I know that guy? Why? Where was I?*

17

I was dazed; I was numb. I hung upside down in my rear seat safety harness.

In a few moments my vision reconnected with my brain, and I began to understand the sitrep. My fingers acted without my thinking, found the door's opener. I leaned my weight into it, pushed against the weight of the Escalade's armored body.

After I forced an opening, the challenging work was getting into a position to get out. Gravity lent a helping hand with my sudden plummet down to the Escalade's ceiling.

I rolled out of the vehicle and onto the wet pavement outside. I couldn't stand up on my own. There was no easy way to get myself vertical. I pulled myself up on my feet by using my hands to pull me up a nearby No Parking signpost.

Andriy!

The driver's door was still closed. No police or fire yet; just onlookers with video phones.

"Andriy!" I called. My knee was locked, and my right foot dragged across the pavement on my way to his heavy door. I braced my feet on the concrete for leverage to yank it open, but my shoes slipped on the water and oil.

I positioned one foot on the driver's rear door and the other as firmly on the ground as I could. I gave the door handle a yank, then a heavy heave. When it cracked open, I let go of the handle and grabbed the door itself. I pulled until it relented and groaned as it opened.

Andriy's body hung upside down in his driver's seat. He was strapped into his restraint apparatus behind an inflated airbag. I reached in to touch his motionless shoulder.

He turned and faced me. "Kemosabe!" he exclaimed. A trickle of blood lined the corner of his mouth. "You, OK?"

I was shocked, surprised, and almost angry at the same time. When I broke out laughing with relief, it hurt like hell. My guts felt like I went several rounds in the octagon, with both hands tied behind my back.

I managed to speak between gasps for breath. "Only a Kemosabe would keep from killing you right now. You had me worried."

Several people gravitated toward us, away from the onlooker crowd. They shuffled over and examined us, at arm's length. More phones were being used as video cameras than as communication devices that made calls to 911.

I helped Andriy release the harness, then aided his descent to the pavement. "That would make two times this morning. Only killing attempt once per day, please," he said.

A white MPD squad car pulled up; its red and blue roof lights spun and flashed. The meat wagon wasn't far behind.

Through heavy-lidded eyes, I studied my reflection in the rain-spotted dark windows of the police car.

My suit began the day out-of-fashion, but now it was destroyed. The jacket was ripped apart on one shoulder; grease marks made black smudges and streaks. Two buttons on my jacket sleeves and one from its front were torn off. My forehead was scratched, and a bloody gouge lacerated one cheek. My hair looked worse than if I just woke up.

At least I looked better than I felt.

A voice behind me asked, "The medics are coming, pal. You gonna be all right?"

My body identified as Rigor Mortis; it was painful to turn to reply. My head and neck were crimped and only moved as if glued together into one piece, at a weird angle.

"I don't think I'm winning any popularity contests," I said. I tried to manage a smile, but my face hurt, too.

The voice belonged to a cop. I said, "Thank you, Lieutenant ... " I looked at his brass name badge, "Dili -"

I couldn't control it. I fought as much as I could. But - those sumptuous poached eggs, buckwheat pancakes, spicy sausages, and the Miller beer decided to spring back to life and leap into the world outside. They broke loose and projected their presence directly onto the splendid and pressed dark blue uniform of ...

"Oh, Roscoe! I can't believe he did that! I'll get you a towel, bro!" said his appalled, uniformed partner.

Lieutenant Roscoe Diliberto. I hoped Roscoe was the good twin.

Roscoe was as by-the-book as his brother, Sal. He wiped himself off as much as circumstances allowed. He took my report and contact information, along with Andriy's, and cut us loose to the MICU.

The good people in ER bandaged me and injected me with some overpowered painkillers. But the lady who won my heart was the doctor who administered her "Magic Shot" into my neck muscles. In the old days, we got cortisone and lidocaine. She described as an updated more advanced version; it felt like the touch of an angel.

After the blowup, my head only turned if I rotated my entire torso from the waist up. Twenty minutes after the doc's injection I felt like I could perform gymnastics.

They wanted me to hang around for observation, which flew with me as far as an anvil. I told them thanks, but I was out of there.

Andriy was cleared to leave as well. His company delivered a replacement vehicle. My replacement driver was Taras Valdemar, a Ukrainian ex-Spetsnaz.

He was dark-haired and rough looking, a chiseled guy with a five o'clock shadow who served in explosives and demolitions forces. And he was not amused.

At 11:35 a.m. I trudged up the 365 front steps of the U.S. Capitol toward the office of the Speaker of the House. I walked up about 20 steps at a time before I needed to stop and rest. My recovery lagged, and my guts felt like hammered minced meat.

I wished Taras had known about the east front plaza of the U.S. Capitol at First and East Capitol Streets. The street level entrance would have been a lot easier.

18

I deposited my ordnance with the Capitol Police and went through security. The long blue carpet of the Speaker's Lobby on the third floor provided a welcome softness beneath my feet as I trekked forward under chandeliers that hung from the painted vaulted ceiling. My back and legs were tight; I lumbered my way toward the office of Speaker Evans.

I had plenty of elbow room; the large hall was the place where the term "lobbying" originated. Back when congressmen were only provided with their desks on the chamber's floor as offices, this Speaker's Lobby was the area where they met with constituents to negotiate their deals.

I shuffled and dragged myself down the infinite hallway, past the portrait of every Speaker of the House in history. Every damned Speaker that ever lived. Finally, I reached the inner sanctum of John Evans.

A movie poster-sized one-sheet outside the office door flashed Evans' toilet bowl white politician's smile. I moved inside and saw the front desk receptionist before she saw me. When I started to tell her about our appointment I was drowned out by a loud call from within.

I recognized the Speaker and his voice as he emerged through the open oak door from his lair. "Julie!" he called. "I need you to go over to Anderson's office and ... "

Speaker Evans looked up from the papers in his hands and observed me in his office foyer. He stopped in his tracks, said with surprise, "You!"

He looked me up and down with a shocked once-over, made smooth no doubt by practice on dozens of cocktail waitresses. "You're - late!"

He regained his composure with the skill of a career politician, then made a display of his overpriced wristwatch. "It's almost noon, sir. Our meeting was at 9:00."

"Yeah," I said. "A funny thing happened to me on the way to your office."

The hazel eyes of his admin Julie stared at me. Her fair skin, still freckled in her late 20s beneath

Irish Setter red hair that cascaded down her back, blushed as bright as a flame. Her mouth gaped.

She stared at my rips, grease smudges, bandages, hair from Hell. The only things missing from my caricature were smoke fumes and some stink flies.

Speaker Evans reached his arm around my shoulder and guided me toward his office door. He thought better of it when he realized the wreckage he touched. His arm drifted back to his side.

He said, "Let's go into my office. I'll manufacture a few minutes." To his assistant he said, "Julie, hold my calls. And bring Mr. Wolfe some water and coffee."

Julie nodded with her eyes still wide.

The Speaker's chambers lofted upward with twelve-foot ceilings. Oak-paneled walls enhanced the spacious floor plan with hunter green accents.

One wall was covered with gilt-framed oil portraits of American political leaders through the ages. A malachite fireplace set into it stood dormant and dark.

Speaker Evans made himself comfortable behind a massive, polished oak desk with leather inserted top. He gestured for me to have a seat in one of his guest chairs.

The office reeked of power. I took my seat in an overstuffed brown leather smoking chair. The legs were lowered a few inches to give the Speaker a height advantage from his elevated seat behind the prodigious desk.

We looked at each other eye to eye. I examined his irises and surrounding sclera. There was no way of getting anything out of this guy by asking civil questions. But under a couple of minutes of good solid torture …

"You made quite an impression last night, Mister Wolfe."

"Thank you, sir. Nice joint. You can contemplate the Washington Monument from here."

The Speaker basked in his elitist position and leaned back in his mustard yellow chair from the 70s. His hands folded in his lap. He swiveled and looked out a window.

"Some of the world's most powerful people visit here, Nick. I want them to feel the quiet power of America when they're in my office. You met Electra White last evening. She's encouraged by your involvement in her son's welfare," he said.

"Which is the only reason I'm in D.C., and I haven't been able to get traction yet. I haven't been here twenty hours and two people have been murdered and my livery service blown up. With due respect to your position, sir, I need to get moving before this thing cools off and gets too far gone."

"Nick, I'm in a position to help you engage at a high level with people involved in the same cause you are. People with committees and connections that can ... "

"That can take up my time," I said, interjecting. "Making a lot of phony contacts while kids like

Nick White go missing to the tune of eight million missing kids worldwide every year."

The Speaker absorbed my comment like a boxer that shrugs off a blow. He continued, "Mr. Wolfe, the person on whom you made the impression was none other than Ursula Schicklgruber."

I could tell he was waiting for my reaction. I didn't know who the Hell she was. I shrugged. "The suave number in the sitting room?" I asked.

He replied with mild indignation. "Ursula Schicklgruber is the U.S. Ambassador from Argentina. She is incoming as the first woman Secretary-General of the United Nations. Ms. Schicklgruber asked me to arrange a meeting with you. She keeps a Washington residence at their Embassy on New Hampshire Avenue."

"So now I'm supposed to make a social call on this lady from llama land?"

"Please restrain your candor, Mr. Wolfe. Yes. Ursula Schicklgruber chairs the Global Council on Missing Children. She's been hailed as one of the world's most beautiful women. She has an interest in meeting you. If you catch my drift."

I asked, "Why didn't she just ask me herself last night?"

Speaker of the House John Evans drew in a breath. He steepled his fingers and looked out his windows as he spoke.

I wished I wore a ring, a huge gaudy gold nugget ring so I could leave its imprint on his skull. I wished I had two of them. No, four.

"Mister Wolfe," he began, "Perhaps you aren't familiar with the protocols of diplomacy. Ursula Shicklgruber would not intercede on the grieving Mrs. Preston White in her home when she is dealing with her missing son. People like the Secretary-General of the United Nations have more aplomb than that."

"You're right," I said. "She's right."

"Tomorrow morning at eleven o'clock, she would like you - "

Julie brushed through the closed double doors to the Speaker's office. The silver tray she carried with the coffee service and shortbread cookies almost knocked loose from her hands. Her engagement ring caught the pot's handle. It rocked and came close to giving the Speaker a bath in hot java.

He looked up at her with surprise, as if to say, "This better be good."

"POTUS," she said.

"What?" asked the Speaker.

"The President. On the phone. For you …" She looked at me, "for him - for you! Right now. Like, now!"

The Speaker picked up his Congressional desk phone and pushed the button that blinked red.

"Yes, sir," he said. "Yes. Yes, he is, sir."

Julie wasn't about to leave. She stood between Speaker Evans and me, still trembling as she held the tray.

Speaker Evans said, "Yes, sir," and replaced his phone. He looked down at his desktop. "The President. Wants to see you. This minute."

"Excuse me?"

"Nick, tomorrow morning at eleven o'clock see Ursula Schicklgruber at the Argentine Embassy. I trust you'll be prompter than you were for our meeting. Right now, your presence is requested by the President of the United States."

He thought for a moment. "Why don't I go with you. I have more experience at these things."

"No," I said. "I'm good."

The Speaker didn't look happy. He muttered, "You'll need to take the Deep Underground Bullet Express."

He turned to Julie. "Julie, use your security clearance. Get Mister Wolfe on the DUBE."

My midsection ached, but I also felt hunger pangs. I hadn't eaten since early morning, and I used that *smorgasbord* to accessorize the uniform of

Lieutenant Roscoe Diliberto. "Your subway to the White House is called the DUBE?"

He replied, "Mister Wolfe, see Ursula Shicklgruber tomorrow, then get back with me. She is emerging as a global power. We want to help you."

On a nearby table, I noticed Julie's tray with the coffee pot surrounded by assorted cookies. Five of them found their way into my pockets.

Julie and I humped it for the unmarked entrance to the DUBE - a two-mile underground express beneath Pennsylvania Avenue between the Capitol and the White House.

We took a secure elevator down two floors. When we got out, we approached three U.S. Capitol Police who guarded the entrance to the restricted tunnel tram.

Julie flashed her security credentials and told them I was summoned by POTUS. They wanded me and had me walk through their x-ray machine. Then they patted me down 42 ways to Sunday.

A minute later, I rode with my Capitol Police escort on a secure tram cart. I shuttled my way underground to meet the most powerful man in the world.

19

When I arrived at the White House end of the DUBE, the secret service frisked me. They debriefed me as I got re-wanded and scanned. I exited from the lower area of the White House beneath its southern doors. Two agents escorted me halfway on my route across the south lawn.

As I walked alone across the manicured grass of the White House south lawn, I wondered what in Hell was happening. 36 hours ago, my Treasury corruption case was wrapped up and hog-tied; literally. All I had to do was go home. But I played a game of catch in the rain with a kid I didn't know.

The next thing I knew I was in a street fight to the death with a pair of heavyweight pedophiles, met two of the most gorgeous women I had ever seen, rounded the bases with one of them when I narrowly avoided murder in my hotel room, got blown up in my vehicle blocks from the U.S. Capitol, met with the Speaker of the House and was walking across the White House grounds to shake hands with the President of the United States of America.

Teresa used to say, "It's all part of life."

President John Jackson stood on the verdant grass near Marine One. The big helicopter rested on its three concrete pads. Its entrance was guarded by a Marine in full-color dress uniform 30 feet from POTUS.

As I approached, President Jackson dismissed a Naval officer with a salute. He turned to the helicopter's skipper and motioned with a whirl of his hand and extended forefinger for them to start the rotors. The big blades rotated into life above us.

He was without a doubt, The President: traditional navy-blue suit, white shirt and solid red tie, topped by his white POTUS ball cap that sported the presidential seal.

"This is an honor, Mister President," I said as I offered my handshake. He was a big man and looked at me eye to eye.

"Look ..." he began. Then he paused, leaned back and surveyed my condition. "You look like Hell. You, OK?" he asked.

"Nothing I can't handle, sir."

"Figures," he said. "Nick, you've been brought to my attention by some important people."

"I've been getting that a lot, lately," I said. "Forgive me sir, but I played catch with a kid in the rain and a day and a half later I'm meeting with the President?"

The steel blue eyes of the President bore laser beams through mine. "Excuse me. When I speak, people generally listen."

Oops. I was so out of place; you don't just walk up to the Chief Executive and say, "Hey, bro, how's your hammer hanging?"

He said, "I wouldn't be alive if not for your father, Dean."

Dad was the head of DIA, not the Secret Service?

He read my internal confusion from my furrowed brow.

"You'll have to pry it out of him, or somebody; I don't have time to narrate your family history."

He looked at his watch, then over at the steps that led up into the helicopter.

"Look; your dad saved my life in North Africa. Preston T. White supported me since my first political race. You and your actions caught the attention and remark of powerful people. I'm afraid, on both sides."

"Sir?" I asked. I flinched. I didn't want to get eye-tasered again by The Boss.

He nodded.

"What sides?" I asked.

He laughed. "Good versus Evil, Nick. You've stepped into the middle of an age-old global civil war. You are awakening a dark, evil, filthy worldwide beast whose stench has been kept under a lid for a long, long time."

I said, "With all due respect, all I did was take out a couple of goons and tell a distraught widow I'd do whatever I can to get her little boy back."

"And those are the crossroads you've stepped into." He paused. "Nick, besides going after the son of Preston T. White, that little girl you rescued is the daughter of the Ambassador from Japan."

"So, this is growing into some pretty tall cotton," I said.

"Nick White, Aki Suzuki, Electra White, John Evans, that UN Argentine lady ..."

"Schicklgruber" I offered.

"That one. Me. Not bad work in 24 hours."

Then he said, "Nick, you're in a position to blow the lid off something I want ended. It's vile and disgusting. It ruins millions of kids and families. But I've got to hop over to meet with Russia, China and Iran. Three of my favorite peoples. Our country needs me to do that. I need you to do this."

"Sir, you've got MACV SOG that can make minced meat out of something like this … I'm not in law enforcement. I'm independent. I do things my way."

"Military operations require oversight. We have over a million officers in law enforcement, Nick. LE doesn't get this job done. Too nasty. I need a trench fighter, a mucker. A guy who gets the job done. Under the radar."

"I'm always under the radar, sir," I said with a confident smile.

"Sure, you are," he said. "Like the Goodyear blimp. Secret Service has your guns from the Capitol Police. They'll return your crazy .45 automatic, your hammerless .38 and that other contraption when you leave. You were almost murdered in your hotel last night, and your jacket's still smoking because your ride to see Evans this morning exploded like you were in Kabul."

I stood, stunned.

"I support you but can't provide oversight. I'm kicking you up to The Boss."

When I replied, my voice carried an involuntary incredulous tone. "The Boss?" I asked. "You're - POTUS."

"I am the King on the chessboard."

"And?"

"There's one king, and there's one queen. FLOTUS. My wife Yvonne is expecting you."

With that, the President turned and stepped toward the Marine that guarded the chopper's entrance.
He stopped and looked back toward me. I barely heard his words above the sound of the rotors.

"Wolfe," he paused for a quick moment. "Your father was right ... Look, that business with you and Hunter ... I don't like Hunter. He's a drug snorting whore banging dick. Civil servant holdover. But tied to his bed with a gun up his ass?" He shook his head. "And two agents in traction? I want you to take it easy on my federal boys, Nick."

He saluted the Marine on guard and disappeared into Marine One. I turned and walked back to the East Wing entrance with propulsion help from the chopper's swirling turbulence. I couldn't have been any more blown away.

*   *   *

The name badge of the tall, slender White House escort who waited for me outside the door said, "Liv."

I said, "Tell me, Liv. Where am I headed next? The Cone of Silence?"

She lowered her head and gave a delightful high-pitched Scandinavian female laugh. She tilted her head to the side to indicate our new direction together. She said with a smile, "*mer eller mindre* — more or less."

The willowy girl with a short blonde wedge cut led me to the White House North Wing, and a massive steel portal. We passed from daily reality into the subterranean super security zone of a gargantuan bank vault. I moved from the DUBE to the DUCC – Deep Underground Command Center.

We descended a wide staircase to a stainless-steel elevator door. The stairs continued, but we rode down in a massive steel cage to the bottom, five stories below. When the steel doors opened, we approached the desk of a Sergeant of the White House Military Office.

Our next portal was the entrance to the White House executive emergency bunker. This was not the old East Wing Presidential Emergency Operations Center. Following 9-11, a new model was dug under the North Wing in 2010.

Somehow, my progress forward took me 3,500 feet below the surface. There seemed to be no bounds to the range of my Odyssey to find little Nick White.

For a moment I forgot all about my pain, my appearance. Ahead of me sat the First Lady of the United States - in the President's emergency security bunker.

20

I felt like a first grader who looked at his first movie star in person.

It was obvious in press pictures and videos that Mrs. John Jackson was attractive, but cameras didn't capture the additional allure of her energy's radiance. Yvonne Jackson, First Lady of the United States, captivated my attention.

Her pronounced cheekbones framed soft, light brown eyes in the oval face of a Polynesian beauty. Silky black hair that shimmered in the light draped down every inch of her back. It graced the curves that swept outward, below the curves that a man's hand would caress inward.

When she rose behind the bunker's Spartan office desk, she stood 5'8". She extended her slender arm and hand. I took it, but I'm not French. I shared a firm handshake with a vision dressed in black high heels and a shape-hugging knee-length black dress made famous by Madame Chiang Kai-shek.

"Please, have a seat," she said and resumed her position behind the gray desk. Her soft finishing school voice bewitched me further. Gentility and grace embraced her like family.

"My, you are a mess. Would you like a drink? A Miller's, perhaps?"

I brushed my clothes and looked at my watch. Mid-afternoon. Instinctively, I said, "Miller."

"Excuse me?" she asked.

"I ran into Chill Wills once in the TV bar in downtown Dallas. Some guy ordered a Miller's. He said, 'Son, they pay me a million dollars a year to say, Miller'."

She buzzed her internal intercom that connected outside the sealed door. "Sarah. Bring our guest a - Miller."

FLOTUS turned and faced me. She straightened herself in her chair, addressed her full seated height. She drew her body back and upright with a deep breath, looked me in the eyes.

Her long thick hair spread wide across the latitude of her shoulders, like a sable hood. I felt in danger of being hypnotized by the world's most alluring black cobra. She spoke without so much as batting an eye:

"Nick Wolfe. You are six feet four inches tall. You weigh 243 pounds. Your hair is brown, eyes blue, birthday July 14, 1980. Special Operations Forces in Afghanistan. Your father was Director of the DIA, and your mother ran the CIA's Special Collection Service. Your fingerprint type is a central pocket loop. You live in a four story warehouse by the East River in the Lower East Side that you share with your sister and pet mountain lion. You smoke, Marlboros, and you run your private investigation business – *El Peligro* - from your 21st floor office, also on the Lower East Side. You've had a knee meniscectomy, a bullet wound in your right chest, and a knife wound ..."

She leaned forward across the desk, calmly reached out, touched my left shoulder. "Right about - here," she said. She gripped my left trapezius. Her fingers sunk into the gap made by the recurved blade of a Gurkha Kukri.

Five years ago, I would have winced. Over time, it healed and reduced itself to just a gap between some muscle tissues.

She sat back, relaxed in her chair. "You obtained your New York private investigator's license by dubious means that have yet to be determined. But you did succeed. You succeed in the face of adversity a lot, Mr. Wolfe."

"I'm flattered, ma'am. But that's public information."

"Let's talk about your marriage to Miss Texas, Teresa Veracruz -"

"Let's not," I growled.

She looked away a brief moment. "Of course not. Mister Wolfe, I don't mean to appear adversarial. You are exceptional at what you do. You're a black and white person. Our operations with FLOTUS involve more situational logic."

I could listen to her all day. I could look at her all night. But the subject of this conversation irked me like a burr under a saddle.

"Is that why I'm getting ping-ponged around from one Washington big shot to another? Because of some esoteric fluid logic? Yes, I'm particularly good at what I do. I get results. Guaranteed. But not if I'm pulled from one office to another to sit around and yak all day long. I still don't get why I'm here?"

She purred. "You just said why, Nick. I can call you Nick?" A subtle catlike smile curled her full lips. She wore the slight scent of Hawaiian Hibiscus like a *lei* draped around her neck.

I rested my eyes on her and replayed my mental transcript of our conversation.

"You get results," she said. "Guaranteed."

Sarah returned through the secure door. She was a 5' 1" pixie with a cute pug nose and shoulder-length dark blonde hair that bounced when she walked. She smiled when she laid the First Lady's silver service on my side table. It held a chilled Miller High Life bottle with a Presidential seal glass.

I wondered how the beer would go down. It tasted cold and good, and I finished the bottle *sans* glass more quickly than I should have.

"You're a rare breed in today's culture, Nick. I know your work. I know your operation in Manhattan, your methods, your father's history with my husband …"

"Seems like everybody knows that but me," I said. My lips needed a napkin.

FLOTUS was shocked and amused at the same time. "You mean, you don't know?" she asked.

I reached for the tray to deposit my empty beer bottle, shook my head.

She observed my condition for a split second and remarked, "You're famished."

A few minutes later I dined on the most luscious pancakes, the thickest crispiest bacon, and the richest poached eggs I've ever tasted. And coffee. I had my own personal White House coffee service full of fresh, hot black American coffee.

As I chowed down on my victuals from the White House kitchen, the First Lady observed me with polite curiosity. She leaned forward and commented, "You're in incredible shape. Have you considered a healthier diet?"

"Like what?" I asked.

She smiled. "Oatmeal, fewer animal proteins and fats. More greens and fruits?"

"Somebody already tried that with me," I said.

"Unsuccessfully, I take it. Why?"

"Canine teeth. Top carnivore," I said.

She nestled back into her chair and spoke as if she narrated for a magazine story.

"It was 1976. My father-in-law was an American diplomat to what is now Djibouti in northern Africa. John was riding in a bus with 30 other military children."

My body's remaining energy transferred from my brain to my stomach to settle the food, beer, and coffee. I felt tired. My head bobbed to nod off.

"The bus was hijacked in Djibouti by pro-independence activists and taken to the border post of Loyada. Negotiations stalled and the children stayed on the bus overnight. The next day, your father's parachute brigade of the French Foreign Legion assaulted the bus and killed the kidnappers."

"Your father Dean, shielded my husband with his own body during the firefight. He dispatched two of the kidnappers himself."

I snapped back into consciousness. *What'd she say?*

"Of course, your father's later leadership in intelligence followed that. John holds him in high regard," she added.

I recovered with, "But why all this? Why me?"

21

I watched as the First Lady of the United States considered her reply, then said, "My husband has his causes. Important causes that make world headlines. Causes where people register their approval with their votes. My causes are not as highly visible. In many ways they are larger in scope."

"And those would be?" I asked.

"Children, Nick. And animals," she said. "Both groups are defenseless, and both are victims of man. They have no choice in what happens to them. And they are both horribly mistreated."

My body slowed down. The digestion process of food after a long morning of explosion, regurgitation and revulsion talked to me about how nice a comfortable bed felt.

"Do you know how many children are abducted in our country each year, Nick?" I shrugged.

"Every 40 seconds a child is abducted in the United States. 2,000 per day. 750,000 missing children every year. And one in six is likely to become a victim of sex trafficking. It's a horrible epidemic and it isn't just here, it's global. Millions disappear every year, worldwide."

"I'm no expert," I said, "but isn't it usually done by family members?"

"Nick, this has become a 150-Billion-dollar profit industry. 25 million cases worldwide. These children are sent to massage parlors and nail salons to sell their bodies or move them around. Not long ago, U.S. Marshals saved 39 lives in 7 states when they took down just one ring."

"Those are big numbers, ma'am. But I'm not pulling down the pillars of any temples. I'm just trying to save one little boy who played catch with me. I don't get all this high-level treatment."

"Electra White is a friend of mine. I know her son. Nick is a good boy, just like 60,000 others who are sold into sex slavery every year."

"I'll get him back, ma'am," I said. "But I need to get on it."

"We have the FBI to handle kidnappings, Nick. They're exceptional at it."

"Now you're pitching me a curveball," I said.

"You can do more than that, Nick. I know it. My husband knows it. The forces he has at his legitimate disposal can be encumbered at times by rules of engagement and legal processes."

"What's this leading up to?"

"Are you at all aware of the world you are entering, Nick?"

"Ma'am, I've been globe-trotting ever since I hit D.C. a day and a half ago."

"Do not underestimate your situation, Nick. What you are about to challenge is no pizza parlor."

"I was hungry," I said.

"And the incident in your hotel room last night? And your cab ride to the Capitol to see Mr. Evans this morning? Do you think these events are unrelated?"

"Occupational hazards."

The media loved to give coverage to Yvonne Jackson. Before she met the President, our First Lady attended Swiss finishing schools. She earned a degree in international business from her native University of Hawaii. She spoke seven languages, partied in Monaco, appeared on late-night television shows.

"Do not be glib with me, Nick."

"No disrespect Mrs. Jackson. But it's true."

"I have my special attachment of select operatives. My husband and I believe you will make a quality addition to my team."

"Your team?"

"F.L.O.T.U.S."

"I know every law enforcement and military operation in the world. I've never heard of F.L.O.T.U.S."

"Of course, you haven't. We are a special assault team with unlimited lethality, but we're an all-civilian operation."

"So, if anyone is caught or killed nothing can be traced back to our government."

"And here you are. *El Peligro*. Literally delivered to our doorstep at exactly the time you're needed. I don't believe in coincidence. We are the Federal Lethal Operations Team of the United States."

"What do you do?" I felt my phone vibrate in my pocket. Fortunately, it was muted.

"We are not America's front line. We are not America's last line. We are America's bottom line. We get results. Dangerous results."

This sounded too good to be true. Work with the White House, take out bad guys with POTUS and FLOTUS oversight.

"Madame First Lady, that is the highest honor I've ever been given."

She enjoyed a demure smile that belied its self-satisfaction.

"But I have to decline." My phone buzzed again and continued its bothersome silent vibrations against my aching chest.

She recoiled in her chair. Her head moved back as if pushed, her eyes widened. She was speechless. *I don't think anyone's ever turned her down before. For anything.*

I spoke with as much grace as possible. "Madame First lady, I'm like Groucho Marx. He said, 'I refuse to join any group that -'."

She interjected with a swift cutting motion of her hand. "Enough! I'm well aware of the witticisms of Mister Marx," she said. "You aren't asked to join F.L.O.T.U.S. You don't turn down F.L.O.T.U.S. You are F.L.O.T.U.S. Nick, you are one of eight people in the world, now nine."

"You're setting out to save a special little boy. But if you're successful you'll go up against people and things more powerful and unscrupulous than you can imagine. This isn't at all a case of one little boy you're dealing with."

"Child sex trafficking has become woven into our society, despicable and demonic. Law enforcement can only detect it at its bottom, like you did the other night. I want it destroyed from the top down. And you have appeared at the right time, at the right place, with the right abilities to do just that."

I pushed my last remaining calling card out of its case and handed it to her. She rolled it back and forth in her palm.

"Quaint," she remarked. Then, "How did you get this past Secret Service?"

"It isn't live, just an engraved cartridge case and bullet. See? No primer."

"I have something for you in exchange," she said.

She reached for a jeweled clutch in the shape of a leopard. When she opened it and reached in, her hand came out holding a small teardrop shaped amulet on a slender black neck cord.

It was thin and unobtrusive, gold, with a small round red button in the center. When she extended her hand and presented it to me, she said, "Keep this with you. When you need us, press the button."

"And what, 'I've fallen, and I can't get up'?" I was getting drowsy again. I had half a pot of black coffee in me, and I was fighting off sleep. And losing.

"And we will be there. We support you."

I began to ask through heavy eyelids, "How will you know …?"

I heard her interject, "We will know. That is your Triad. It does three things for you."

She continued her detailed description of the little doodad, but her voice faded into an echo. Meanwhile, my body wanted to sit down under a shady tree and lean against it for a nap. My dopy thoughts ran wild. I tried to figure out any kind of angle on the kid's disappearance.

I sensed that my breakout lecture on the device was over and said, "Thank you, ma'am." Beneath my eyelids that that kept trying to close, I slid the thing into what was left of my pants pocket.

"You are now F.L.O.T.U.S., Nick," she said. "We don't call you. You call us."

With that, she rang for Sarah. "Bring Mister Wolfe's belongings, please?" she asked with a smile.

When Sarah returned with them, she handed my satellite phone to me and laid my smartphone on the desk. Mrs. Jackson pulled a phone from her clutch and touched it to mine. With that, she rose from her seat. She offered my phone back with her left hand and took my handshake with her right.

"*Aloha: Malama pono Akua, Kapu,*" she said. "Go with God, Mr. Wolfe."

I said, "You don't know half of it, ma'am."

Sarah turned me over to Liv, who escorted me back to the East Wing exit. When we reached the doors, I said, "*Tak so mucket*,"

Pleasantly surprised at my Swedish, Liv said, "*Du tala Svenska?*"

"*Jag*," I replied. I indicated my tattered condition with a smile. "*Nar du har din helda, du har just om allting!*"

She laughed. "Yes! When you have your health, you have just about everything!"

The wipers of my waiting replacement bulletproof Escalade kept a slow intermittent rhythm in the sprinkling rain. I climbed in and asked Taras to give me a minute before we set out.

I mentally compartmentalized everything that happened in the past eight hours. Too many compartments. I redirected my mind to what brought me back to D.C. in the first place.

My smartphone showed one voice mail message and one text from Victoria. She sounded excited and happy.

"Nick! I can't believe it! I make a good detective! I have a thumb drive with a video you'll want to see. I got it from the Chinese Laundry. I have it someplace special for you in my gallery."

I said to Taras Valdemar, "Drop me at the Victoria Taylor gallery. How are you fixed for tonight?"

"At your service," he replied.

22

This time, the place was quiet, but Victoria told me it was closed today. It was late in the afternoon when I pushed through the front glass doors. I hurried through the foyer of art that was so bad, it could only have been created by the purple-haired guy I saw there the night before.

Soft jazz music on the speakers invited me inside. I stepped into her initial showroom and announced my presence. "Hey, Vic -!"

And stopped.

My foot kicked into the body of a man who laid face down on the gallery's floor. A massive wound split his cranium open like a monk fruit. His head of close-cropped black hair was the centerpiece in a pool of his thick red blood.

The blue velvet bulldog sculpture I saw the night before lay nearby. It looked even weirder, split apart into two pieces on the floor.

A white pearl-handled switchblade glinted on the polished onyx showroom floor a few feet away.

The guy still breathed. With each desperate intake he made a hoarse, raspy gulp to capture air one last time. I leaned over him and studied his face and frame.

No sunglasses, but other than that he resembled the guy that wore the cyclops shades. Close cropped black hair, tightly drawn tan skin, medium sinewy frame. I nudged him with my foot, then toed him over so he faced upward.

His features were hard to distinguish through the gore of his split skull. He coughed and gurgled with blood in his throat. It wasn't Blue Turtleneck.

His pockets didn't yield a thing: pants front and back, shirt, jacket inside and out, crotch, socks, inside and under his shoes. Not a thing, except a quarter in his jacket pocket. One lousy quarter. One measly, stinking quarter.

I stood up and tried to sort things out. While a hundred thoughts crashed together in my brain, I flipped the coin in the air. Then I used it as a thinking stone and rubbed it between my thumb and fingers. Something didn't feel right.

When I brought it up close to my face for a better inspection I saw why. Stamped into the middle of George Washington's profile was a clearly defined symbol. It matched one of the symbols I tried to make out that night in the pizza shop.

I leaned down and whispered, "So, how much cash do Eurotrash hitmen get these days?"

He spewed blood and saliva from his lips when he spit out his accented retort. "Fuck you!"

"Who's paying you to kill me?"

His mouth sputtered his reply through terminal chokes and gurgles: "Fuck off!"

He blasted more intimate words of affection my way through lips that foamed with crimson spittle. I looked away to avoid his spray and saw her across the room in a corner.

Victoria lay face down, with her arms spread apart above her head. Her face was turned to one side. She wore a red 80's pantsuit with padded shoulders and red sling strap heels. A sanguine pool of blood around her lips glistened, thick and glossy in the bright directional lights.

Victoria's jet-black hair spread around her beautiful bone structure. In the gallery lighting, its sheen matched the glossy *noir* showroom floor that stretched out beneath her. It was difficult to define where one ended, and the other began.

Rage consumed my mind and body. I reached down for the near-dead hitman and yanked him off the floor by his jacket lapels. He couldn't stand, but I didn't want him to stand.

I held him up, dangled him in the air before me because I wanted him to look me straight in the eyes. I wanted him to see Death staring back at him. I wanted the sick bastard to feel what his shiv victims felt when he looked them in the eye and slipped his switchblade between their ribs.

I wanted him to know it was coming, and most of all, that it was coming here, and now, and from me and from my hands.

At first, he showed defiance. Then he locked my eyes. His irises darkened and matched his dilated pupils.

"That's it," I coaxed. "Get mad. Get real mad. Come on. Fight. Fight for your life." I watched as the panicked realization of death in his eyes spread across his features. He tried to scream but he only choked on his blood and his body stiffened in my mitts.

Call it professional courtesy. I did him a favor and snapped his neck.

The dirtbag hit the floor with a crumpled thud. I turned toward Victoria's fatal corner of the gallery.

Not wanting to believe that what I saw ahead of me was true, I crossed over to her. Victoria's red suit cut a vivid contrast to the high gloss black floor.

My hand reached out to touch her, but I stopped, then pulled it back. I didn't want to confirm by touch what my eyes knew had to be real.

I held Teresa in my arms and returned her stare of disbelief. Then I suffered that crushing, hollow, helpless feeling deep into your soul when you hold someone dear as their life leaves and their body falls limp in your hands.

You can get used to many of life's tragic adversities, but if you're sane you don't get used to the feel of death. I didn't want to experience that intimate touch of finality.

After I studied the countenance of her tranquil profile, I looked around and found a telephone. Mine was in my pocket, but her hardline would register all her data to 911.

A couple of steps away a futuristic Lucite writing table held a high-tech, low-tech hardline telephone. The actual telephone unit was a solid red design, inside a clear Lucite cylinder lit with red light from its ends.

A small hologram floated above the desk, the two of us from the party. The isolation image of us in full color slowly revolved around an axis so we were visible in 360 degrees. Victoria was stunning in her indigo beaded and sequined dress. All 360 degrees of her. I looked like I'd been hit by a train.

I inhaled and recalled the tuberoses in her Boucheron perfume.

"My life is an art gallery, Nick. With nice, quiet, creative, artistic people. Harmless people. I need to go back there."

Near the *Avant Gard* phone and out of place in this roomful of chrome, glass and tri celluloid acetate, rested a roughed-up horsehide baseball. A red thumb drive held it in its place. When I walked over and picked up the baseball, I saw the red pretzel **W** on the sweet spot.

"I have it someplace special for you in my gallery."

I figured the thumb drive to be the one Victoria talked about. The baseball with it could only be little Nick's.

I inserted the thumb drive into a nearby laptop. The video was from a high altitude high-definition night vision security camera. It focused on the front of the Chinese Laundry just down the street.

In a few seconds, the kid entered the frame. He walked alone down the sidewalk in the rain, plunked the baseball back and forth, in and out of his mitt. A pizza delivery van zipped into the frame and splashed gutter water up as it pulled alongside him. The marketing skin that covered its entire body advertised its name: Bolide Pizza Boutique.

The driver was the guy I just gave a fatal case of whiplash. As the van pulled alongside, a painted side door slid open and Blue Turtleneck jumped out onto the sidewalk behind little Nick. He bulldogged the kid like a roping steer and threw him into the van as it rolled.

The kid's baseball bounced out of the van and dropped into the street's gutter.

I figured the FBI boys had the video. I banked on them doing their jobs, so I pocketed the thumb drive and lit up a Red.

The crime scene surrounding me had to be called in to the police. I picked up the phone. The baseball rolled around in my fingers; I stared at the pretzel **W** as I dialed 9-1-

"What are you doing?" It was a woman's voice, and I'd heard that same voice say those same words before.

23

I looked up in shock. I still had ringing in my ears from the explosion. The ER people that morning warned me that I might hear things for a while. I replaced the red handset.

"You don't have anything better to do? A grown man?" she asked.

I looked over at the woman's body on the floor, then turned in the direction of the voice. Victoria Taylor stood behind me. But the standing version didn't wear a red eighties one-piece jumpsuit.

Her raven hair shone wet with perspiration. A loose-fitting fuscia pullover top bounced around the voluptuous body beneath it, above cheetah print yoga pants.

Her skin glowed beneath light, glistening sweat. That, with her relaxed attire, gave the appearance of someone who finished an intense workout. But this workout had been a struggle of life and death. Her movements were calm, but she was far from relaxed.

She stood in ballet slippers, raised a couple of inches to her tip toes and looked at me eye to eye. Better yet, she held a fresh cocktail in her hands. "I was in back, passing out don't you know," she said. "I made a drink. Want one?"

A long time ago a guy climbed outside onto a ledge, and I was elected to talk him back in. His voice then sounded like hers did now. Her words made all the logical, rational sense in the world. Except she was out of her mind with shock and wouldn't remember tomorrow anything she said today.

I nodded toward the body of her doppelganger in the red padded shoulders on the floor. I asked, "What the Hell is that?"

She replied with a voice of forced calm that restrained her fight-or-flight adrenaline. "That," she said, "is what we in the business call, Art. It was just delivered today."

She indicated the pieces of the broken bulldog on the floor, raised her drink in a mock toast. "Old Blue, I'm afraid is a different matter. Dead

181

loss. Poor little guy. A lot of things dying around here, lately."

She tossed back half of her cocktail without tasting it. "You know that little guy was priced at $50,000. Now I can have the artist sign both halves and get $50,000 for each one. I mean, now it has a history."

"Victoria," I said. She cut me off, said, "Of course, first it will have to be impounded as evidence in a murder scene." Then she lost it. "A murder scene!"

I drew in a soft breath and moved across to hold her in a reassuring hug. She stiff-armed me and forced me away with her head down. She cried. "Please! Take that video - whatever it is - and go."

I backed off my attempted embrace and spoke in earnest. "Victoria, I -"

"No," she demanded and briskly backed away a step. Her eyes were wide, but unseeing. I talked to a 5' 8" doll.

She was terrorized. Fought for her life and won. I wanted to help her, remove some stress, so I offered, "I'll call 911 and handle the police when they get here."

Her eyes jumped back to life and glared at me. Her voice came out strong as her vision came into focus with reality. "Like Hell, you will."

I was speechless.

"That guy came into my place. He attacked me. I defended myself. I smashed his head. I'll call the cops. I'll tell them about it. And I'll handle it, thank you very much."

"Victoria …"

She averted her eyes and turned away. She tried to use the same voice she spoke with the afternoon when we first met. But this time, her timbre was different. She couldn't hold back her tears. Without looking at me, she said,

"No. I will not have dinner with you. I will not laugh at your … I will not date you. I will not sleep with you … and I mean it. Please. Go."

So, I left.

It was only a few blocks to the Hotel Washington. I told Taras Valdemar and his motorized luxury beast to scram for the night. I decided against going straight back to the hotel. There was one quick detour I wanted to take. Besides, I needed time to think.

I took my time and hoofed it down the sidewalk. I tossed little Nick's baseball back and forth between my hands as my mind battled between thoughts and feelings.

My head was caught between two classic warring parties, one on each shoulder. The angel on my right pressed for my mind to concentrate on the clues I had. It told me to focus more on little Nick's path down the street. The left one wanted me to recognize Victoria's feelings and process the loss of her, that I hoped was temporary.

We'd only known each other 24 hours, but I felt drawn to her. I recalled the night before: her smooth skin and silky hair that smelled of floral perfume. The seductive passion I felt in her body that night in my hotel room. And a dream I'll never forget: Victoria sat up in bed, the lines of her body, fluid in the moonlight.

It only took one coffee conversation to appreciate her quick mind and razor-sharp wit. Victoria Taylor was a lot of woman, and I wanted every ounce of her.

I hoped the proverb, "Time heals all wounds" was true. I planned on returning after time allowed emotions and memories to fade. This one was too good to let get away.

* * *

Only three people had my satellite telephone number. James Murgatroyd Fontenot was one of them. His ringtone reminded me I hadn't checked back since I left. I was sure there were messages on my cell phone and my hotel room voice mailbox.

I looked at my watch: happy hour. I sat down on a covered bus bench and took his call.

James opened with, "I'm about to clock out and head to Vic's Vodka Lounge. I thought I would inquire about why our account just received an electronic deposit of a half million dollars?"

"I have no idea," I said. "What's the identifying bank and routing?"

"That's just it. There isn't any," he said. "I traced it back to the bank that issued the payment, or I tried to. Nothing. This isn't my first rodeo, hombre. I can work bank scams. This is as unidentifiable as it is legit."

I was impressed and smiled. "Wow," I thought out loud. "They work fast."

"Who?" James insisted.

I thought out loud: "F.L.O.T.U.S."

"We're still speaking English, right?"

"FLOTUS. The First Lady. We met this afternoon. I'll catch you up later. I'm going inside on a lead about the kid. They're about to close."

James' voice almost knocked me down over the phone. "You met Yvonne Jackson! For gorgeous! And so, so …"

"Elegant?" I offered.

"Yes! Where? When? What was she like?"

I reflected for a moment on the vision I met with only hours before: the power and poise she exuded from behind that metal military desk, her Swiss boarding school charm, the enchanting Polynesian beauty of her light brown eyes, cheekbones, skin, hair, and the tall athletic figure that filled out her Madame Chiang Kai-shek dress.

"Nice rack."

"You're an ass," he said. "Maybe she'll introduce you to the President."

"Yeah," I said. "Maybe. Look, I'll call tonight. I'm checking out this Chinese Laundry."

"Nick - I keep telling you, you can't go around using stereotypes like laundries being Chinese. Call it by its name, not its ethnicity. Jeez."

I looked up at the sign above my head that ran the full 30-foot length of the storefront. Large bright red letters flashed their message to the street in all capitals: CHINESE LAUNDRY.

"I'll get right on that." My satellite phone showed it was down to 5% battery power. It featured an instant GPS locator button, and its global range was the best in the business, but its battery wasn't, with only 30 hours of standby time.

The owners of the place were a likable couple. I caught them as they puttered around and closed their shop at the end of the day. Thick glasses obscured her eyes, but not her beaming smile. I perceived him as better looking at his current age, handsome with features created by character, than the countertop picture of him when he was an undeveloped young man.

They knew nothing. The baseball was in the gutter when they opened their store early the morning after Nick disappeared. Victoria ran through their security videos with them and edited the segment I saw onto the thumb drive that I had in my pocket.

They said they were happy to give the ball and video to her. That was evident now with me, as well. They were excited by my local celebrity, Capitol Hill's new "Mr. Pizza Chop Chop."

One interesting detail came out by accident during our conversation. The FBI never came calling. Victoria had the only copy of the video other than the Changs' original.

24

I thanked the Changs for their help, pushed out the door to the descending twilight and mist on the street. My next destination was a couple of blocks away. I deferred to the logic and reason on my right shoulder and parked my feelings on my left.

The cop on duty outside the Bolide Pizza Boutique kept watch from inside his MPD-mobile. I ducked under the wet yellow caution tape and approached his car.

"Lieutenant Diliberto!"

He turned, looked out his window at me. Through the glass, I heard a muted, "You!"

I waited until he rolled his window down part way. "I get that a lot lately."

"Get away from me!" He pretended to go for his console-mounted riot gun.

I protested. "Lieutenant. Listen to me."

He said, "I had to go back to the lockers and take a shower." He looked me in the eyes, then closed his and drew in a breath. "Don't tell me you just came from the Victoria Taylor Gallery."

"That's quick, Roscoe. I'm impressed. Your buddies should be there right now."

"I shoulda figured you'd be involved."

"I'm not; just a passerby. Victoria Taylor is. She whacked an attacker that got between her and a blue bulldog. I walked in to see her right after. I read the scene and left. She wanted to handle the 911 call herself."

He looked me up and down, wrinkled his nose. "I'm not the only one who needs clothes and a bath."

"Isn't this a long shift for you, Roscoe?"

"I volunteered. Long day. I just wanted to sit someplace quiet. Alone!"

"I know the feeling. I want to go in and poke around."

He looked away with a grimace. "Why not. Everybody else has. But don't be all night."

I was sure that everyone from the MPD to the FBI to Whistler's mother turned the place over since my impromptu pizza party.

I opened the glass doors that pictured little kids who romped and played among geometric shapes. When I entered, I left the dim pall that blanketed D.C. The blazing whiteness created by overhead lighting that bounced off the tile walls and floor created unpleasant memories.

Everything behind the counter was examined, photographed, and any potentially meaningful evidence collected and removed. So, they'd say.

Dried fire extinguisher foam spread in and out of the police outline markings on the floor where my tango partner from the day before cashed in his last dance ticket. I examined tables, benches, chairs, trash bins. All picked over. Good. At least somebody was doing their job.

The bathroom looked like a scene from a B crime movie. Chalk body outline of Shanghai Pat in the hallway, fingerprint dust all over the place. Still, I gave every row of white tile a thorough inspection. Nothing.

A small storage closet on the other side of the short hall provided a lot to look at. But it was just a lot of shelves that held cleaning supplies and maintenance tools.

I surveyed the pizza-making ingredients on the shelves. Some on-the-spot practice as a pizza chef called to me. I was starved, but my guts were so sore I felt no desire to consume anything.

The thick door to the walk-in refrigerator pushed open. It remained fully operational, along with the ovens, appliances and lights. Not the lights.

The fridge was the only room that was dark. I flipped the wall switch. Nada. Zippo.

I thumbed my lighter and torched up a Red. Shadows flowed around on the walls and floor like dark liquid from its flickering light. This place looked the same as the other rooms, except these items needed cold storage. Stainless steel shop racks held boxes, plastic containers, some sealed, some opened.

Suddenly, the flame from my lighter pulled forward from me and down, as if someone opened a door. I looked behind me. The fridge door was still open. I closed it, leaned forward and held the flame down in the blackness, in the direction it pulled before.

A few seconds later, it reached further forward again, and down. I got down on the floor. On both knees and one hand, I held the lighter aloft with the other.

It was in the corner, beneath a couple of stacks of boxes. The trap door's front lip aligned with the front edges of a pile of stacked boxes. This even pairing of edges made the covered opening almost impossible to notice, even when I looked straight at it.

The large boxes on top of it marked, "Pepperoni" were instead packed with white lies: Styrofoam cups. I slid the featherlight boxes off the big lid and lifted it. My lighter only showed that its flame was too weak for me to see what was in the pitch-black depths below.

Unfortunately, satellite phones do not download apps, so no flashlight. But my standard smartphone did. I activated its flashlight and looked below.

As far as the light carried forward, I saw a brick tunnel with a dirt floor. It ran in two directions directly beneath the pizza shop.

I propped the trapdoor open behind me. I toed my way, step-by-step down brick stairs that showed recent use, wear, and no dust. As far as I could see, the tunnels were arched, standing height, made of brick. In both directions they stood about one person wide.

When my shoes thumped down on the dirt floor, I looked down the tunnels both ways. I reached out and ran my fingers along one wall. These weren't the Tiber Creek tunnels from D.C.'s cholera epidemic. They reminded me of the countermines in the Petrovaradin Fortress in Serbia. The superb brickwork made them at least 250 years old, built before the 1863 aqueducts.

It had to be a system of underground countermines. They would have been used to protect Capitol Hill and the surrounding area of innermost Washington, D.C. If they were installed after August 24, 1814, they were useless; if they were dug before that, they weren't used. That's the date the British burned the U.S. Capitol and the Presidential Mansion.

Civilization and Progress must have forgotten about them and paved them over. This ancient passage wasn't referenced in any tourist's guide to D.C.'s underground. I crept forward about 80 feet and came to an intersection with an adjoining brick tunnel that led off to the left.

I had a hunch I was on the main highway and decided to keep moving in my same direction. I also wanted to remember how to get back.

An abrupt suction of air pulled me forward, followed by the most chilling sound I've ever heard. It cut through the stale air like long cold knives.

25

An ear-splitting shockwave of terrified screams echoed down the old brick tunnels from in front of me. Panic-stricken cries of desperation wrenched themselves loose from the lungs of children. A lot of children. I couldn't estimate how many. I heard the rattling and clanging of metal cages.

I stood rooted to the floor, confused. Hell, I was horrified. And I felt fear of the one thing I can't control: the unknown.

Before I had time to think about it, I raced down the tunnel in the direction of the screams. The light from my cell phone's flashlight bounced off the walls. I chased it past another dark and empty underground connection to the left. Soon, I came to the end of my tunnel.

I slowed to a stop and looked out at an immense underground cavern. The voices ahead of me died down to moans and the anguished cries of kids sobbing.

I made a mental note; I passed two dark offshoot tunnels on my left getting there. The stairway up to the hatch was about a hundred yards behind me. I left the hatch open so I could find it again.

In the grotto ahead of me, the light was a bleak green that glowed throughout the chamber. The flashlight from my phone changed from being a welcome friend to an enemy that betrayed my presence, so I killed its light.

I paused to give my eyes a moment for visual decompression., then peered from the end of my tunnel into the vast chamber ahead.

The fully bricked and arched cavern that opened before me could house a pair of hot air balloons. What it held was beyond awful – beyond disgusting. But real, and in front of my eyes.

I steadied myself with one hand on the dusty brick wall. I leaned out and surveyed the vast subterranean space, aghast. Not one conscious muscle of mine moved, but I felt my blood boil inside my veins.

Before me, a system of steel framework shop cages rose from the brick floor, one row atop another. The structure was four cages high, four cages wide and two rows deep. Some steel structures were empty, but half of the metal cells imprisoned a terrified boy or girl.

Nobody guarded the dungeon prison. Apart from the captives, the place was empty. Beyond and around the structure, I made out five more tunnel openings like the one I stood in that led away from the roundhouse cavern. Each one exited in a different direction.

On a wall across the massive hall, I saw a large white dry-erase board. On it, an administrative grid system laid out the position of each cage.

Every square on the board showed a cage position grid code that identified each cell. An additional hand-marked code for F or M plus a number like 6, 9, 10, 12 completed the squares that held kids. The only other feature was a large round red industrial button mounted alone, a few feet away on the wall.

I took a step inside the cavern toward the structure, then stopped. What my eyes picked up in the topmost, centermost cage, sucker punched me in my gut.

My previous emotional trio of, "stunned, confused and horrified," vanished. The taste of acid filled my mouth. A hair-raising adrenaline rush of battle lust started at my back and spread like fire beneath my skin. It coursed throughout my body like a wild animal, raised its hackles from my feet to my butt to my fingertips to the back of my neck.

The kid in the topmost, centermost cage facing me was Nick White. He still wore his torn and dirtied Senators jersey and ball cap. My jaws clenched and my fists balled tight. I was about to blast past ballistic and go nuclear.

This time my arguing entities on each shoulder fought it out over fight/flight emotional response versus cooler heads prevailing. It was a struggle, but the cooler heads won. I looked across at the large white board grid. Nick was identified as A-1-B-9.

I sneaked toward the cage, motioned to the kids not to make a sound. They shared a collective stunned silence at the sudden appearance of a benevolent stranger. I focused on what I needed: stealth, search, escape.

Their cages' outward-facing doors were locked, but it looked like there might be another way to reach little Nick. Each cage had a trapdoor in its bottom. Two cages below him were open, and I could get to them by angling my way through two others to one side.

The kids kept quiet behind their hushed sobs. I got down on my hands and knees. I crawled and barely fit through the door of the first cell on the bottom row. I squeezed through to its adjacent cell to one side, but I needed help with my contortions.

I twisted around, collapsed my shoulders, pushed with my legs, and stood up. It took a moment for me to catch my breath. I was standing straight up through two cages directly beneath Nick.

He gripped the rods that made up his cage as he watched my struggle to reach him. When I got to a position close enough to hear, he leaned down to his floor toward me. He whispered, "You played catch with me." I nodded. Then, he asked, "Why did you do this to me?"

I looked up at him from the constrictions of my temporary imprisonment. I almost yelled. "What?" I whispered, much too loud. "I've been killing people for two days finding you, kid. I'm here to get you out. Just do what I say when I say it."

The kid gave a silent salute without a word.

You could say I was in a tight spot. The openings for the cage doors, top, bottom or sides were kid sized. My arms were jammed down against my sides so all I could do was stand, look around and talk.

It looked like I could open the latch on the kid's bottom trapdoor from my cage beneath him, but my arms were locked down at my sides in the narrow space, out of position to do it. I needed to drop down and reach back up -

Clang! The bottom row cage door I crawled through to stand up slammed shut by my feet. I heard it lock with a following click.

26

Dozens of kids screamed again. They grabbed their cage bars and shook them without restraint. A thunderous clamor echoed off the walls of the cavern. I jerked my head around to see the source of their fears.

He stood at the board with the grid chart. The cyclops thug I identified as Blue Turtleneck looked at his smartphone. This time, he was dressed for a party: black leather pants and jacket, red turtleneck and red cyclops shades. *In this dimmer than dim ghoulish green light, he wore red cyclops sunglasses.*

He touched the screen of his phone. The lock on a floor level cage door near me clicked open. He flashed a sickening jagged smile in my direction, then walked to the cage adjacent to my feet. Its occupant was a cute little black-haired girl in a pink and white polka dot dress with a pink ribbon in her hair. He laughed when he opened its door.

She screamed as he snatched her arm. She fought; she grabbed her cage; her arms showed the red from his grip's pressure against the fairness of her juvenile skin. The little girl hung on with her fingers as long as she could. The children screamed and shook their subterranean prison when they rattled their steel structures.

Eventually, his strength outlasted her desperation. Cyclops dragged her, kicking and screaming for all she was worth, through the entrance to a tunnel across from ours and was gone.

Nick whispered, "What's going on?"

I said, "I don't know, and you don't want to know."

I wriggled around in my destroyed jacket but to no avail. The bandages over an exhausted body from a long day held me tight. And I was pinned into place as I stood up in the two vertical cages.

"Are you sure you're the one doing the killing?" he asked. "You don't look so good."

"Kid, I've got two phones on me. One of 'em will get us out of here. But I'm pinned; I can't get to them. You'll need to do it."

I stood as tall as I could to get the inner pockets of my suit as high and near him as possible. Nick reached down through his cage's floor, stretched further. I felt his fingertips when they touched the top of my shoulder. I tiptoed as high as I could; he shoved his shoulder hard into the steel bars of his floor and stretched his fingers for my jacket.

When I leaned as far as I could to one side, he reached a hand into one breast pocket and barely – almost dropped it – slid out my phone. He gripped it with the fingers of both hands and guided it to the bars that separated our cages.

He made sure he had a secure hold on it and moved it up toward him. The cage bar openings were close to the size of my phone's girth. When he pulled it up and through, I saw that he'd lifted my satellite phone.

I said, "Look, there's a button on that thing marked -"

He held the phone in one hand and pointed at the GPS button with the index finger of his other hand.

"Press that and four people will immediately get our exact location and know it's a call for help." *Four people will look for us — above ground, on a street or in a store, whatever is at street level above us.*

He pressed it. Nothing. No buttons responded. Battery dead.

I remembered Yvonne Jackson's amulet in my pants pocket. I contorted my shoulder and arm and lifted my hand near my pocket opening. My fingertips clawed their way inside it when the cages shook again. I lost my footing and my hand jerked loose.

Cyclops returned. The kids screamed. He strolled around the portable prison in a slow, cocky manner with a twisted smirk on his cruel lips. In one hand he brandished a black anodized aluminum nightstick. He pushed a button on it; blue sparks crackled from its end.

He neared me, leaned against the cages with one hand. He drummed his fingers as he spoke. I thought I heard the voice of a mynah bird or a cockatiel with its high-pitched, squeaky voice.

"The others are for them. They gave you to me."

He jammed the end of his electrified nightstick into my left calf. A paralyzing jolt shot up my leg through my spine and into my brain. My body convulsed and I lost control. Only the restriction of the tight walls in the small cages held me up.

I was conscious, but in excruciating pain and powerless. He zapped me again on the other leg. His shrieking laugh tortured my ears like a marine air horn.

"Five million volts, cowboy!" He hit me again.

Through bleary eyes I saw the horror-stricken look on the kid's face. I watched the dim green light fade. The shock burned its way through my body and brain again. And again.

I lost count of how many times he shocked me. I didn't feel anything anymore. My vision faded. I fell into a deep blackness as if I plunged toward oblivion. I couldn't see, couldn't hear, couldn't feel. Didn't care.

I was lying down on my back and tried to sit up. An invisible immovable force held me down. I tried again. And again, I was held down.

This was the purgatory of my worst childhood nightmares. I laid in bed, feeling the silent pressure of an unknown force suspended over my head like the Sword of Damocles.

The only way to get rid of it was to defeat it and to do that I had to sit up. Every time it appeared, I tried to sit up in defiance. Every time, it held me down into feelings of claustrophobia. I couldn't sit up until I reached down deep inside, decided to give it everything I had as if my life depended on it, and bolted upright for all I was worth. I often awoke in the middle of the night, sitting up in bed, dripping cold sweat.

I was back there again, only this time it was no dream, no nightmare. This time I knew it was real. It knew it, too. This time was The Showdown.

I never knew the dark force that was behind my nightmare's overhead demon: never saw it, never heard it, and only felt its omnipresence.

This time it spoke. In a voice as powerful and frightening as can be imagined it declared, "I am evil incarnate."

That did it. Beaten up, blown up and shocked, I was filled with battle rage. I felt the power in my chest and arms grow from adrenaline. My lips still worked, and I spoke out loud: "All right, motherfucker," I said with disgust. "I'm sick of this shit. I'm ending it now. Come on; let's go. I'm going to rip off your head and shit down your neck."

I felt it before I finished my soliloquy. The relief. The quiet. The calm. The peace. It was gone. Everything was gone, the pressure, the fear, the sweat. I was alone, but I'd won. It quit and split, like all cowards do when confronted face to face.

I came around to consciousness, but I didn't want to. It felt good there; sleeping was comfortable. I'd had enough exercise for one day.

When my eyes opened, I tried to remember where I was. I looked around at myself, tried to figure out why I was confined.

Nick White sat above me in his cage, cross-legged atop the bars that made up his cage's floor. He fiddled with something in his hands. "Dude, you've been out for a couple of hours."

27

I was still woozy. I said, "Is that my phone?" My head wanted to droop. I fought back puking; my guts were too sore. It wasn't pretty when I retched and heaved, but I was victorious over regurgitation. "Give me a minute and I'll get us out of here."

"I'm ready to get us out of here now," said the kid. "I've been waiting for you to wake up after I got your smart phone out of your jacket." He turned it around and showed me its face.

"See? I've watched them. This whole Jungle Gym is controlled by an app. They use it to run the cages. I know my position and number, A1. Now that I have a phone, I think I can open the door at your feet."

I indicated the wall with the white board and controls. "That big button must be a master emergency switch for a mass release. Get me out of here. I'll go hit it and get us all out."

He punched the phone with his finger. The door by my feet swung open.

It was difficult enough to get up to the kid going forward when I twisted my way through the cages. Getting out backward after playing shockwave with Cyclops got me thinking about taking up croquet.

My jacket got caught on a cage corner; my banged up knee didn't want to bend at the obtuse angle I needed it to. My lighter fell out of my pocket. It clattered down through the cages to the floor below the little black haired girl's cell. *My grandfather's Zippo.*

I clambered out and fell onto the floor of the pedophile prison. My fingers clutched the cold steel of the cages' bars. I pulled myself up off the floor by climbing up the cage bars with my hands. I was exhausted from pain, but I clawed my way to a standing position.

I took a big, expanded lung intake of foul air and stretched. My eyes searched the floor in the dim green light for my lighter. I looked up for a moment. The cages stood directly in front of my face.

Children. The eyes of children widened by fright they'd never known. They reached out to me through the cage bars, tried to pull me to them for help. These kids were horrified; their fear stifled their voices. They stayed silent with only quiet whimpers.

I turned and looked across the expansive room at the big board and red button. I walked, halfway doubled over, clutching my stomach with one hand. My other hand pulled my .45s from its holster.

My unsteady locomotion across the packed dirt floor almost failed. When I reached the big red button, I searched around to see if there was any way to determine its function.

The Hell with it. I didn't have time for 20 questions, and I was pissed. And packing. I hit the damn button.

One by one the cage doors swung open; eventually, all of them. Despite the fact that they were all little kids with constitutions of cartilage, it took a few moments for their mobility to get going again. Their unfortunate bodies were cramped in those metal cages for God knows how long.

I motioned to them to keep quiet with my index finger to my lips. With my gun hand, I waved them along to follow me. The kid stayed at my side. He asked, "Is this the way out of here?"

"Just follow me," I whispered.

The kid noticed the big double-barreled automatic in my hand. "Wow!" he said with a restrained voice.

Six tunnel openings gaped open in all directions, 360 degrees around us. I knew the direction I came from and paused at the entrance to the tunnel. My head was still foggy, my muscles were cramped and sore and my stomach felt like mush.

I used the flashlight on my phone and headed into the tunnel the kid at my side. About two dozen other kids followed. They had no choice but to trust me and keep quiet as we shuffled forward together along the dirt floor.

We moved ahead about fifty feet when I saw a light that spilled into our tunnel from the right. It could be either good or bad. I immediately shut off my light. *The two tunnels were dark and empty when I came in earlier.*

I motioned to the kids to stay put, handed Nick my phone. I gripped a pistol in each hand; my back pressed against the brick tunnel wall. I sidestepped forward toward the lighted opening.

A few paces ahead, I paused. After a couple of seconds and a deep breath, I peered around the corner. The source of white light that overflowed into our tunnel was not from another tunnel but emanated from another large domed chamber. It was big, bright, and ghastlier than anything I've seen in fiction or fact.

28

The first thing that hit me was the odor. The stench of recently opened bodies in a closed space permeated the dank tunnel air with the smell of Death. If I had an airline bag, I might have used it. Some of the kids behind me stifled gags. One of the bigger boys held a pre-teen's hair as she hurled onto a brick wall.

Unlike the gloomy pedophile prison yard, this room blazed with light that illuminated everything I wish I never saw. Dozens of torches burned on the walls and in the hands of people who stood below me.

It could have passed for a typical production lab, but here and now it was a rendering plant for humans. Young humans. Homo Sapiens veal.

A cold storage machine displayed plastic-wrapped body parts through its glass doors: hands, feet, heads, organs. Some people inside the big room wore brown hooded robes. They unwrapped some of these monstrosities and passed them around. They smiled and laughed when they devoured them as *hors d'houevres*.

A production line consisted of gurneys, tables, cutting machines, a band saw, weigh scales, cabinets and a standing industrial packaging plastic wrap machine. These were surrounded by a sect that celebrated a gruesome event of child sacrifice.

From my elevated position, I had to exert extreme mind control to partition my shock and horror. I needed to concentrate and pick up details of the scene before me.

At least fifty people gathered in a semicircle and faced outward toward me and their leader, who stood in their center and presided. He wore a robe of black satin, with a red symbol of angular magic on the back and red lining inside the hood. I almost got a glimpse of his face, but he turned away.

A couple of dozen men and women in brown robes clustered around their leader. They held their hands high in a worshipful stance. More underlings in white robes ringed outside the brown robes to complete the unholy congregation in their subterranean temple of evil.

I quickly scanned the brown robes because all their faces were visible with their hoods down. When I realized that I recognized many of them it made me feel sicker.

Inside this chamber of horrors, a half-circle ring formed around the one who wore black and red. And I recognized every one of them: department directors, senators, actors, all part of the D.C. power structure.

No rendering workers were present to produce shrink-wrapped pediatric body parts for storage and delivery. That work was complete. Tonight, this chamber housed only those who celebrated the fruits of those labors.

Their chanting in monotone unison echoed off the vaulted brick walls. One of them moved aside; I got a direct look at the object of their attention. In front of the figure robed in black, a little girl lay naked on a table before them, vivisected.

She was drugged with massive local anesthetics throughout her body parts. Her conscious face was forced to watch as the ghouls dipped inside her opened body and dined on her live organs.

The voice of the black robed ringmaster proclaimed, "Tonight we near a hallowed moment! Halloween is anon. We are rich with sacrifice for our dark lord! This is the first night of sacrifice to he who rules below and will soon rise above!" His followers chanted and ohm'ed. Soon, we will rule the world!"

With that, the fiend bent over and, with a huge gleaming ceremonial blade, decapitated the little girl. He lifted her dripping, gory head and held it high to the exultations of his evil congregation. The little black-haired girl's pink ribbon was still tied in her hair.

When the murderer in black and red threw his head back in heinous glory, I got a dead solid look at his face: Speaker of the House, John Evans.

A flash of bright white light blinded me in the darkness. It didn't come from the chamber below, but from us. I looked down. The kid stood beside me with my smartphone. He looked up at me in shock. "I was videoing – the flash went off!"

I raised my arms and motioned back toward the direction we came from. "Back!" I yelled. "Everybody back! Run! Run!"

The kids screamed and ran back to the entrance of the tunnel and the chamber of cages. When the room widened, I rushed past them and found my original tunnel on the opposite side. I was too woozy earlier to register the 180-degree discrepancy.

I roared at Nick, "Run for about a football field! Pass two tunnels on your right! Trapdoor's open at the top of the steps." He ran off and led the kids into the tunnel's darkness with the phone's flashlight in his hands. I turned around with two handguns in mine.

Behind me receded the sounds of footfalls made by a score of terrorized children. Before me clattered a wave of white robed ghouls that wanted to eat them.

I needed to conserve my ammo, so I held my fire. I backed down the tunnel toward the kids. The ghouls would come at me any second, but they were confined within the tunnel walls. I'd be shooting ducks in a barrel.

Here they came. I heard their footfalls and waited to hear gunfire. They weren't carrying guns; they didn't think they'd need them at their unholy safe zone. I saw the glints of their blades in the lights of their torches. They wanted to hack us to apart.

The sounds of the kids' footfalls behind me were gone, drowned out by the bringers of my impending donnybrook. I backed down the tunnel with my guns ready and waited for the pedophile parade to march into my optimum firing range.

First, I saw the lights, then the torches, then the blades, ahead of the white robes. Their hoods flew behind their bouncing heads as they rushed at me, compressed by the tunnel's walls into single file.

My Italian-made .45s bucked in my right hand. The double-barreled semi-automatic handgun by Arsenal Arms fired two .45 ACP bullets with each trigger pull. The first runner blew back into the first runner-up behind him.

When my target crumpled into a heap on the dirt floor, his ardent follower crashed down on top of him.

In the lights that fired forward from my barrels, I saw the second one hit the dirt. I fired a pair of slugs into his head. It exploded into a water balloon of blood when the cannibal that ran behind him crushed it beneath his feet in his haste.

He and his blood-soaked foot tried to evade my fire by running up on the wall of the tunnel at full speed. I pivoted to my left; my .38 barked out another flash in the tunnel's torch lit obscurity. He clutched his guts and crumpled to the floor with a yelp.

I backed down the tunnel further toward the kids, my eyes as wide as I could hold them to gather light. Several more freaks rushed at me out of the darkness. I tasted the adrenaline in my mouth.

I blasted the .45s into the first one, fired another shot from the .38 into the next, the .45s again, then the .38. In the flashes of my guns, I saw the bodies hit the dirt as more white robes flew at me over them.

If I ran out of bullets before they ran out of bodies, we were headed for a bloody hand-to-hand fight I didn't look forward to. A few seconds later I backed into a kid.

I yelled, "What the hell are you doing here? Get up the steps!"

Nick's voice called down from the top of the steps at the trapdoor. "We can't!" he said. "It's blocked shut!"

Another robe charged me with his torch and shimmering assassin's blade. My left fist shot forward and sent a .38 hollow point bullet into his chest. A crimson stain spread across the robe's whiteness - between a pair of tits. Big tits. The hood fell back from the red-headed female ATF Director who face-planted in the dirt at my feet.

I listened for footfalls and didn't hear any. I scrambled up the stairs past the kids. Nine-year-old Nick took my guns in his hands so I could use both of mine to press upward on the trap door. It was as tight as if latched and weighted down by a gang of lead.

I looked down at the terrified faces of a couple of dozen kids. They pressed together in the tunnel as close to the stairs as possible, as far from the rampaging ghouls as they could get. I wasn't about to get this far and lose it all now.

Another pervert crept toward us over the bodies of his dead pals. He clutched a massive blade behind the scant protection of his torch. A shot echoed down the tunnel walls. He hit the dirt and raised a dust cloud in the throes of his anguish.

The kid aimed my .38 and squeezed the trigger again. The resounding click of the gun's hammer told me we he was out of ammo. It also showed me that the kid didn't flinch. A moment later the guy stopped his gastrointestinal suffering and laid still.

I fumed with frustration and anger. "Michael," I said. "You're pissing me off. Get us out of here!"

A little boy below me with freckles and glasses looked at the other kids, then stared up at me. His voice trembled. "How do I do that, mister?"

I stood up and slammed my shoulders into the door. It didn't budge. I slammed it again as hard as I could, reared back down and hit it again. Nothing. It might as well have been a solid concrete ceiling.

My ears picked up another set of dirt-muffled footfalls headed our way down the tunnel. My eyes watched the faces of the kids as they looked at me with pitiful combinations of hope and fear.

I didn't want to do it, but I had to. The straits were dire, and it wasn't just me; there were a couple dozen lives at stake. I reached inside my pocket for my Triad and pressed the red button.

WHOA! An instant surge of energy shot through my body. It began in my heart and raged outward to my toes and fingertips. I felt indestructible. I could lift mountains. I drew in a breath and filled my chest with air.

The palms of both my hands pressed the trap door; I braced my feet on the step that gave me the best leverage upward. I jammed my eyes shut and readied every muscle. My body felt invincible. I took a deep breath. One ... two ...

I slammed upward into the hatch with everything I had. The door flew open above me. It smashed against the floor on the other side of its hinges. I sprang upward through it like a high jumper on a trampoline.

My body seemed to float for a second above the trap door opening, then I came down on the floor of the walk-in fridge, flat on my two feet. I looked through the darkness, right into the face of Lieutenant Roscoe Diliberto.

29

He was as surprised as I was to see each other. He barked, "About time! Where the Hell have you been? I heard you banging in here -"

I said, "We've been *in* Hell! Get these kids up and out of here!" I jumped back down through the trap door. I bypassed the steps full of terrified kids scrambling upward when I dropped 15 feet to the floor below. It felt as if I dropped six inches onto a featherbed.

One by one, I helped each kid scramble up the brick steps and outside to freedom and safety. Lt. Diliberto used his flashlight and helped pull the kids out from above. The kid handed my guns back and bounded upward and out of sight.

Another freak came at me with his torch and blade. My .45s fired, then hung open, empty on both sides. In the double-barreled flash, I watched Percy Hunter slam back into the wall from the impact of the twin exploders. This just wasn't his week.

Blood gushed out of his mouth and over his lips; the crimson fluid spilled down onto the front of his white robe. He convulsed from the shock of the pair of half-inch holes that opened the front of his stomach and the vacuum left behind when his guts blew out his back.

I helped push the last couple of kids up through the trap door. The last one was on the top step of the walk-in when the shrill screams of a Banshee cut through the tunnel's blackness. I faced down the shaft full of dead bodies and backed up the steps through the opening. I held two empty pistols in my hands.

The shrieking thing came at me down the brick shaft with amazing speed. My phone's flashlight clicked on behind me. What it revealed made me grimace with revolt.

Whatever it was, it had never seen daylight. Its entire body and face were pale white, with scant, random outcroppings of fine black hair. It came at me on four legs like a dog, then moved from four legs to an ape-like biped up the steps. It stood erect at the trap door and glared at me with red eyes and hideous pointed teeth.

And it stunk. My God, but it smelled foul. Its stench was more overpowering than its hideous presence was fearful. Kearny, New Jersey smelled better on a hot day.

All I had left was my derringer: El Diablo, a 12-gauge sawed-off shotgun black powder pistol in a cross-draw rig. The creature charged up at me through the opening in the floor. I fired both barrels one at a time point-blank into its face and watched its head explode as it fell backward down the stairs. "*Sayonara*, bitch."

I slammed the metal door shut and latched it. I covered it with the heaviest objects I could find, the same heavy boxes that were moved into place after I went spelunking. This time, with the power delivered through my Triad, they felt like they were the boxes of Styrofoam cups.

The kids circled up in the empty pizza joint's seating area. Lieutenant Diliberto held his collar squawker near his mouth as he called in to his police service area office. "Wait!" he said. "Who am I talkin' to here? You ain't MPD. This is a secure police line, lady."

He paused, fumbled as he plugged an earphone into his shoulder mounted squawk-box. "Say again, lady? First Lady? Yeah, and I'm Christopher Columbus. Look, get off this frequency. You're gonna get arrested."

Nick rushed up to me. "You, OK?" he asked. I groaned when I got down to talk to him at eye level. My smile made me wince, but I managed to say, "I'm buying the ice cream."

He leaped up and threw his arms around my neck. His embrace was strong, and he didn't want to let go. I peeled his arms apart and took a quick inventory. Three empty pistols. Satellite phone. Smartphone... "Where's my Smartphone?"

He held it out before me. "I got it all on video!" He replaced the phone and pulled me to him. He whispered into my ear. "Let's get out of here!"

I returned the whisper. "Let's get out of here!"

My visual and mental acuity due to the Triad's wonder drug were amazing. I made a quick scan of the room. Without effort I assessed the overall situation, heard every word of Lieutenant

Diliberto's conversation, took a total head count and assessed the face of every kid.

I had never done any recreational or performance enhancing drugs. Maybe I was missing something, because I had to admit, whatever the F.L.O.T.U.S. Rx was, it was a wild ride.

The kid snuck over to the front door and held it open. He waved to the other kids to follow. I replaced him, held the door wide. Outside in the dark, I whispered just loud enough for them to hear, "I'm buying us hot dogs and ice cream!"

Inside among the bright white lights, the good Lieutenant closed his eyes in concentration. He held one ear shut with the index finger of his hand as he managed his squawk phone with the other.

Practiced by now at silent exodus, our gang of escapee kids snuck over to the door and out into the street. I kept my eyes trained on the preoccupied Lieutenant. He jabbered on his squawker.

The reflections of red and green traffic lights shimmered on the rain glazed avenues beneath our feet. We inhaled refreshing clean air as we speed-walked away from the place. Nick's little footfalls came at me from behind. I stopped and braced for impact.

He jumped up, clambered up my back and sat on top of my shoulders, ready for a chicken fight. He called back to his fellow inmates. "Follow us, guys!"

I looked up at him and said, "By the way: Happy Birthday."

He laughed. I couldn't help but laugh. Two dozen kids and I doubled up and howled until we worked through our group's cathartic release. "Best birthday present ever!"

The compression of laugh muscles cut through my drug induced temporary pain relief. My guts hurt like Hell from my recent hazing by the Cyclops, on top of the pummeling and bomb attacks from before.

In a sobering moment, I remembered the sight of the kids behind in the caverns who didn't make it with us. It took me away for a moment. I said, "Come on guys. We're going to Nick's place. It may not be a White Castle, but it is the White Mansion."

The kids and I trekked the next few blocks together, down the middle of the street. There were few cars at that hour; we didn't obstruct anyone; and we didn't care. After the lurid stench of the tunnels and caverns, the positive ions in the rain washed air smelled delicious. It was a pleasure to breathe.

In a few minutes we approached Pennsylvania Avenue and 15th Street, N.W. As I anticipated, my personal pocket-sized FBI agent greeted us in the darkness between streetlights with his usual endearing bedside manner.

He took a quick survey of the situation, then demanded, "You can't come here. This is an FBI zone. What's with all the kids?"

He clicked his flashlight to make out the face of the only adult on the block other than himself.

"Who are you?" he asked. His flashlight shot up to Nick on top of my shoulders, then dropped down to me. "You gotta be kidding."

A voice above me said, "My name's Nick White. Please move. We're going to my house."

Agent Johnson's mouth gaped. He knew he should be happy, but he wasn't. He was so consumed with venom toward me he could only fume with frustration. A nervous tic began its uncontrollable twitch on his nose as he escorted our gang to the front doors.

I stopped at the front doors and waited. Every kid pressed up against us. They laughed and jostled, ready to explode through the doors together. When the gang's pressure reached critical mass I pushed the doorbell button and waited.

I commented back over my shoulder. "Hey, kids. I lied." There was a sudden silence. "Nick's mom is buying the hot dogs and ice cream."

Horace answered, dressed in his formal black tie and unprepared for the tidal wave of youth that burst into the massive foyer of the home. The squeaky-clean young man jumped aside. He held the door wide and watched in amazement.

When he saw Nick, he forgot about everything and ran across through the gang of kids to him. They hugged without words. When they loosened up, Nick looked at me. "My brother," he said.

"Half-brother," added Horace.

"Yeah, half is plenty," quipped Nick. Horace joked like he wanted to backhand his brother.

Again, on cue, that ingratiating soft Texas voice emerged from the nearby sitting hangar. "Horace? Everything all right? What's the ..." She paused with astonishment at the overwhelming sight before her. "... commotion?"

Electra White stood frozen as she tried to comprehend the scene that played out before her. About two dozen other kids who looked like they'd been through Hell, which they had, ran about and played with childlike abandon. Her son, Nick, was back home, and stood in the middle of her foyer with Horace.

There were also looks of bewilderment on the faces of the resident FBI guys. And then her eyes found me. And there I stood, trying to comprehend Electra White.

Casually immaculate in every way, she rushed into the heart of our joyous melee. She was drop dead gorgeous in her pair of polished brown leather riding boots, Doeskin Jodhpurs and a white cotton sleeveless blouse.

"Nick?" she asked with near disbelief.

Mother and son came together into a moving embrace. She looked up at me over his little shoulder and smiled. Tears formed in the corners of her eyes. Her south Texas accent showed, even when she mouthed silent words across the commodious room, "Thank you."

Agent Brunneman surveyed the day's catch. He sighed without taking a breath. "I'm looking at these kids… I don't get it. A bunch of them are kids we've been trying to find for weeks."

Electra, beside herself with a mother's relief and joy, said, "Yes, it took Mister Wolfe two whole days to find them all." She finished with a laugh that showed it hadn't sunk in yet.

It was such a vision of triumph I wanted to stand by and enjoy it. But the physical and emotional stress and taxation of the past couple of days poured over my body like a slow heavy waterfall. As long as I kept running, my fatigue couldn't catch me. But now that I stopped, it caught up and slammed into me from behind.

I wanted to stay, to watch this sight of jubilant children. The charming woman who looked at me with damp dark brown eyes tried to tell me something. My eyelids became burdens to hold open. In my peripheral vision I saw an approaching dark blue uniform.

My body collapsed. I recognized the feeling. In my younger days I took a knockout right cross straight into my face in a heavyweight bout. My mind was aware of my condition and the surroundings, but there was nothing I could do to hold myself up.

I hit the deck. In the middle of everyone's ecstasy, I didn't feel my knees when they hit the floor first before my face followed suit.

The last thing I remembered was the sound of Lieutenant Roscoe Diliberto's voice. "MPD, Mrs. White. I'm sorry, ma'am. I got to take him in. He's wanted for the murder of one Victoria Taylor."

30

Everything was white. Everything, except the angel's face that gazed at me with admiration. She wore the look of a princess who beheld the peasant that snatched her pet puppy from a pack of wild dogs. Only an angel could be that stunning.

My eyesight was bleary after being out for a while. The objects of my vision appeared as if somebody hung gauze around my visual lens.

The vision before me sat at eye level. She wore an elegant winter white wool suit with the slightest suggestion of enhanced shoulders. Yvonne Jackson's smiling face welcomed me to the land of the living as she came into focus. "Good evening, Mister Wolfe," she said.

I tried to speak but my tongue wore a hard coat and my lips stuck together. "Nick will do fine," I said with a growl. *Great; I just growled at our First Lady.*

Every morning, my shaving mirror reminded me that I've never been asked for autographs because

I looked like a movie star. Sometimes I thought it'd be better if I covered my scarred mug with a full beard. And I was certain that my current condition didn't qualify me to pose for any glamor shots.

The etiquette of FLOTUS was too refined to be bothered by my coarse response. It seemed she enjoyed an opportunity with me that was unique in D.C. The ability to speak openly with someone who did the same. She said, "It appears each time we meet you look a little the worse for wear."

"I'll tell your husband we've got to stop meeting like this. Where am I, anyway?"

"You're in the White Mansion, in the visitor's Presidential Suite. Your biggest fan, Mrs. White, had you installed here immediately. The White House doctors tended to you while you rested."

I looked at the IV stuck into my wrist and the beeping medical machines behind me that monitored my vital signs. "How long was I out?"

Some of my mental fog lifted and my clarity returned; I took stock of the room. The dark suits of two secret service agents stood out like oversized crickets against a white cyclotron. One stood across the room by the white door while another leaned against a not-too-distant white leather chair.

Somehow, the enormous room provided a feeling of security and intimacy. White walls with cream-colored beams, baseboards, and trim featured French doors that opened to balconies on the outside.
A crystal chandelier scaled for hotels competed with natural sunlight that streaked through the windows, dressed in rich gold drapes and gold sashes.

One original Frederic Remington painting and two by Charlie Russell added classic and expensive western touches to the ambiance of the room. A fully stocked cowhide bar stretched the length of one wall. It welcomed occupants with lighted shelves of seldom used but sparkling clean bottles and glasses.

A writing table with side chairs stood across from the bar. It provided everything you'd need to pen a letter home to Aunt Edna on White Mansion stationery. The ceiling resembled the night sky with constellations, like Grand Central Station.

The room's principal asset was silence. Absolute silence. Though I watched an ambulance that roared past a block away, beneath a plane headed for Reagan National Airport, not one sound reached my ears that did not emanate from within the room.

"How long was I out?" I asked.

"You're probably hungry. You've missed breakfast, lunch and dinner. Twice. But Electra's kitchen is on standby to make anything you want."

While we waited for my late-night breakfast, my Commandress-in-Chief briefed me. I asked, "I'm sure I dreamed some ridiculous things while I was out. I thought I heard MPD come in?"

"That's been cleared up," she stated. "There's nothing for you to worry about. But every media outlet in the world is on the front lawn waiting for you to appear."

"I'm not talking to those parasites."

She gave a slight shake of her head. "I've never heard it put quite that way."

"Forgive me, ma'am, I know they're a way of life for you. But not for me. They're parasites by definition. They don't do anything. They don't create anything. They produce no commerce. All their "content" is only a vehicle designed to sell and provide advertising revenue. They can only subsist because of the life energy of someone else who does do something. They have to rely on someone else's life energy to feed off it in order to survive. Textbook definition of a parasite. No thanks. You don't want me talking to them."

"Jess Blasdell has been handling them well in your behalf."

"The White House press secretary is keeping the press off me?"

She smiled. "I told you there were perqs to F.L.O.T.U.S."

I smiled at this particular perq. "I need to send him some steaks. Who's working on my car bombing? MPD? And the couple murdered in my alternate hotel room?

"Metro Police are investigating everything, including your tunnels." She waited for my response.

"Did I hear him say, they thought Victoria was killed?" I laughed, then felt a painful reminder that it hurt to laugh. "It fooled me, too. That's a sculpture on the showroom floor that looks like her. Bad taste, but just bad art. Probably expensive as Hell. They should know that isn't her." I took a drink of water.

The elegant woman's harmonious Polynesian features turned down. "They do," she said.

Her innate gentility made her delivery of even the worst event feel as if conveyed via velvet gloves. But she might as well have punched me in the stomach with brass knuckles.

I was stunned. I was fully aware of Yvonne Jackson's presence and calm detachment as she sat by my bedside in silence, but it didn't feel real. The white room wasn't real either. I wasn't there, wasn't anywhere. I didn't see anything, didn't feel anything.

I stood inside her gallery. She stood before me with a drink in her hand, with her doppelganger prostrate on the floor behind her.

"She took out that killer by herself," I said. "I walked in right after. She was in shock. But she dealt with it, cocktail in hand. Wouldn't let me call it in, handled it all herself." It was the second time that the incredible woman died in two days.

I looked into the eyes of someone who didn't want to tell me what I didn't want to know. She said, "The police had nobody else to suspect that night. You told the Lieutenant on duty at the pizza shop that you were the last one who saw her up to that point."

"I'm sure I was, other than her killer. So, if they don't have him, why don't they have me?"

"Your friends Mr. and Mrs. Chang - at the Chinese Laundry. They came forward and witnessed that you were in their store with them before they closed the shop at 5:00 and for a while after that. Time of death was about 5:00 p.m."

I didn't look at her. "How?"

She said, "I met Victoria Taylor at some National Gallery of Art events. And Electra knows of her gallery, too."

"How."

Again, she paused. She said with a subdued voice, "It was a garrot."

I sat, silent. I wanted to lose control. I was angry; I wanted violence, wanted the bastard's throat in my hands, just for a warm up. And that's just what they'd want. Get me to twist off, do something stupid, take me out of the situation, set them up to win in the end.

I didn't move. In my quiet thoughts I watched five different ways I would destroy the son-of-a-bitch that killed her.

Yvonne Jackson said, "I can feel the shock wave of an H-bomb inside you from where I'm sitting."

I didn't look at her. I was preoccupied with visons of the torture and Hell I was going to put the bastard through. I reached across the bed for my Marlboros and Zippo. I was about to flame on but held off.

"Oh, go ahead. I'm not royalty." She tried to diffuse the room's energy with a demure chuckle. "Nick, don't you think you've done enough for one week? You rescued your little baseball friend, plus all those children. You brought down a huge pedophile ring. It almost killed you."

I didn't like the look I gave her. Neither did she. But she got my message.

She asked, "Who?"

I said, "I know who."

I mentally wiped my calendar clean. I had one mission: heal up and get my hands on the stinking son-of-a-bitch that I knew killed her. With maximum prejudice.

"Nick," she said. "We were glad you used your Triad."

"Not my style," I said, not growling. "But there were kids involved."

"It isn't any good if you don't use it," she replied.

"Now you sound like my father," I said. "I'll tell you one thing – it gives a wild ride."

"I take it you know how the Nazis stormed across Europe in World War II? The blitzkrieg?"

I nodded.

"They did it by providing unlimited amounts of methamphetamines to their entire army. The invading Nazi armies were meth addicts, on Pervitin. They outworked, outran and outfought everyone, as long as their drug-induced states held up."

"Thanks for the history lesson." I asked. "So, my Dr. Strange talisman gives me a meth hit? That's great."

31

Yvonne Jackson turned toward her nearest secret service agent. The white wool of her suit stretched tight against her curves. I studied her body's poetry in motion as it fought against the fabric.

"Jason," she said. "If you would be so good as to admit Mrs. White."

She turned back and caught my involuntary once-over. She blushed.

I made the First Lady of the United States blush! The smugness of a boy with the hots for teacher flushed my body with heat from the hot faucet side, cooled down by the cold faucet guilt of a critical adult.

She concealed her embarrassed smile with a quick comeback. "Well, it doesn't give you x-ray vision," she quipped. "But it does make you nearly invincible."

"Now, I'm interested," I said. I caught the slowdown in my words; I already felt tired again.

I strained to hear her voice while I fought eyelids that a distant hypnotist told me were heavy. "Your Triad performs three tasks. When you depressed the red button, you instantly absorbed enough Meth-Adrenaline Delta 9 to significantly increase your strength and speed for half an hour."

"So, it blasts my engine with nitrous oxide," I said, beneath droopy eyelids.

"It simultaneously signals us from anywhere in the world via satellite. We pinpoint your exact GPS coordinates. That's how we knew where you were when you came out of those wretched tunnels. It's how I was able to talk to that MPD Lieutenant at the pizza shop."

She paused and leaned back in her chair. "It's unfortunate you didn't use it when you were trapped in those cages."

This time I was the one who smiled. It didn't feel good. I was sure it didn't look good, either. "My hands were tied," I said.

"We know," she replied. "Nick and the children told us about your painful ordeal getting them out."

A sudden burn shot up my arm. I winced.

She waited. "Your Triad also serves as Top Secret security clearance, White House Top Secret security clearance. You are admitted onto any U.S. military installation or into any government office. Everyone else clips on their red Top Secret badge. This is two levels above that."

"All that, in this little thing, for little old me?"

"It's fortunate we have that flash drive with the video on it showing the abduction. The Changs were burned out of their shop. Their servers were destroyed, as well as the security videos on them. You had the only copy. Of course, it's copied and secured now."

"All they wanted to do was help," I said. "What the Hell is the FBI doing on all this? I see MPD doing the heavy lifting and the fed boys are standing around getting their pictures taken."

"John is meeting with the FBI Director when he returns from his Russo-Chinese Summit in Air Force One."

"Pardon my French, but it's time for some heads to roll," I said. "How are the Changs?"

"They're fine. It happened in the early hours of the morning. Don't worry. They have our help; if you know what I mean, and I think you do."

I touched her wrist when she rose. "By the way. Thanks for the donation."

She looked at me with genuine false modesty and a cat-like grin. "I don't know what you're talking about."

"What about the other video? From the tunnels?" I asked. "I don't relish seeing it, but the rest of the world needs to."

"We haven't seen it yet. Your little namesake won't let us. He says it's your phone and his video and he needs to discuss it with you first before anything is done with it."

"Smart kid," I said.

"Nick." Her voice dropped an octave with dewy earnestness. "You have no idea the global impact you've made because of what you accomplished."

Here came the gooey stuff. Please, no gooey stuff.

"Besides your little baseball teammate, you rescued the daughter of the King of Sweden, the sons of two ambassadors to the United States and children of many more VIPs. Children - any children should never experience that."

"But because of who these are, they were especially designated to be sacrificed on their heinous Halloween night *Walpurgisnacht*. You got the job done. You located them and got them out."

My mind recalled the sight of the little black-haired girl with the pink ribbon in her hair who fought so hard for her life in the cages next to me. "Not all of them," I said.

The towering floor-to-ceiling doors opened. Electra White strode in past the secret service guys. The sound of her tall western boots was muffled by a pricey thick middle eastern rug beneath her riding heels.

Today's walking full page fashion ad involved her hand-made boots worn outside skintight, waisted jeans, a burnt orange gingham checked shirt, and a smile bigger than Dallas.

"Is it true?" she asked with a playful tone. "Is the Pied Piper of Washington aroused?"

Yvonne Jackson stood at my bedside and waited for the lady of the house to join her.

My eyelids grew heavier. "I wouldn't exactly say that." I raised my eyebrows to keep my eyes open. I wanted to stay awake to talk with these two incredible women, but I was fighting a losing battle.

Electra mimicked the voice of a South Texas diner waitress ordering Adam and Eve on a raft, wreck 'em. "Now you just open your eyes, Mister Wolfe! We're burnin' daylight and you've got a chuck wagon breakfast headed your way on a blue-plate special."

I forced my eyes awake as if I came out of a drugged stupor. It wasn't far from the truth. I wondered what I'd been pumped full of in those IVs. I forgot all about it when I looked up at the bounty of beauty on display before me on both sides of my Presidential suite bed.

On one side stood FLOTUS, one of the most elegant and beautiful women in the world. Also, one of the most powerful, as I had come to know in the past few days.

Opposite her on the other side of my covers, my eyes explored another vision. Electra White was one of the wealthiest people in the world, if not *numero uno*. She stood and observed me with a smile, an auburn-haired Texas drink of bourbon and branch water on 35-inch stems.

Electra White took care not to drop the morning newspaper with any impact when she laid it open on top of my stomach. The front-page two-inch headline of the *Washington Post* proclaimed, "The Pied Piper of Washington."

A high-angle street security CCTV image four columns wide nearly filled the page. Nick the kid rode on my shoulders, followed by the other kids around us. A map inset showed our pilgrimage from the Bolide pizza shop to the White Mansion. Several inset photos featured the pizza shop trapdoor and the underground tunnels.

Electra engaged Yvonne in a mutual smile and said, "Of course, you know who's just dying to run in here and jump up on your lap."

"The President?"

I studied the pair of soft-focus portraits before me as my lights dimmed. I smiled and enjoyed fantasies that took place behind the doors across the wide hall from mine. Electra's voice said something as I drifted off into a quiet place where I didn't see anyone. *There's a bee in the meat ...*

"Well, before my Nick runs in, your friend James is here. If it's OK, he has some important business for you, and then my boy wants to ..."

32

Something poked me in the side, then again. Its prodding brought me into semi-consciousness. I peeked through one eye out of annoyed curiosity to see what it was.

I much preferred the feminine sights that greeted me the previous morning when I woke up. This time, an overweight guy looked down his nose at me through a pair of tortoiseshell reading glasses.

He wore a gangster's three-piece worsted wool navy suit with wide silver pinstripes and a French blue shirt under a solid black tie, with black wingtips. A Phi Beta Kappa key hung on a gold chain that reached from one pocket of his vest to the other through one of the buttonholes.

The instrument he used for my wake-up call rested on his lap with a newspaper, a silver flute.

As I moved about, he leaned back in his chair. The highball glass in his hand was wet with condensation, a tall violent looking Bloody Mary.

I said through parched lips, "What's up, Murgatroyd?"

"Nice digs. I've got to hand it to you," he said with a chuckle. "Only you can take a detour through Hell and wash up on the shore of the world's wealthiest estate."

I asked, "Hey, I need some food. What's with the flute?"

"You haven't eaten properly in three days. IVs have kept you going. I heard you left a perfectly good Metro breakfast abandoned on its plates yesterday."

"Let's get some coffee," I said. Then again, "So, what's with the flute?"

"Surely, you jest," he said. James held up the front page of yesterday's *Post*, courtesy of Electra. He indicated his flute. "I'm taking these back for a framed display in the front office."

I said, "What a bunch of crap. The media has to create something to sell their ads, I guess.

That's fine if they tell the real story behind it. But they won't."

"Now, now," he said. Murgatroyd pushed the bedside button. A professional housemaid came in, uniformed in traditional light grey with a white apron and headband. She left with our orders, which included a pair of Bloody Marys, and a lot of coffee.

He produced a pair of 50 ring Churchill cigars from inside his breast pocket. Then he clipped the end of one and handed it to me. I borrowed his lighter.

"I'm not going to start worrying about my social skills now," I grumbled.

"Speaking of which, I've already thanked Mrs. White," he said.

"For breakfast?"

"For the money."

"What money?"

"The $500,000."

"Is that where the $500,000 came from? Electra White?"

"Yes. But not the money you're thinking of."

"I'm going to throttle you."

"The first half-million is untraceable."

"The first?"

"The second half-million that posted this morning."

"What second half million?"

"That's what I'm talking about."

"'One of these days I'm going to break you into little pieces!'"

"In 25 words or less: you've been floating around the universe on morphine and better living through chemistry for a couple of days. During that time, your pro-bono Pied Piper show with the children of Washington increased the *El Peligro* bottom line by a cool total of a million bucks in the bank account. From two deposits."

I laid back into my pillow and contemplated the sky on the ceiling.

"From what I saw when I walked in, I'm going to take a wild guess and say I just passed by your two new benefactors."

"They love my ass," I said.

"I can see tomorrow's two-inch front-page headline: *American Gigolo does D.C.*"

"What about T and C?"

"They're fine. Your sister wanted to jump on the train down here with me, but everybody assured us you're going to be fine. She was working on a commissioned piece and stayed back to take care of Cody. And Winston."

"You're right. I've been away," I said. "Cody will want some rough play. Don't let him near any raw meat until I get back."

The staff rolled in a huge breakfast-in-bed table. We got our rudimentary orders of business out of the way during the morning meal. When we were caught up, I said, "OK, I need to talk to the kid." Murgatroyd caught the train back to the Big Apple.

A few minutes after he left, the doors to the room flew open. Little Nick ran across to my bedside, with his mother in tow, behind.

"My turn!" he laughed. "Finally!"

Electra took quick stock of my healthy diet and recovery regimen. "Now that's a man after my own heart," she said. "Recovering in a hospital bed with plates full of cardiac arrest, a cold drink and smoking a cigar."

It's a fact that our eyes are naturally attracted to motion and bright colors. But despite the kid's active body that flashed a vivid green and white striped rodeo shirt, I had to work to keep my eyes off his mother.

Electra White arrived at my bedside in a winter white chain knit turtleneck sweater and long cream twill culottes. She acquiesced the moment in favor of little Nick. The proud mother stood beside her son with her hands clasped in front of her.

He was beside himself with excitement, an oversized new Rawlings outfield mitt clutched in his hands.

He blurted, "I thought you'd never come around! You were out a couple of hours the first time down there. Then you were out a couple of days this time! I have your phone. Mom has your pistols. Can we play catch again? Are you going to stay in D.C.? Do you want to see my horse?"

"Whoa there, pilgrim," I said with a laugh.

Electra said, "You know boys. He's been pacing like a caged wildcat outside your bedroom door."

Little Nick turned to his mother and addressed her in his best grown-up delivery. "Nick and I need to talk about some business."

She said, "Of course you do. Don't forget, tomorrow night is Halloween. We have the White

House function to attend so you'll have to watch your time with Mister Wolfe."

I looked at her. "A function? On Halloween?"

"You know how it is," she said, with a note of apology. "The start of the social season."

"Yes, I do," I said. I turned to the kid. "You think your mom would let us go out trick-or-treating for real? Flying solo?"

The kid was stunned. So was his mother.

"For real?" he asked. "No embassies, dinners, or bodyguards? Costumes? Candy? Kids? Really?"

He gave his mom the universal little kid look, guaranteed to deliver an instant guilt trip. "Can I, mom? Can I? Pleeeeease?"

The features of her face furrowed, but in thought, not consternation. "There's so much evil out there."

The look on my face bordered on being incredulous. "Really?"

She smiled again. "If you take him yourself, you can take him anywhere you want Mr. Wolfe. He couldn't be in safer hands."

The kid hugged his mom, then he tried to hug me. Because of the expanse of the big bed, he had to settle for cranking my neck in the crook of his arm. He held the new baseball mitt out to me.

"This is for you!" he declared. "How are you feeling?"

I started to slide out of the bed. For the first time I made a conscious mental note of the ivory silk pajamas I wore. I held the new ball glove to my face and inhaled an aroma that took me back decades to sand lots and outfields.

Electra looked me up and down and shrugged. "I hope those PJs are OK. It's the best we had on short notice."

Little Nick, already across the room, held his ball and glove. The moment he released the ball from his hand he called, "Catch!"

33

My hand wasn't in the new glove, so I caught the horsehide bare-handed.

Electra bit her lower lip in a way that accentuated the tiny cleft in her chin. "What am I going to do with you two?" she asked. "Nick, you know you play ball outside. Why don't you take Mister Wolfe to your playground to throw?"

I turned to her, "I'm Nick, too, by the way."

I made a quick change and we went outside for recess. Little Nick's playground on the estate was a full-sized soccer field, with aluminum sideline bleachers. I assumed the cheerleaders and fans had the day off.

We practiced curve balls and sliders until my insides reminded me that I was bed-bound in recovery for two days. I walked to one of the bleachers. The kid followed.

I took a seat and said, "You told your mom we needed to talk business. Let's talk."

"Your phone's safe, in my room," he said. "Nobody's seen it yet."

"Good. I don't want you to see it, either."

"I already have," he said. "I couldn't wait … I'm a kid!"

I looked at him, suppressed a smile. "Yes, you are. And?"

"That wasn't real, right? It was AI or something?"

"Let's go get the phone," I said. "I need something to eat." We headed back inside the Mansion. I said, "I've got a couple of places to go tomorrow. We'll hit the streets together Halloween night."

"I can't wait!" he yelled, slapped me with a little kid's high five.

Electra, Nick and I shared a servant-delivered, chef-prepared lunch on their Austin stone patio. We discussed everything in the world of politics and baseball. Nobody mentioned the intense violence of the past few days.

Nick handed my phone over and I returned to my Presidential suite.

I shouldn't have eaten. My memory shielded me from what I witnessed live and in-person back in the tunnels. The scene I revisited on the video made me make a stiff drink at the bar.

There was only one visual detail before my eyes that didn't make me sick. All the predatory ghouls faced my camera from behind their ringleader, as if they sang in a bandshell choir. Each face that wore a brown robe was identifiable in the blazing torch lights.

These elitist sycophants gathered ringside around the Speaker in his distinguishable red and black. They wore their hoods down. Only the white robes that ringed the outside of the semi-circle of insanity were hooded.

I recorded notes of every face I saw this time: the FBI Director, CIA Director, National Intelligence Director, and the former National Security Advisor. There were congressmen and women, senators, plus several actors who wouldn't win any more Oscars. Plus, I gunned down the red-headed ATF Director in the tunnel. And at the focal point of the macabre event stood my personal favorite, the Master of Ceremonies for the gruesome sacrificial circus, Speaker of the House, John Evans.

I narrated a quick introduction and shared the video with a half dozen trusted sources: FLOTUS, Murgatroyd, Margo, my law firm, an old girlfriend who had a popular podcast, plus the *Washington Post* editor who broke the coverage of The Pied Piper of Washington.

When I fought my way through heavy action in Afghanistan, I saw bodies destroyed; friends cut down in bullet hailstorms. I learned to handle that. But that was war. These were innocent little kids betrayed by adults, to their horrific tortured destruction.

I knew about these perverts but never got involved. That was different now. These VIPs, these egotistical elitist bastards, believed devouring children's organs and bodies made them supernatural and super-powered.

These ghouls believed if they harvested adrenochrome from the adrenaline gland of a frightened, tortured human body and self-administered it, it was their fountain of youth. And they preferred children because they thought their energy was fresher, cleaner.

They took pleasure in dining on the organs in the little girl's body before Speaker Evans put her out of her anguish. They had a full production lab for body parts and celebrated vivisections.

I read the stories. I saw the newscasts. One Hollywood producer launched a single-camera video of his talking head that went viral. He spoke to the camera for half an hour and told of the incredible number of predatory violations that occur there every day.

I watched a leaked video of an ABC TV network reporter. On a hot mic on set, she talked about how they had the goods on a bunch of these pedophile psychopaths years ago. She named several names, big names, and said they had the evidence, but network executive brass shut the stories down.

So, the public was kept in the dark by a conspiratorial mainstream media, Hollywood celebrities, and politicians. Until now. Because when even the *Washington Post* headlined their rag with the Pied Piper story, people sat up and took notice.

As I watched through horrified eyes, I remembered how much I wanted a pair of shotguns in my hands that night. But the ghouls had more resources, humans and otherwise, than I had bullets. "Every good general knows when to retreat." Especially with a couple of dozen tortured and freaked-out kids under my wing.

The minimal exercise of playing catch with Little Nick, along with the coaxing of my stiff drink, did me in. I passed out and slept through dinner until sunrise.

* * *

The next morning, Electra escorted her handmaid into the suite with my breakfast. I was finding it easy to get used to her charming face each new day. It was getting easier and easier to picture how much fun it would be to play Romper Room with this pistol-packin' mama.

I ate, showered, shaved. I found my suit in the suite's walk-in island closet. It was cleaned and pressed and hung up. It may have been cleaned, but it looked like it caught the Concorde to the 80s and back - on the wing.

Taras Valdemar pulled up to the White Mansion entrance through mobs of press corps in his gleaming black armored Escalade. Security staff from the White Mansion held the scribblers at bay on each side of the short walkway.

Electra escorted me out through the front doors and to my awaiting caravan. Glints of red shimmered in the sunlight through her auburn shag.

She asked, "Will you be back in time for dinner?"

"What time?"

"Six o'clock. That should give you two boys plenty of time to go carousing out on the town tonight." She flashed an ingratiating smile. "It's all he's talking about."

Taras held open the door of my Escalade; I turned to get in. Venus from the Lone Star State caught my arm. She turned me to her and embraced me in a hug. She whispered, "Be careful. Come back alive, please?"

Flashes went off that I didn't see; reporters yelled questions at us that I didn't hear. "I'm just running out to the hardware store and seeing a couple of old friends." I touched my suit's rips and tears. "Maybe I'll get some new glad rags."

"Mm-Hmm. I guess most men need armored trucks and armed bodyguards to go shopping."

"I will return, dressed for dinner at six," I said with a mock salute.

She turned back to the front door and walked through her security ranks as we drove away toward my first whistle stop. "When the going gets tough, the tough go shopping, eh Taras?"

34

We cruised the four-block distance to the Brioni house on Pennsylvania Avenue. *Paparazzi* chased behind us on a purple Vespa. They parked and followed us after we pulled in.

I got out and approached the store. A couple of minutes later, Taras caught up with me. I checked the street before we entered. Not a single *paparazzo* to be seen. "I like your style, Taras."

The Brioni street front windows displayed their tasteful suits on forms. We entered and I explained my circumstance. When my bodyguard stood behind me and held up yesterday's *Washington Post* front page, the tailors couldn't scramble fast enough.

Since my childhood I have wanted a suit that bore the Brioni signature. It isn't the kind of attire worn much in my line of work, but my circles had expanded. My thrift store 80s suit was out of date and ripped apart. Some finer threads wouldn't hurt when I operated at these levels and now, I had the money.

Two hours later as I rode away, I wore a new Brioni single-button navy suit. Its brother in sharkskin gray hung near me behind the back seat. This was an incredible feat, considering the significant tailoring needed to disguise my concealed artillery.

I needed the first new monkey suit for my next destination, the Argentine embassy a little north of us at New Hampshire Avenue and Q Street. The ambassador from the Paris of South America was the second personal meeting I'd missed in as many days.

On the way, I made a secure call to an old colleague, Mr. Allison at NSA Headquarters inside Fort Meade. We'd meet in the "red corridor" there. He said he'd bring his aid.

We arrived at a massive four-story stone structure. Its masonry wings extended down two streets from the front door, situated at their intersection. Seven dormers on the fourth floor spread themselves down both streets.

The street-side iron gates were open; Taras pulled into the semi-circle drive. The celeste blue and white flag of Argentina drifted in the breeze above the black iron front door. I got out three steps away and pushed through to the foyer.

A pair of young, blond, blue-eyed Eurotrash punks approached me across the foyer floor and arrested my entrance. Like Nordic bookends, each one was tall and slender with angular features. Twins.

80s Eurotrash thugs? Today? Really? Was I in the right place?

Behind them, a gang of school-aged kids crowded around the bottom of a large stairway. The sweeping staircase wound up a long curving wall to the second floor.

I recognized her by her unique hair color. Ursula Shicklgruber stood halfway up on the staircase red carpet. She spoke with an assistant while they reviewed details on a clipboard. They both stopped and turned to look at me with surprise when I came through the door.

The aristocratic lady cried, "You!" She turned toward me in her colorful Hermes suit. If she could have fired daggers from her eyes, I would have been a dead man several times over. Her voice was strong, throaty with an aristocratic foreign accent.

My eyes swept the impressive entrance foyer that stood open before me. Aside from the group of kids, large steamer trunks created a formation like soldiers in black. They stood at attention in rows, accompanied by as many similar suitcases, briefcases and pouches.

I asked, "You wanted to see me after we didn't meet the other night?"

It was the first time I noticed her intense, unwavering, hazel eyes. They glared at me as she forced herself into her composure. She descended the winding stairs and feigned a smile when she nudged and moved some kids out of her way. Her words came at me through teeth that were clenched in tightened jaws.

"Of course," she said. By the time she stood before me, she relaxed her demeanor down to a state of controlled indignation. "You were to see me here two days ago. We depart now for New York."

She was attractive, except for her crazy stare. There was something about the way she looked. I couldn't put my finger on it.

It could have been her designer suit, her halo-twist hairstyle, unique hair color, vivid hazel eyes, posture. Her tall, lean Teutonic features were enough. Hell, I couldn't pin it down.

But I was sure of one thing. She was nuts. *I bet she's great in the sack.*

I said, "Yeah, well a funny thing happened on the way to the Forum. Look, I live in Manhattan. We can meet there."

Her demeanor changed, took on a different, more convivial tone. She looked up at me through eyes that turned friendlier. "Really?" she asked. "I followed with interest your recent exploits in the news. You must tell me more."

"Nothing to tell. I helped your friend, Mrs. White and her son down here, and I live up there. I saw you at Electra's the other night and Speaker Evans said you asked to have me meet you here."

"And you've been quite busy since then. You're currently at *'Electra's'* I believe you said?"

"I'm staying at the Washington Hotel. The White House and White Mansion have been hospitable in my recovery from some altercations."

"How charming," she replied. "I'm sure she has."

"I make good on my commitments," I said. "Sometimes that gets in the way of other opportunities."

"Indeed," she said. I watched as her mind contorted itself with girlish conniving. "Then you can commit to being with me when I address the United Nations General Assembly next week. In New York."

"Wouldn't miss it for the world," I said.

"I will arrange seating for you to attend the General Assembly as my guest, Mister …?"

"You know my name," I said. "Day and time?"

"Friday morning, 11:00. Birgitta will arrange UN grounds pass for you. You will have a VIP Pass waiting for you to enter the General Assembly room."

"I'll brush up on my Spanish." I turned to leave. "Or would that be German?"

Ursula's penetrating voice called from behind me, "*Auf Wiedersehen, Lebensgefahr.*"

* * *

We stopped at a corner mom and pop hardware store. I got what I wanted and dropped it inside my jacket pocket. While I was in the D.C. area, I wanted to look up an old friend.

We were entering the Baltimore Washington Parkway to Ft. Meade, when I had Taras pull over at a roadside stand. This wasn't your everyday truck garden produce stand.

The happy bald guy in a soggy stained apron sold freshly caught Chesapeake Bay Blue Crabs. Taras and I loaded four bushel baskets of the crawling critters into the truck.

We drove east 22 miles up highway 295 into Central Maryland. Late October rain dampened the sounds outside as we headed north. Leaves on trees finished their autumn turns of color. The change of seasons in this Scotch mist provided me with a brief pastoral interlude.

I thought about Victoria, Electra, Teresa.

Eastbound traffic on 295 had a marked exit directly to the NSA. All gates required security clearance to get on the base, except this one. It was open to the public for access to NSA's National Cryptology Museum and visitor center. I chose it as the easiest point of entry.

At 13 stories, the OPS2A building is the tallest NSA building at Fort Meade and houses most of the agency's operations. It's also the office location of Mr. Allison in Antiterrorism/Force Protection, and its "red corridor" is accessible from the visitor center.

Allison had access to things that I didn't, but I had four bushel baskets of Chesapeake Bay Blue Crabs.

Normally, it would have been easy to pass through the visitor's gate. Normally, I wouldn't arrive at NSA HQ with three guns, with a former Spetsnaz operative as a chauffeur. The guard waved us over and asked our stated business on the base.

I showed him my IDs and paperwork, then I volunteered my three handguns, plus Taras' 9 mm Makarov. There was no way we were getting on base carrying loaded weapons and we didn't have any place to rest them. The corporal held our collective arsenal in silent astonishment.

He asked, "Why are visitors going to the visitor's center carrying so much ordnance, sir?"

35

I said, "I'm going to have lunch with an old friend in the cafeteria. I have a little surprise for him." I opened the door and showed him our baskets full of scrabbling Blue Crabs.

Meanwhile, exit traffic ceased on the other side of the guardhouse. His partner stepped over and joined us. I looked at him and smiled. "Call Mister Allison. NSA Antiterrorism/Force Protection. These are going to him. He'll give you all the clearance you need, at least for visitors."

His guard gate partner grabbed his arm. A second later he pulled him aside. "Didn't you see the news? That guy's "The Pied Piper of Washington!"

Our guard looked back and examined me from head to foot. "Sorry I didn't recognize you, sir. You're a national hero, sir."

Finally, a breakthrough. I gave a humble nod and sat back to drive into the base. "Thanks."

"But I'm still going to need to see some kind of

security clearance for you and your - friend - to come on this base, sir."

I slipped my Triad off my neck and handed it to him. I said, "Wave this at your Top-Secret card reader."

He turned the Triad over in his hands and examined it. He looked back at me as he moved toward his security card reader. I hoped it worked.

When he held my Triad in front of the reader, its screen popped alive with a flash. The background turned solid gold and stated, "POTUS Top Secret" with a white ghost image of the White House in the background.

He returned with a flabbergasted smile. He said, "Mister, I don't know who you are, but this is better than *carte blanche*." He turned to his partner. "This is *Carte Gold!*" He turned back to me. "My apology, sir. What can I do for you?"

I indicated Taras behind the wheel. "A red visitors badge for him and a Top-Secret Clearance badge for me. Just for today, and a parking pass. Hold our guns until we come back through. Thanks, corporal."

"Yes, sir." He handed Taras our badges and a "Reserved, VIP" parking pass. "This will get you into reserved parking for VIP visitors from the private sector." He paused. Then, "Those must be some special crabs."

The "red corridor" inside the NSA's version of ABC's Black Rock building is a visitor-friendly area. People can pick up light fare at concessions, among other things. I had an American black coffee at a kiosk. In a few minutes, I saw them approach around a corner.

Mr. Allison and I went back together to my days in Afghanistan SOF (Special Operations Forces). At the time, Mr. Allison operated within "the activity", the most top-secret group within the Joint Special Operations Command that the government does not acknowledge exists.

He also coordinated several high-level Combat Search and Rescue operations. I reported enemy positions back to him at Shahbaz Air Base when I was the point man on LRRP missions.

He was now NSA's new Boss of the Antiterrorism/Force Protection division. He stood a towering 4' 2" back then. And that counted his full head of thick black hair. He hadn't grown. But he had lost some hair.

His massive albino aide more than made up for his diminutive size. He looked like the good twin of the monster in the pizza shop who tried to body slam me to China. This one had fewer scars atop his shaved white head.

We slowed our mutual approaches, stopped five feet apart and stared. I said, "Well cut off my legs and call me shorty, it's Sky Lo Lo and The Albino Hulk."

His eyes dropped toward his shoes, he said, "That's why you could never be part of an agency, Major." He looked up at his escort and said, "One day back in Jacobabad, Major Wolfe here and one of his friends -"

I interjected: "Who shall remain nameless -"

"As I was saying," he continued, "Major Nick Wolfe and Rusty Dennis posted handbills throughout the offices in Jacobabad -"

"Ha, ha! In Asscrapistan!" said his genius colleague.

Allison continued. "... handbills that promoted their "nipsky contest" to measure the diameter of our women's nipples."

The great white hulk looked confused.

"Different times," I said. "Want to know who won?"

Mr. Allison frowned. "To what do I owe the great honor of a visit from the Crown Prince of Intelligence after what, ten years?"

I proffered my paper cup and asked, "You want a cup of good old American black coffee?" He stared up at me. His oversized muscle stared down at me. There was a whole lot of staring going on.

I explained with innocence, "I closed a case in D.C. early. So, I rented an inboard motorboat, got a guide and some nets. I went crabbing under the roadway piers on the Patuxent River. They're ripe for the picking right now."

Mr. Allison spoke an aside to the giant beside him, "He plays at being a private investigator. Lots of free time." Then, to me, "Common decency forbids me from conjecturing how you scammed a New York p.i. license. Did you just come here to taunt me?"

"Of course not. I've got a car and driver waiting outside with his motor running. We can make a break for it and take Mr. Allison's Day Off. Plus, the Wizards play the Celtics at home tonight."

He tried not to frown. "You know I can't go."

"Why? You're the Big Dog now."

"That's why I am the Big Dog. I don't go crabbing at the drop of a hat; I do my job. End of month reports due tomorrow. Plus, Q4 reconciliation to finish out the government's fiscal year."

I bit my upper lip with my lower teeth. "Come outside with me." I beckoned him and his comical sidekick to follow as I turned toward the exterior doors.

After a quick text to Taras, the big black Escalade wheeled around a corner and rolled to a slow stop in front of us. The NSA's tag team followed me to the curb.

As I opened the side doors, I turned to Mr. Allison. "Chesapeake Bay Blue Crabs. Just caught today. Hell, some of them are bigger than you." To the giant, "Not you."

Mr. Allison showed little emotion about anything, good, bad, or horrific. On top of that, he was trained in espionage and counterespionage to always maintain complete control. But we formed a tight bond in some critical conditions during our time overseas and I knew him as well as anyone.

I knew he exhibited strong mimetic desires from the times we shared officer's mess hall. I also knew his passion for these local delicacies. When his eyes took in four bushel baskets crawling with Chesapeake Bay Blue Crabs, his mouth gaped. For an instant, he registered human emotion. I had him.

I said, "The problem is, I'm headed back to the Big Apple and don't want to mess with them. So, I brought them to you."

He straightened up and reverted to spy mode. "What do you want?"

"What do you mean?" I asked. "My war buddy, after ten years. Just rekindling our friendship with something you love that I'm delivering before I head back to the Lower East Side."

Mr. Allison's mind was a lightning-fast information processor that was suited for the most advanced cryptographic work right out of school. That was before he honed his skills with decades of face-to-face experience. He gave me a once-over and blinked.

"What do you want?" he asked again.

"Well, now that you ask …"

He cut me off, said to Goliath, "He also thinks because his father became Director of DIA for the President, and his mother ran F6, he can just swing by here any time to exact special privileges."

"Only on Tuesdays," I said. "But now that you mention it, there is one thing I can use some help with. It's tiny."

Mr. Allison tried to bore holes through me with his eyes, but I was jiu-jitsu eye-shape after my one-on-one match with POTUS. I fired right back. We continued our visual wrestling match until he broke off with a grin. "Delbert, take the baskets up to my office."

36

Taras Valdemar dropped me off at the White Mansion in time for dinner. I carried my new gray suit as I emerged from the truck. The kid ran out of the mansion, baseball and gloves in hand.

He threw my glove to me only a second before I caught the pitch that followed it.

I reached in my pocket and spiffed Taras a wad of C notes. He thanked me and said, "You almost blowing tonight with little man. If Allison says *da* to going basket balling tonight ..."

I said, "I can play Mr. Allison like a fiddle. I wouldn't ask you to take us out tonight, Taras. Don't you have kids of your own?"

"For you and your kids, Taras Valdemar being on duty 24 hours. I get dinner. Wait here. You come. We go."

I said, "He isn't my kid, Taras." Then I turned to the kid. "You ready for dinner?"

"I'm ready for action!" he said.

"Good. You can go wash your hands." We went inside.

"My, don't you clean up nice?" came the voice from the foyer inside the Mansion. The huge Bois d'Arc doors were held wide by Horace in his formal day wear.

The ubiquitous Mrs. White seemed always present on cue. Electra stopped in the open front doors of the massive building, perfectly framed in her couture party dress. She looked ready for a high fashion photo shoot.

Over dinner, Electra was curious about the events of my day. I told her: the hardware store, the suit shop and taking some Blue Crabs to an old military friend wasn't very exciting. Little Nick's body and verbal language assured me he was ready for the night of trick or treating that lay ahead.

I changed back into my street gear. While I was out, Electra had my overcoat reconditioned by Washington's finest leather repair shop. I was afraid it would be stiff as a board from the soaking it took.

I wanted the kid to see real life for a change. We drove north out of the beltway suburbs through Upstate Maryland to a small town near the Pennsylvania border. Taras drove us into a large residential neighborhood and parked.

He held the truck at idle at the end of one block while we fell in among some local kids and parents and walked the rows of homes. We were neighborhood party crashers, but nobody seemed to mind. Little Nick had fun and made new friends in his favorite superhero costume.

Meanwhile I hung near him, wearing my full armament. The three of us enjoyed a good old-fashioned Halloween night among the homes and people in the neighborhood. The candy was good, too.

Taras Valdemar may have had the most fun of the evening. Little Nick donated some chocolate bars from his trick or treat bag for Taras to take home. But he especially enjoyed the phenomenon of the great American drive-through fast food windows.

We arrived back at the White Mansion near midnight. I cut Taras loose and carried a sleeping little boy inside. The excitement of his new experiences, fresh air, plus all the fast food and ice cream caught up with him before we got back to the beltway.

Horace took him from me and carried him up the massive staircase, passing by Electra as she descended wearing a flowing silk-satin dressing gown. She checked on little Nick, asleep in Horace's arms.

The lady of the house had a body that was meant to play, and she knew how to work every inch of it. She kissed her boy on his forehead, then drifted my way. She stifled an involuntary yawn and asked, "Is big Nick turning in for the night, too?"

"Later," I said. "I'm going out for a walk." I handed her the kid's trick-or-treat bag full of good stuff. "He had a blast. You'll probably want to have this stuff scanned."

"You're going out again? Now? Will you be safe?"

I didn't respond, checked the ordnance inside my trench coat. She laughed. "I'm sorry," she said. "Will *they* be safe?"

Our eyes met. I wanted this moment and dreaded it at the same time. Electra softened, leaned forward, and let herself lean into my arms.

I held her as we searched each other's eyes for something; we had no idea what it was or if it was. But we looked for it. The search alone felt nice, warm.

"I'm heading out," I said. "I'll be back later."

Electra said, "You are the most freewheeling man I've ever known. And I grew up with cowboys. I'm not surprised it took a Miss Texas to throw a lasso around your neck."

I turned to leave. "I won't disturb you when I return," I said.

Her fingers caught my coat. She said, "I'm sorry. That slipped out."

She looked up at me like a little girl who got caught with her hand in the cookie jar. It was a nice look. I kissed her cheek.

She knew damn well where I was going. So did he. I knew he'd be waiting, and he knew I'd come. This wasn't war. It wasn't business. This was personal, and it was about to become fear and loathing in the D.C. tunnels.

37

As I walked down the glazed empty streets of the city, I came upon the charred remains of the Chang's Chinese Laundry. I paused. Rainwater poured onto the floor inside the smoldering roof. Rivulets of water streamed down clothes sheathed in transparent plastic that still hung on racks.

I turned and looked in the direction of the Victoria Taylor Gallery.

Further ahead, a donut shop's windows were beginning to bake for the morning's early crowds. Among blocks of darkened storefronts, it's windows were the only ones that cast light onto the sidewalk. I tapped on the glass and pressed a C-note to the window.

The MPD officer who sat in a squad car outside the Bolide Pizza Boutique worked on a laptop when I approached. He looked up as I neared his car, cracked his window open against the rain. I said, "Diliberto get the night off?"

He said, "He needed it. Long days, long hours." He checked me out through the rain on his windows. "Aren't you…?"

I nodded, showed him my ID. "Here, these are for you," I said, and handed him a couple of dozen fresh hot donuts, along with one of my .45 caliber calling cards. "They're safe," I said. "You know where to find me." He rolled his window down and took the boxes.

"I need to go back below," I said. "I dropped something important."

He said, "The FBI and MPD combed the place. They probably have it."

"I hope not," I said.

"Thanks," he said, indicating the box of sprinkled goodies. "Go ahead. If anybody has a right to the place, it's you."

Items in the store's walk-in refrigerator were visible now, lit by a temporary shop light that hung from the ceiling. Also, the hatch entrance to the tunnel below was braced open. I descended into the hellhole and retraced my steps through the brick tunnels.

My cellphone's flashlight led the way as I looked for bloodstains in the dirt but saw nothing. No blood, weapons, torches, robes – no tracking spoor.

I reached the end of the tunnel and looked out into the vast cavern. Everything that was there before was gone. Cages, gone. Whiteboard, gone. Release button, gone. Only the ubiquitous eerie green light remained.

With Caution at my side, I crept into the cavern. I paced off the distance to where the cages had stood. There were markings dug into the brick floor, to be sure. But they could have been made by anything. The place was picked as clean as bones in a desert.

I inspected the floor. *Dammit.* The cop might be right. *If they cleaned up this meticulously, they probably picked up my Zippo, too.* I knew precisely where the cages were that confined me. I kicked at the holes in the floor that anchored the apparatus, toed my way around the dirt and dust atop the bricks.

Nothing.

Then my flashlight's periphery registered a glint in a recess of the floor across the room. I kept the light focused on its muted reflection and approached it. It was dirty and dusty and dark with its black crinkle finish, but its case was steel. With its lid open, the shiny inside reflected enough light to find its way back to me.

My grandfather's nickname was Pony because he liked to play the horses at the tracks. His WWII Zippo lighter was my lucky family heirloom. Pony was sent from the Battle of the Bulge to Stalag IX-B to endure the worst POW hardships of the European war. He became one of only a couple of hundred survivors of the Berga labor camp. There was no accounting for the number that died.

A secret satellite of Buchenwald, Berga served as a Nazi slave labor camp for American POWs. More than 70 out of 350 died of malnutrition, pulmonary disease from the mines, and merciless random beatings.

The conditions were worse than at any other Nazi POW camp. Every day they limped through the snow for two miles to their destinations. They blasted their way forward underground and built secret Nazi tunnels. This was where the Germans hid their hydrogenation production to turn brown coal into fuel for their military weaponry.

The Nazis doubled Berga's inhuman value by also using it for extermination through forced labor. There was no medicine, no food, no clothes. Men kept warm with shared body heat and ate the lice off their bodies for food. When anyone collapsed because they breathed dust and dirt caused by the tunnel explosions, they were cast aside, left to die, and replaced.

Pony told me of the European Jews he saw. He described them as a mass of humanity in blue and white striped pajamas, the most emaciated people he had ever seen. They had huge eyes and didn't make a sound. They just stared at the Americans when they arrived, like they were from another planet.

It wasn't long before he identified with them. When Pony entered Berga he weighed 157 pounds. When he was liberated, he was down to 85. He never talked much about the war, but he said the possession of his lighter was the only thing that kept him alive. When I read *Man's Search for Meaning* by Victor Frankl, a book written by another Nazi POW, I understood why.

I bent down and picked up my battle tested heirloom. I rubbed off the dirt, closed it and tucked it inside my shirt pocket, sealed with a Velcro flap. I crossed the rest of the grotto to the recessed chamber where I witnessed the horrors we captured on video.

My back scraped against the bricks as I crept near the torture chamber/dining hall. I prepared myself to be repulsed and peered around the entranceway. Pitch black. Dead silence. There was no choice but to use my flashlight to see down into the subterranean scene of slaughter and sacrifice.

I flicked it on. The sight of the ghostly cavern, now vacant and still, appeared like video footage of a spooky sunken shipwreck. In the eerie light and shadows, there were no signs of life.

Only the rows of empty tables remained, and the standing plastic wrap machine. Other than that, the place was as empty as the cavern behind me.

Then it came; I knew it would. From the eerie grotto, it echoed down the tunnel through which I just walked, a mocking, screeching high-pitched laugh.

38

My head jerked around in response. My body left my thoughts behind; I ran down the tunnel at the source of the shrieks.

My .45s were clenched in my left hand, my derringer in my right. This was game face time, and the mug that psychotic monster was about to see wouldn't grace any magazine covers.

I reached the tunnel's opening that looked out on the dim grotto. I paused; my back pressed tight against the wall. Two shots exploded like cannons. The bullets smashed into the bricks beside me. Shards and grit shattered into my face and hands.

He called to me in that painful, screeching excuse for a voice: "Guns? You? Me? No ..."

I peeked around my corner's edge. He stepped from the shadows into the vacant greenness of the cavern. He stepped to the center and laid his pistol down on the bricks, a Smith & Wesson .500 X Frame. "You came to fight," he said with a shriek.

My trigger finger on my .45s itched like it had eczema. *I don't play fair. I don't play at all.* What an idiot. I wanted to blow his head off and get it done, but I had bigger plans. I stepped out into the archway of my tunnel.

I said, "Don't flatter yourself, psycho. I came back for my lighter." I unsnapped my shirt pocket, pulled it out and clinked it open. To my surprise, it still lit a flame. I fished out a companion Red, lit it, snapped the lighter shut and secured it back inside my pocket.

"You came back to die!" he screeched.

He took off his jacket and tossed it aside. He wore only black combat boots and a tight-fitting black body leotard. And his Cyclops shades. Tonight's flavor was vanilla. He stretched his arms out and slowly twisted around both ways to show he had no weapons.

I checked his proximity to his gun. He checked my vision's path and before my mind registered its conclusion, stepped two paces farther away from it. I took a couple of steps out and dropped my overcoat; I was down to my special ops ballistic black gear.

I kept my eyes on him, lowered myself forward and laid my guns on the ground. My index fingers touched their triggers until I was convinced there was nothing in his boots or up his sleeves, and that the place was empty. I still had my hammerless .38 in its holster behind my back.

I walked into the bricked grotto. Before I launched my first attack, he slammed two powerful blows into my chest. Then he vanished from his position directly in front of me. By the time I looked up, he stood in front of me again and grinned through his jagged teeth.

I felt a cut on my cheek. Then another on the back of my hand. I flicked my cigarette butt at him – missed. He giggled with an ear-splitting squeal.

My right and left shoulder angels argued:
I'm going to kick his ass.
Keep your head.
I'm going to kick his ass.
You know the drill.

I don't care, I'm going to kick his ass.

No matter what I did, it was like fighting a quicker opponent, blindfolded. Every blow I made struck empty air. I was swinging, but the *pinata* slipped my blows.

I listened to his air movements. He swished around me and cut the back of my neck. I heard him move and saw him stand in front of me again.

He drew himself up and lifted his arms high. His hands were open, pointed down at me, when I noticed his fingernails. Classic White Crane. His long fingernails were perfectly manicured to sharp points and edges. He used them to perform the crane beak that would peck out my eyes or slice my skin to ribbons.

OK, Crane. You take the high road; I'm going to kick your ass.

I rushed the sadisic assassin to tackle him - but when I got there, he was gone. He whipped behind me again and cut the back of my neck. I felt the coolness of the blood trail from his slice. I didn't care. *I'm going to kick his ass.*

I took the fight to the center of the chamber, ducked when I heard his movement just in time to avoid his long nails shredding my face. When I reached and grabbed to give him a head butt, I clutched two handfuls of air. Then his second punch hit me before I knew his first punch had already landed.

I couldn't see him, but I could see his punches coming. The problem was, there was little I could do about them. Too many. Too fast. He flurried me with a series of Wing Chun attacks.

The son-of-a-bitch was a whirling dervish. He punched me and cut me from all angles, high and low before I knew what hit me. He tried to take my legs out but bounced off, then continued his attack.

He stood before me with a shit-eating grin and adjusted his white Cyclops shades. He said in his irritating screech, "You're weak. 20 minutes for your lady to die."

He joined his hands together and slid them apart. One hand gripped a small blowgun the size of a large straw he'd hidden up his sleeve; the other hand held its glittering short dart. His leering smile sickened me.

In a flash, he whipped the blowgun to his lips, popped the dart into it and blew. The missile glinted in the dim green light as it zipped across the room. I watched it hit home.

Its impact was strong, like getting poked in the chest. But that was it. I looked down. The dart hung from my shirt pocket, with no penetration. Pony's lighter saved another life.

Cyclops charged; he attacked me with another flurry of blows and cuts. He was all around me, all over me, punching me, cutting me.

I stuck out my leg. He tripped and smashed headfirst onto the brick floor.

I pounced on him like a lion and grabbed the back of his neck with both hands. His short dark hair served as handgrips for my fingers as I bashed his face into the deck again and again until blood covered the bricks. Then I smashed my right fist as hard as I could into his lower right back for a devastating kidney punch.

He clutched his side in agony and writhed in the dust, gasping for breath. I hammered my fist into his kidney again with everything I had, with the knuckles of my middle finger extended. He shrieked from the intense agony and fainted. Cyclops lay face down in the dust, unconscious and at my mercy.

I zip-tied his hands and feet and collected my guns. I replaced my pistols, slipped back into my coat and added his .500 S&W to my personal collection. Despite being unconscious, he groaned with pain when I threw him over my shoulder and carried him like a rolled-up rug.

I made sure he got plenty of happy bounces from the spring in my step as I carried him out of the grotto. My first destination was straight back to the chamber of horrors. A piece of equipment there was waiting to be repurposed.

The large stretch wrapper they left behind rotated objects while it covered them completely in cocoons of clear plastic wrap. This industrial-sized unit was scaled to process pallet capacities that weighed up to 5,000 pounds.

I dumped Cyclops from my shoulder to the deck where he landed with a dusty thud. The pickings were slim, but I found one cracked blue metal and plastic chair that got kicked under one of the tables. It positioned well, centered on the stretch wrapper's rotating platform.

The unconscious Cyclops slumped in the chair as I lashed him into his seated position with the machine's plastic. I stepped across the platform and pressed the white Power button on the control panel. It lit up, active.

I pressed the green Start button. The big machine whirred the platform around with Cyclops in his chair on top of it. I let it rotate 20 times until the clear layers stopped just beneath his chin. Still unconscious, he puked. And puked. Then puked again.

Now, with everything under control, I did something I wanted to do for days. I reached out with both hands and slid off his shades. There was no way I was prepared for what I saw.

39

Cyclops suffered from anophthalmia, the rare instance of being born without one or both eyes. Literally, Cyclops had one eye.

There was no prosthetic for the second eye socket that had sunken back into his head. Instead, he wore his cyclops shades. It wasn't a pretty sight, and I was going to have to look at him for a while. I slid them back on his face.

Time to wake up. I smacked his cheek. Then again. Then I grabbed both his cheeks with my hands and motorboated him like it was high tide in Smuggler's Cove. Nothing doing.

I raised his shades and thumped his eye with my finger. He chomped at it with a bite that a snapping turtle would envy. "You die!" he screamed.

"Maybe. First, we're going to play 20 questions."

He struggled against his full-body plastic bonds. "I kill you!"

"Here's the deal, Cyc. I'm impatient. If I just wanted to listen to you ramble on about anything I ask, I'd use sodium pentothal. But God, I hate your screeches. If I had time for psychoanalysis, I'd use sodium amythial. But then you'd just clam up."

He tried in vain to twist with his shoulders; he snapped his snaggled choppers at me. "So, that leaves us with good old reliable scopolamine. Maybe you know it as hyoscine." I reached into my coat pockets and produced a special syringe in one hand, along with a clear glass ampule of the colorless, odorless, tasteless liquid in the other.

His eye widened. He screamed in fear and used every ounce of adrenalin he had to break free of his plastic prison. He failed.

Cyclops watched my syringe slowly draw the scopolamine hydrobromide from its glass vial. "Maybe I should have given it to you before your little spin around the world here. Might have kept you from getting so seasick. Oh, well. But as you and I both know; the key is injecting it. And where. When shot into the spine even the most hardened criminals tell the truth 95% of the time."

I pulled out the Buck pocketknife I bought at the hardware store and walked behind him. The big knife sliced an opening in the plastic near the base of his spine. This did not make him happy.

"Of course, as you also know this causes excruciating pain." I smiled at him. "You're gonna love it."

I noticed a thin silver chain around the back of his neck, so I cut its cord and liberated it. His neck chain was attached to a round medallion. I examined it in the dim light. About an inch in diameter, it was black enamel with a gold inlay of a complex design. The symbol of Angular Magic.

In my hands, I held the ID of an ONA assassin. The Order of Nine Angels was the most evil society on the face of the earth and my direct celestial foe. FLOTUS added me as her ninth operator. I had just taken down one of ONA's Original Nine Assassins.

My curiosity licked its chops. He would be privy to the highest echelons of the satanic cult.

Something was going on that I couldn't fathom. I felt like I was standing in the middle of a giant 360-degree jigsaw puzzle. All the pieces flew around me and some of them paired up to make sense but most of them confused the landscape. The few that fell into place and stayed there didn't make sense. Hopefully, a lot of new pieces would fit together in a few minutes.

I stood up and placed myself in front of him so he could watch me squirt a test drop out of the syringe's needle. "The medical journals say not to use this if you have narrow-angle glaucoma. Do you have narrow-angle glaucoma, Cyclops? No, I guess that isn't an issue in your case. Having any trouble urinating? You shouldn't use scopolamine then, either."

I indicated the puddle on the deck at his feet. "Oh, no, I can see that isn't an issue. Never mind."

He screamed. "No! I kill you!"

I said, "Tell it to the little girl in the pink and white dress, you son-of-a-bitch." It was tricky delivering the serum into his spinal column from his incarcerated sitting position, but I was motivated.

After I shoved the needle into the base of his spine, Cyclops suffered violent convulsions and a borderline seizure for half an hour. He succumbed. I stood before his bowed head and, with sarcastic confidence, quoted Lewis Carroll:

"The time has come, the walrus said, to talk of many things. Of shoes and ships and sealing wax, of cabbages and kings ..."

I patted his cheeks, and we were about to begin chatting like old drinking buddies when a youthful voice over my shoulder broke in and said, "and why the sea is boiling hot, and whether pigs have wings."

I spun and looked behind me. Little Nick stood there; I had no idea for how long. He looked at me with his arms akimbo in his sneakers and PJ bottoms, beneath a T-shirt and **W** ball cap.

I moved toward him. "What the Hell are you doing here?"

He shrugged. "I followed you here when you weren't in your bedroom at home."

"Kid," I said, "I'd much rather be there than here. How'd you get past the policeman?"

He shrugged. "I'm a kid."

"Don't give me that." I turned him back into the tunnel and pointed him toward the grotto. "Get yourself back up and out of here like there's no tomorrow. All Hell could break lose any second and I don't need you here to get hurt."

He looked back at me. "You mean, like when I shot that guy in the tunnel? Hurt like that?" I loved this kid and wanted to smack him at the same time.

I grumbled as I plucked my hammerless .38 revolver from its holster in the small of my back. I slapped it into his open hand and smacked him on the butt. "Get out. Now! Run up like you're being chased and stay in that cop's car with him until I come out. If I come out and you're not there, that's it between you and me. No more us. Understand?"

I watched his flashlight grow faint as his little legs carried him out of my sight down the tunnel. The light bounced forward into the grotto and toward the tunnel on the other side. A long breath of exasperation escaped my lungs as I focused my attention back on my subject.

> "A wise old owl,
> Lived in an oak.
> The more he heard,
> The less he spoke.
> The less he spoke,
> The more he heard.
> Wasn't he a wise old bird?"

I listened. He talked. And I recorded everything.

Cyclops sang for an hour, and his screeching speech was as sweet to my ears as a tenor on stage in *La Traviata*. I recorded stories that involved specific Senators, Congressmen, Congresswomen, movie stars, foreign heads of state, billionaires, VIPS – all pedophiles to an extreme degree.

It went beyond sexual slavery; it involved vivisecting, dissecting, producing body parts for sale on the dark web and websites about "recipes to cook girls." It made me want to puke.

In its twisted way, it was politically connected and motivated. Because it was all about power. That materialized when we discussed financial aspects like pay-to-play deals and influence peddling. These occurred at the highest levels, ranging from lobbyists to heads of state.

I made a note to thank Mr. Allison with more Chesapeake Bay Blue Crabs. The scopolamine worked with greater detail than I hoped. I double-checked to make sure I had it all recorded on my phone, so I could report every granular detail.

Especially the specific offshore bank accounts and numbers.

Cyclops connected the dots between their charitable foundations that took pay-to-play payments. They lined their pockets through laundered money sent to multiple hidden bank accounts in Switzerland and the Cayman Islands.

How do you launder dirty money? Buy and sell "art." Create empty shell corporations. Play the tables in casinos. There are a hundred ways.

When we finished, I felt exhausted and exhilarated at the same time. I stood and observed my antagonist in his captive state. He was born deformed; he had those horrible jagged pointy teeth - and that voice. I almost started to feel bad for him.

Then I remembered the little girl in the pink and white dress, and her vital fight against him for her life. I remembered the innocent weird couple in my Washington Hotel room next door. I remembered my ride to the Capitol blown into attempted oblivion on Pennsylvania Avenue. I remembered the video of little Nick's abduction in the van. And the Changs.

I thought about Victoria Taylor.

I reached into my jacket pocket and again removed my purchase from the hardware store. I planted myself in front of him and opened the blade in my hands, moved it before his face. Cyclops' eye enlarged as if inflated.

I touched the golden earring in his left ear. "You won't be needing this anymore."

He screamed.

40

The Mansion's heavy wooden doors swung open before me in the morning's dark hours. Horace tied the sash of his floor length quilted robe and wiped sleep from his eyes. Together, we snuck the kid up the sweeping stairway to bed before mom came around.

After we tucked him in, I stepped light down the hall. Electra's bedroom suite towering doors approached on my right. *Not gonna happen.*

My Recovery Room's chandelier shone 50 lights, enriched by gold leaf linings in their individual shades. They glinted off the cuts of my Waterford crystal old-fashioned glass at the bar. I grabbed a decanter and poured myself a bourbon and water.

A nearby chair made of cowhide and cow horns invited me to park it. I fished out my smartphone and yawned. The full recording of my fireside chat with Cyclops transmitted from my phone to FLOTUS, Murgatroyd and Margo. I yawned again. My law firm received it as well.

It might or might not be admitted in court as evidence, but that didn't matter, and I didn't care. It gave dead solid clues. What it provided was information to be identified, researched, verified and expanded upon. It was evidence that would send a dozen office-holding and unelected elitist perverts to jail for a long time. And wouldn't they have a fun time in prison.

Sleep didn't come easy. I felt like a kid who counted jumping sheep until Christmas morning. At sunrise, I showered, shaved and slipped into my new sharkskin Brioni suit. The aroma of a full force Metro Diner breakfast filled my senses; I followed it downstairs to breakfast.

The White Mansion staff gift-wrapped a candy box for me in Halloween colors while I made a breakfast-to-breakfast call across the street.

I forgot that kids don't sleep late. Mrs. Jackson and I discussed the morning's agenda when the pitapat sound of little feet charged in my direction. They padded across the forward zeppelin hanger, down the hallway, and into the Cattle Baron's Diner. That was my name for the first floor apartment set aside for morning meals.

Its long 19th century farm table seated 20 yet was dwarfed by a wall-to-wall enneaptych of large framed black and white photos. In every 4' x 5' framed picture Electra's dad stood beside a different Grand National Champion Steer bred on the McDonald cattle ranches.

They showed the late Winfield "Rip" McDonald as a tall, lean Texas string bean. Rip was every bit the aristocratic statesman that someone like John Evans wanted to be. Plus, Rip punched cows and criminals.

He embarked upon his life when he joined the Texas Rangers in 1955 for what he called his first and last real job. Company D out of Weslaco was his home. Rip McDonald learned to love the local land that was officially classified as uniquely subtropical, also semi-arid, and the people who were the same way.

Rip's parents were poor and attended the Welhausen School in Cotulla. Their teacher was Mr. Johnson, a man who inspired the youths and taught them to pursue their dreams with near ruthless commitment, to never give up. He taught them the meaning of the Latin phrase, *Carpe Diem*.

That schoolteacher went on to become a U.S. Senator from the Lone Star State, Vice-President, and eventually President of the United States. The elder Leander McDonald passed these lessons on to his son, Rip.

In 1956 word got out about a movie made in Marfa with Elizabeth Taylor, Rock Hudson, James Dean and Chill Wills. Rip McDonald had a hunch. He sensed a Texas boom on the horizon and bought up all the south Texas ranchland that he could not afford, as fast as he could.

Several years back, Rip was run down for six months with idiopathic pulmonary fibrosis and passed away. His Creole wife Francoise Sabine McDonald and her daughter took over the operation.

According to articles in *The Cattleman* magazine, they ran commercial crossbreds that wore their running **M** brand. These grazed on a half million acres that spread across Uvalde, Zavala, Dimmit and Maverick counties. Plus, that little 1,000-acre ranchette southeast in Jim Hogg.

Electra ran the McDonald's *vaqueros*. They waged firefights against rustlers, human traffickers, and drug smugglers that poured across the southern Texas border. And "they" included her. She could ride, rope and shoot.

Little Nick climbed up on the primitive bench in his blue and white tracksuit and sat beside me. He asked, "What are we going to do today?"

That ended my call with the White House. I closed my eyes, inhaled a semi-deep breath. I slowly let it out between my lips. "You, young Nick, are going to school," I said.

"School," he said. "What are you going to do?"

"I am going to have tea with the Queen."

As if on cue, as if somehow always on cue, Electra appeared. She stood behind her son in a pink silk nightgown beneath a matching robe, in matching satin wedge slippers. "I prefer coffee," she said.

She gently massaged her son's shoulders. "But if Mr. Wolfe prefers, I'm sure Henri can brew some organic herbal patchouli tea especially for his sophisticated Manhattan taste." She looked at me from behind and above the kid's head and wrinkled her nose.

I wrinkled my nose back at her. Nick looked confused. I whispered in her ear. "And my coffee has a shot of Bourbon," I said.

She smiled and replied, "Somebody's feeling better." Electra sat on the bench across from me. She unfurled her napkin and laid it across her lap. Within another minute her staff delivered her favorite breakfast, the kid's favorite, and mine.

Electra pursed her lips, blew across the top of her black coffee. "So," she said. "What is it you have on your agenda today? I'd like to tag along."

Little Nick chimed in with, "That's what I was saying!"

"Sorry. Private party. You'll know all about it tonight." Again, I got the wrinkled nose treatment. "Timing is everything. I don't want to ruin the surprise."

Electra still retained flashes of a college girl look, and on such a beautiful woman I found it irresistible. "Electra," I said. "Why doesn't Horace join us at these family breakfasts and dinners?"

She grinned. "I suppose that does seem a bit out of place, doesn't it? Why don't you tell him, baby?"

Little Nick dropped his fork into his huevos rancheros. "Mom. You said you'd stop calling me, 'baby'."

She looked at me. "You say that today. But I'll bet Mr. Wolfe says different."

The younger brother began to explain. "What happened was ..." Electra reached across the table with gentile grace and covered his hand with hers.

"He lost a bet," she said. The kid laughed.

She was a mother who loved her son, and she looked for ways to have some fun. On my way out I received a pair of full force hugs and kisses on the cheek. The second set was from little Nick.

It must have been a slow day for news. The world press covered the White Mansion's front lawn in a mob; actually, several mobs: reporters from multiple news and gossip channels, their cameras, their crews and vans with satellite uplinks.

I emerged into the clear bright sunlight on that crisp November morning. Despite the media vultures, I paused and indulged in the gorgeous air that followed the night's rains. Andriy rolled up in his armored SUV through the press mob.

But which one was he? I didn't expect his comrades Victor and Sergei to follow suit in their matching black armored Escalades.

The Mansion guards' security line stretched from the carvings on the massive front doors to the open entry of the center Escalade. My ears caught the shrill voice of a female reporter above the din. "What can you tell us about the video that's gone viral this morning?"

Andriy positioned his SUV to provide me with man-in-the-middle security. He stood ready and waiting beside the opened passenger door. "All this for little old me?" I asked as I climbed in. I noticed that Andriy & Co. had upgraded their armaments. Kalashnikov tactical shotguns with extended magazines stood on the console inside each vehicle.

"Your Mr. James," said Andriy. "He is telling us. Big day today."

Three armored escorts for a three-block trip. I played a game of catch with a kid - and became a rock star.

But that morning I could have ridden a bike and been safe. My immediate chief threat was out of commission and my forthcoming attack would be a surprise. Still, I couldn't help but scrutinize the landscape and surroundings on both sides of the street as we wheeled along.

In the back of my mind, I searched for Cyclops' shades among the sidewalk crowds. My Spetsnaz entourage played a rolling shell game as we rolled down Pennsylvania Avenue toward the Capitol. Our vehicle started in the middle, moved to the back, then to the front, then back to the middle, in steady, smooth maneuvers.

Instead of mountain climbing the steps to the front doors, at 10:30 a.m. they deposited me at the east front plaza of the U.S. Capitol at First and East Capitol Streets. I would have arrived earlier, but the liars, cheats and thieves wouldn't have been in their offices yet.

I expanded my lungs for another deep breath of the morning's crisp autumn air, then began my stroll. I walked toward the U.S. Capitol Building along the concrete football field known as the East Front Plaza.

On each side, a pair of impressive fountains launched their aerial waterworks skyward into the sunlight. The plants on their bottom levels enjoyed a constant misting taste of water. I flicked a butt into a sand trap trash can on my right, moved on toward the imposing Columbus Doors of the east entrance.

I could have passed through security based on my new Pied Piper celebrity. Or I could have simply invoked my new Top-Secret clearance. But it was a beautiful morning and there are so few things worth savoring.

I stood by while the security detail scanned me. A young Capitol Police officer with a pronounced limp on his right side and only four fingers on his right hand inspected my gift-wrapped box.

He looked at me, then carried it off to the side where he placed it under an x-ray scanner. His face tightened into a twisted combination of confusion and disgust.

"Halloween," I said with a shrug and a smile.

He didn't smile back and handed it to me. I carried my gift box past the girls at a couple of tour kiosks on my way to a slow climb down the stairs. There, I entered the grand and impressive Capitol Visitors Center.

41

I picked up a cup of U.S. Capitol black American coffee and strolled through Emancipation Hall. I paused to appreciate the statues and toasted the massive bronze of "The Last King," King Kamehameha, with my cup of Kona java.

Half an hour before noon, I made my way down the running length of the Speaker's Lobby once again. It was a quiet morning under the rotunda and before long I stood before the doors for the office of the Speaker of the House.

I studied the pompous pose of John Evans on the 27"x 42" one-sheet poster outside his office. Capitol business was slow and in the office entrance, Julie flipped through the pages of a magazine at her desk.

I moved inside, said, "Hi, Julie." The pert redhead looked up from the pages of her glossy rag, behind large octagonal reading glasses. "I need to borrow a black Scripto pen. Do you have one?"

Her eyes looked greener than hazel through the lenses as she studied me, confused. "I've cleaned up since you saw me," I said. "I smoldered more a couple days ago."

Her memory returned and she scrambled to lose the cheaters. She slapped her *Cosmo* shut and shoved it into a drawer. I reminded her about the Scripto.

As she rummaged through her desk, I broke out a broad, televangelist smile. I said, "If you'd tell Speaker Evans I'm here to see him. He's going to be just thrilled."

Her hands were spasmodic. In what resembled a bad relay baton handoff, I obtained the pen from her. She glanced at my gift box.

I said, "A Halloween gift for the Speaker."

Julie hastened inside the Speaker's sanctorium. "Yes, Mister Piper. I mean, Mister Wolfe. Mister Pied Piper Wolfe." If she ingested a heaping tablespoon of raw niacin it wouldn't have made her fair-skinned face blush any brighter.

She disappeared into his office for a minute. I stood beside her desk when she returned. "Speaker Evans will see you now," she said.

I laid her Scripto on her desk and walked inside. John Evans did not rise from his chair. He kept his hands folded on top of his desktop's leather inlay and glowered at me. His coiffed silver locks looked like he slept in a hair net.

"You don't just waltz into my office any time you want. I am not some wet behind the ears freshman. I am the Speaker of the House."

I sat down and faced him across his desk. The gift box rested in my lap. I reached into my breast pocket, lifted out my deck of Reds and Pony's Zippo.

He studied the smoking paraphernalia in my hands. "You ignored the meeting I arranged with Ms. Schicklgruber. I'm afraid that's all I can do for you -"

I said, "But I come bearing gifts." I placed the orange and black wrapped box on his desk and pushed it across to his clasped hands. "Trick or treat."

His eyes looked down his nose at the orange and black package like it was a regifted fruitcake. He read the granite in my face across the poker table that was his desk. His fingers grasped the corners of his gift.

Off came the ribbon, then some tape, then the crinkling decorative wrap. He let the papers fall to the floor and looked down at the candy box. The resentment he showed in his eyes when he looked back up was the product of many rehearsals.

His glare was meant to intimidate me. I said, "How many times have you practiced that look in a mirror?"

I wanted to break out laughing with my hand of a royal flush. But this was poker at the highest stakes. I'd wait until the very end to play my cards.

"I take it this isn't candy," he said.

"It's from a friend of yours." He slowly opened the box but never took his non-terrifying eyes off me. I said, "Polyphemus couldn't be here. He's busy feeding the tunnel rats if you know what I mean. And I think you do."

When he looked inside, his expression changed from authoritarian anger into shock and disbelief. He swept the box and its contents off his desk onto the floor and shot up from his chair. He backed away from the objects that lay on top of his carpet, horrified by the images they placed in his mind.

Rolling around on his extravagant handwoven rug were the broken and bloodied vanilla Cyclops sunglasses. They circled until they spun to a rest on the floor. Beside them laid the Order of Nine Angels medallion and chain, and a golden earring.

And an ear. The earring was still attached to its ear.

I asked, "Stylish fellow, isn't he?"

The Speaker's face was contorted with responses he never knew he would have to register. Anger. Hate. Passion for Death. Fear. Vulnerability. It was so hard to choose.

"We talked like a pair of old buddies. And I recorded every word. He recited an impressive A-List of elitists."

I laughed. "You were at the top of his list. He showed an incredible capacity for numbers when he recited explicit Swiss and Cayman bank accounts. So many digits. In such a little brain."

He squinted his aging eyes at me.

"Don't worry. I didn't kill him." I lit up my smoke. "I beat the shit out of him. But when I left, he was alive. I think." No response. John Evans was a pillar of salt. "But yeah. He's feeding the rats." My cigarette ash flicked onto his carpet.

The only parts of his body that moved were his eyes. He stared at me, appalled. "You can't do that in here!"

I said, "Really? This is the least of your worries, pal," I blew a deep, long, large puff of smoke into his face.

He called out, "Julie! Get the Sergeant at Arms!"

"Rufus McShaw? Funny you should mention him. I talked to him this morning. We go way back; ran track against each other – BCC and Anacostia. He's on his way here, now. He's going to take you in. Murder one, among others."

I leaned forward with a look that only Hell could appreciate. "Mister Speaker, this is what you call a NIGYSOB. Do you know what a NIGYSOB is?"

He looked past me and refocused his eyes, eyes that registered extreme angst. Speaker of the House of Representatives of the United States John Evans, second in line to accede to the most powerful position in the world, stood quaking behind his desk.

A strong and powerful voice boomed over my shoulder. "'Now I've Got You, Son of a Bitch'."

Behind the Speaker's desk hung a 19th-century bull's eye mirror with an eagle perched atop its gilded frame. Through its looking glass I saw the reflection of John Jackson, President of the United States. It was a good thing the round mirror was convex. He brought his full entourage.

"I'll see your House Sergeant at Arms, Wolfe, and raise you my secret service licensed and registered federal officers, the Secretary of Homeland Security, the Chief of the Metropolitan Police Department, and the Chief of the Capitol Police."

I stood at attention. This was an All-Star cast I wanted to believe I was seeing.

POTUS said, "John, we've just come from Clinton Moore's office at the FBI. He's under arrest, for accessory to murder and other charges. Things are in motion for about twenty others just like him. And you."

The Speaker of the House found and slumped into his yellow chair. President Jackson continued. "John Evans, you are charged with murder in the first degree. And just to make sure this goes down *According to Hoyle;* these gentlemen provide the incident command for every possible jurisdictional question."

One secret service agent and one Capitol Police officer bent the Speaker over his desk and cuffed his hands behind him. The Capitol officer read him his rights. The Chief of MPD didn't want to be left out. He followed and cited *Miranda* again as they led the satanist leader through the large doors.

Julie's flaming tresses stood out against the deep green velvet drapes behind her. She held up her smartphone, recorded the entire scene.

POTUS gave me a quick head-to-toe assessment. "Looking better than the last time we met," he said.

"Thank you, sir. That's quite some entourage."

POTUS looked back over his shoulder and grinned. "Why should rock stars have all the fun?"

"So, one big roundup at the OK Corral, sir?"

"There's a lot to be learned from The Godfather," he said. "Hit them all at once. Your video is shutting down YouTube's servers with hits. We edited it to be as un-revolting as possible for the public."

"You'd have to black out the whole video."

"What do you know about the blackened tooth and eye patch on the Speaker's office poster?"

"Eye patch?" I asked.

He eye-tasered me again and looked right through me. "Bring Electra and join us for dinner. Tonight. Foursome."

Electra's soft South Texas tones emerged from behind a pair of secret service agents. "We would love to, sir. Wouldn't we, Nick?"

What am I going to say to the President? "Nooooo…"

42

Between the lump crab appetizer and the chef's salad, I wondered what looking glass I crashed through. The mystery of the eye patch on the poster was the lead item of discussion at dinner.

This was a four-person dinner with POTUS and FLOTUS in the White House. The directors of several alphabet agencies and a host of others were just arrested. The incidents made international headlines. But the story of interest over dinner was graffiti.

After two glasses of Italian Barolo wine, the puzzle was solved. If anyone could be sheepish and playful at the same time, it was Electra White. We listened with rapt attention.

Little Nick dogged me that morning at breakfast. It was obvious that he was Hell-bent for playing hooky. While I was escorted past the press corps to Andriy's Escalade in the middle, the kid snuck past and stowed away in the lead Spetsnaz Special SUV.

One better, his mother grew tired of hearing his stories about his adventures with me. Electra jumped into a quick pair of chinos and a canvas brush jacket. Just as we drove off, she ducked into the caboose SUV while the wheels rolled forward.

According to our dinnertime narrator, the pair of amateurish sleuths were challenged staying unnoticed while they followed me. My irregular dawdling pace baffled their timing up flights of stairs and around corners down to the Speakers Lobby.

They peeked around a corridor corner, high and low, and watched me come out of John Evans' office with Julie's Scripto. Mother and son withheld silent laughs as I performed my cosmetic dentistry graffiti on his choppers and waved to the corridor's CCTV cameras.

They watched me return inside, then snuck into Julie's office when we went in to see Evans. Little Nick snatched the Scripto from her desktop and added to my makeover with an eye patch of his own.

The pair of Whites camouflaged themselves within the crowd scene in the Speaker's office. It couldn't have been hard to do, considering the general commotion and confusion. That, plus Electra's personal pull with the VIPs that packed the place.

She wound the story down and looked at me out of the corners of her flashing brown eyes. "And nobody would have known if Jack here didn't bust you on it," she said with a laugh.

The President said, "Nick keeps reminding me how inconspicuous he is."

* * *

I met the kid's new governess when Electra and I returned to her shack. The crisp autumn night air outside was something I didn't want to leave. I lingered behind for a few moments to breathe it in.

Electra went inside ahead of me and as I followed, Aasta rose from her seat, in her comfortable track suit. She was up late and read while she waited in the sitting hangar. As soon as I overheard her speak with Electra, I pegged why her evening attire colors were the red, white and blue.

Electra turned to me and asked, "Can you excuse me a moment?" Any reply was unnecessary. She climbed the winding staircase along its great wall up to the lair of the boy king. I couldn't help but marvel at her dynamic legs, shapely muscles that showed off their definition with each step up the stairs.

Aasta turned to me and asked, *"Du er Herr Pied Piper?"*

"Ja," I replied. *"Mit naven er Nick."*

Aasta's Norwegian cobalt blue eyes flashed with surprise. *"Du snakker norsk!"* she said.

"I *snakker* a lot of things," I said. "But my Swedish is better than my *norsk*."

The massive Bois d'Arc front doors opened. A current of the clear night air blew in with Horace, in his customary black tie evening ensemble.

He was surprised to see us and spoke in a quiet voice. "Oh, Hi," he said. I flared my nostrils and tilted my head back, inhaled a deep breath of the clean night air. Aasta stood beside me in the opened doors and did the same.

Horace took notice and said, "I know. I just checked on the horses in the stables for the night. It's so nice out, I took the long way back here. It sure would be fun to go for a ride."

"Good idea, Horace," I said. I looked at Aasta. She stood about 5' 7", with eyes as blue as Lake Louise in Alberta. Her hair was deep brown, cut in a shining Cleopatra hairdo, *and bangs*. I said, "I agree."

Aasta took a moment to compute what might be going on. Her mind gave her permission. She drew in a breath to reply. "I…"

"You're about to turn in. Isn't that what you told me, Aasta?" With her usual impeccable timing, the ubiquitous lady of the house descended the massive staircase. Her re-entrance from Nick's room down the wide carpeted staircase was a study in the apotheosis of womanhood.

Electra's Command Performance dinner gown was impossible to ignore. The hem of her black, fitted off-shoulder affair allowed a full appreciation of her lovely limbs. Her hair wasn't the only thing taken from magazine covers. Those long slender legs would have earned enough model money on runways to pay for many of the extravagances she enjoyed.

Aasta blushed, turned to leave across the entrance hall. "*Ja*, Mrs. White. *God natt.*"

Electra crossed over to the front doors. She came up to me and took my hands in hers. "Honestly, Nick. The hired help. Whatever am I going to do with you?"

"I thought it would be a nice night for a ride," I said.

She looked at me like a grade-school teacher who knew her pupil was lying out his ass, but she couldn't prove it. "If you play your cards right," she said, "you might just get one."

She said out loud, "Alexa – play *Waltz Across Texas*." The twangy strains of the Ernest Tubb classic filled the lower chambers. We raised our hands into a two-step stance and circled the zeppelin hangar. In an instant we became a cowboy and his bench-front-seat girlfriend in Amarillo.

"You boot scoot good for a Yankee," she said.

"Fort Hood in Killeen. Six months. Ma'am."

The auburn-haired beauty enjoyed a chuckle. "Aren't you just Mr. Road Runner on the high chaparral," she said.

The song faded out. She hooked her arm inside mine. "Buy you a drink in the Long Branch Saloon?"

The entire first floor of the building was paved in white marble. Entrances to large areas were archways 10 to 20 feet high. Every closed room or chamber opened behind massive hand-carved wooden doors like the front entrance, each one Bois D 'Arc, four inches thick.

The main wet bar was a watering hole large enough to open its doors to the public. A full-length hand painted glass mirror behind the smooth wood bar proclaimed in gold leaf: *Long Branch Saloon.*

Fancy saddles perched on top of their strong chrome mounts filled every one of the nine seats at the bar. Electra strode across to a jukebox that played .45 rpm vinyl records in a vertical position. There were professional dancers and track stars who wished they had legs like hers.

I looked closer. She stood before a pristine 1952 Seeburg. The curvaceous muscles of her legs stretched with splendid definition as she leaned over the display panel to examine selections. "Isn't that jukebox like the one they used in, *Happy Days?*" I asked.

"Darling," she replied. "This is the one they used in *Happy Days.*"

Electra pressed a couple of buttons. As the record wowed to life she walked behind the bar and took the position of bartender. She tied a white apron around her waist and placed both hands on top of the polished Birdseye maple surface. She asked, "What'll it be, stranger?"

"How about a tall, slender, auburn colored bourbon and branch water," I said. She reached for a gleaming glass bottle on the top shelf behind the bar. Again, she stretched those long, smooth legs. She poured the dark amber liquid into one of the Waterford old-fashioned glasses. "With 35-inch inseams," I added.

She produced a pair of barbed wire swizzle sticks and slid them into my drink.

43

We shared a polite goodnight kiss in the hallway between our two bedrooms. The shower inside *El Presidente* provided a showerhead on each of the four walls that were crafted by stone masons. I took my time with the relaxing hot water. My back and shoulders loosened, and I let their muscles ease into their sheaths with the help of the hot hydro action of the showers.

When I doused the lights, I felt fresh and at peace for the first time in a week. The fingers of my hands intertwined behind my head on the pillow. I stared into the pitch darkness.

What a week. My rational shoulder angel told me I needed to get back to New York. Get back to the office, my caseload, Murgatroyd, Trouble, Cody. And Winston.

But my emotional angel prevailed this time. I stretched duct tape across the rational one's mouth and let my thoughts play among the positive things that happened.

A million bucks in the coffers, the results of an unpaid non-job. POTUS. FLOTUS. F.L.O.T.U.S. The UN next week with the crazy classy dame from Argentina. Little Nick. Electra.

At that moment, the grand bedroom doors pushed open without a sound. White light from the hallway spilled into my chamber of darkness. Her backlit shadow in the doorframe reached from her feet across the floor until the top of her head touched the foot of my bed.

Neither of us allowed words to spoil the moment. She drew the doors together behind her, closed, but allowing a vertical sliver of light to spill in behind her. Electra's backlit silhouette approached me, a slow seductive runway catwalk that created its own visual music.

The translucent fabric of her nightgown parted. Its backdrop defined the voluptuous contours of an athletic body ten years younger than the numbers on her birth certificate. Her thick auburn hair spilled across the shoulders of her 5' 10" frame, above the kind of feminine curves that inspired designs of Italian sports cars.

Her waist, hips, legs - ankles so thin I could touch the tips of my thumbs and middle fingers around them. They were all exposed before me with increasing detail as she approached.

Her breasts were full and firm, with pink areolas that pronounced themselves through the flowing panels of her sheer nightwear. And she had removed any way to tell if the carpet in her body's temple matched the drapes. She reached the bed and without any pause of motion and climbed up, then settled on top of me.

I said, "Come here often?"

She ignored me and leaned forward. *Coco by Chanel* filled my nose, lungs, brain and memories of passion, and I felt her D cups softly settle on each side of my face. Her twins fell across both eyes, then my cheeks, throat, shoulders, chest and abdomen as she lowered her body down the length of mine.

Just as it was getting good, she rose and got off the bed. She stood beside me for an instant, then touched the center of my chin with her index finger. She turned and retreated toward the doors.

Electra grasped each door's handle and opened them. I surveyed every inch of a body that could make the Pope shell out Andy Jacksons for a lap dance. Then the doors closed.

Across the darkened room, I heard the locking latch click. Then the snap of a deadbolt, followed by a pair of floor bolts.

Il Passione, my fervent left shoulder angel, swung from the floor with a Kid Gavalin uppercut. The rational one bit the dust and was counted out for the night.

We had lap dances; we had cowgirl up; we had reverse cowgirl, bucking bronco and one time that felt like I was steer wrestling. At the crack of noon in the next day's light, I felt like I should have won a silver buckle for Best All-Around Cowboy in the Sex Rodeo.

We ordered breakfast in time for afternoon tea. Little Nick was noticeably absent, considering we were both MIA. Electra unlocked the doors and rang her Ukrainian honor maid.

Daryna appeared in her traditional gray maid's uniform. She informed us that Jasper, Electra's version of Murgatroyd, managed Master Nick's morning domestic activities and trip to school.

We dined on our comfort food, chased by mimosas that Electra kept flowing like Niagara Falls. She curled up against me on top of luxurious sheets like a big tawny cat. My chest became her pillow that she padded with her palm before she laid her head to rest.

I recalled a feeling of happiness and contentment I thought was gone forever. It might have still been gone. I didn't know. But it was there then, that day, with her.

Her open palm made slow circles as she rubbed my chest. "Mister Wolfe," she asked. "Would you permit me one question I'd like to ask, and I'll never ask anything about it ever again?"

I didn't know if I was in the mist, or if I overdosed on dopamine. I heard myself say, "One question."

She traced her finger around my chest. "What happened? That you're not married?"

I asked her to hand me my deck of Reds and my lighter. The tobacco I inhaled was the single best tasting cigarette I ever had in my life.

"I was on vacation in Fort Worth from Fort Hood. I stumbled into the Miss Texas pageant in my hotel's grand ballroom. It was during the talent competition. I watched this one gorgeous girl own the judges and the crowd. She had this incredible trick shot pistol routine."

I pulled a long draw on my cigarette. The smoke I exhaled through my nostrils felt like pure oxygen. "It was never done before and probably never will be again."

I paused and realized that if I had seen myself talk about this, I would have been appalled. But somehow, now, I had no issue with it.

"Teresa got around their safety and projectile clause because it specifically cited fire batons, throwing or twirling knives, swords, and archery. But it said nothing at all about guns. That changed after she won that year's talent competition with her matching staghorn .44s. That was a big deal because talent made up 35% of their score."

I poured more *Dom Perignon* in both our glasses. "She stuck to her guns, literally. I fell in love with her that weekend. It took a while for her to come around to my way of thinking, but I was persistent."

"She must have been beautiful."

She was. "Teresa Veracruz, Miss El Paso. Miss Texas. Second runner up for Miss America. That's how I know how to two-step. And eat chicken fried steak. And ride. And rope and brand and drink bourbon and branch." I took the last draw of my smoke and stubbed it into an ashtray.

"Electra, if you're thinking of hooking up with me, I'll admit I'm a sucker for beautiful Texas women. But you've got to realize, it's been over a decade since Teresa. I've been a lone wolf ever since. The longer I'm that way, the longer I'll probably stay that way."

"Who am I trying to fool? I live with my pet mountain lion in my waterfront warehouse. My housemate is my artist sister. I'm in the private investigative and personal security business. I get shot. I get knifed. And I return the favors."

"How am I ever going to be corralled by someone when that's my style of living? I'm not fearless, but I know I'm successful at what I do because I generally care less about living than the other guy."

"What happened with Teresa?" she asked.

I said, "One question."

"My question was 'What happened - that you're not married?' I learned a lot of wonderful things, absolutely wonderful, about why you got married. But you didn't answer my question. I asked why you aren't."

I lit another cigarette, sat up in bed.

"It was the winter solstice, the longest night of the year, December 21. Teresa was having our baby in a West Texas hospital. Labor was long, complicated, difficult, late at night into morning. She lost a lot of blood. Our unborn son's umbilical cord got wrapped around his neck. We lost them both."

Electra remained silent. She stopped drumming her fingers on my leg. "I'm sorry," she said.

I said, "I don't know if me today would have worked back then, or if me back then would work today."

Electra pushed herself up on her elbows and sat up in bed beside me. She was as graceful and beautiful as a ballerina, with a body put on earth to delight and torment men. And I loved the touch of every inch of it. But right then, that moment, it seemed far away.

She said, "Don't be silly. What's all this metaphysical mumbo jumbo? That's why today is today and why you are who you are. Here and now. Today. *Carpe Diem* and all that. Any six-year-old will tell you that."

Electra White, enlightened Zen master, buttered some toast, had a sip of mimosa followed by some coffee. She reached down and pinched the corner of the sheet with her fingers. Slowly, with tantalizing deliberation, she slid the soft smooth fabric up the soft smooth skin of her leg. She continued upward over her hips.

"You can stop there," I said. She popped the sheet over her breasts with a defiant grin and pulled it up to her neck. There was that tiny dimple in her chin I loved to see when she smiled.

She said, "I know your life is in New York and you have to get back. But we own the White Hotel on Madison Avenue near the Empire State Building. Nick and I usually check in for the Christmas season."

44

Nick's tutors and coaches occupied his energy and attention with normal after-school schedules until we met for dinner. He joined us at the table in his navy wool blazer that bore the crest for St. Albans School on its pocket.

Electra dressed for dinner with a pair of hand-tooled western boots that bore flourishes of yellow roses, worn over her skin-tight blue denim jeans and matching long-sleeved shirt.

"I'm still the BMOC at school," said the kid. "What did you guys do today?" he asked with a cocky smile.

Electra said, "Don't forget to take your supplements. I took care of some things for myself, and Nick did, too. Pretty much. Isn't that, right?"

I took a quick bite of toast, chased it with coffee.

Little Nick looked at his mom. Without moving his head, he redirected his eyes at me, then turned to let his face catch up to follow his gaze. His mother leaned back with calm confidence and sipped her wine.

Nick exclaimed, "You guys hooked up!"

Electra almost shot her wine out of her nose. Too well-mannered for that, she covered her mouth with her hand and swallowed a quick, big gulp. I almost followed her lead with my coffee, but as a delayed reaction of laughter at her, instead of surprise at him.

Reminds me of me.

I needed to saddle up and ride out of D.C. on the iron horse for the Big Apple, back to my business, back to my office, back to Trouble, and Cody. And Winston.

The last thing I needed was to be part of some high-level Presidential Posse. The last thing I needed was to become a Pictionary dinner couple with POTUS and FLOTUS. That would be living too close to the mouth of the dragon.

The Last Thing I needed was to get in some kind of entangled romance. Especially between two cities. Vastly different cities. In New York, on the streets of the city, I knew what the hell was going on. Down in D.C., I didn't think anybody ever knew which end was up.

I watched the kid stifle a giggle, pleased with himself for his brilliant deduction. Electra's blush belied the European influence on her fair skin.

The last thing I needed was to become some kind of Big Brother for a precocious nine-year-old boy in a different city. The last thing I needed was to hook up with a single mom – especially one who was next door neighbors with the White House. Even an incredible, over-the-top woman with a good heart, beauty, passion, style and grace. And more money than God. The last thing I needed was to instantly inherit some sort of family. And the absolute last thing I needed was, "Coco."

"Excuse me?" asked Electra.

"Oh, come on, mom," said the kid. "You can't sidestep that easy."

Electra came alive and looked me in the eyes. She stiff-armed little Nick with a mild Heisman maneuver. "No, wait a minute, baby."

She asked me, "You said, '*Coco*' I believe?"

"I love your perfume," I said.

"Uh-Huh," she said. She studied my face. Her coffee cup was empty in her hands. She slowly circled its rim with her fingers. "Do you love it enough that I should keep wearing it?"

This was the kind of bear trap I wanted to avoid. This was the kind of couple's conversation I didn't like having. Let's get out of here.

"Electra, you're one of the most charming, gracious women I've ever known. And you're stronger than goat's breath."

It was 10 years since I lost Teresa. And her scent still haunted me. I hadn't begun what could have been special with Victoria and her scent was gone forever too, because of me. I didn't need Electra White to become another casualty on my watch.

What the hell did I care whether she wore Coco. It was her life, her decision. And who cared anyway? Why did I even think about this? I needed to catch the train back to New York.

I knew Electra White in 3D, in stunning ensembles pulled from *haute couture* clothiers. At the drop of a hat, she could own the room in whatever she wore. Better, she was ravishing as a gatefold girl in nothing at all. But just then, as she sat across from me in a simple blue denim shirt and matching jeans, she was more beautiful than ever.

She waited. "Yes," I said. "Yes, you should."

Post dinner plans included a full tour of the infamous White Mansion, conducted by none other than Master of the estate, Nick White. Five floors. 68,000 square feet. I had no idea how many rooms. I could move in as a squatter on the top floor, and nobody would notice.

I waited at the open door as mother saw her son into his room and to bed. She came back out into the carpeted runway and drew his doors closed behind her. Electra tugged my jacket's lapels and nuzzled my neck, spoke in a soft voice. "I've given everyone but the head staff the night and day off."

I had wondered what things were like on the other side of those fortress-like doors, carved with red hearts and yellow roses. It wasn't the architecture or the design or the furnishings I contemplated. I wanted to know what it was like to be inside her inner sanctum, deep cleaning her carpets and caressing her drapes.

I found out.

45

The next day, POTUS had a scheduled trip to the Big Apple and offered me a ride home on Air Force One. FLOTUS offered to make Air Force 2 available if that schedule didn't work, with a helicopter from the airport to the Lower East Side. Electra offered to have her tenured chauffeur, Clive, drive us on a champagne-fueled Rolls Royce road trip north on I-95.

I caught a cab to Penn Station and the Silver Star, and not a minute too soon. I was in danger of giving in to the bear hugs of little Nick, the kisses of Electra, the amenities of life at the White Mansion. If I stayed longer, that comfortable inertia may have been too much to overcome.

I knew I was home the moment my feet hit the Penn Station platform and I walked toward the gate. Cabs honked; diesel trucks idled; people walked and talked. The aromas of cuisines from India, China, Italy, Japan, France – and steak houses, presented their earnest greetings in sound and scent. The smells of hot dogs, onions and steamed buns in humid air welcomed my senses.

I closed my eyes for a quick moment. D.C. might have been the nation's capital, but this was New York City. The Big Apple. Home of the Yankees, the Mets, the Giants and the Jets. Central Park, the Met and Nathan's hot dogs.

I stopped beneath the big blue Chase Bank sign atop the station's entrance and flagged down a hack to the Lower East Side. My three-story waterfront warehouse was only a few blocks from our office that overlooked the East River and the Williamsburg Bridge.

I watched streetside coffee shops, convenience stores, hot dog stands slide past my taxi's windows. I was headed home. New York. Lower East Side. Diners. Delis. *El Peligro*. A couple of boys scuffled on the sidewalk.

Genesis

One day at recess in my suburban Maryland grade school, Bobby Clingingpeel approached me on the playground. Bobby was the class tough kid from the local trailer park. He lacked real athletic ability, but his fifth-grade size in our third-grade class made it easy for him to bully other kids.

We were the two always picked first for teams at recess, but that's all we had in common. Plus, the unwritten playground policy that we refrained from playing on the same team.

But that day the Fates decided we'd get together.

Bobby's scuffed and worn brown leather shoes kicked up playground dust as he walked toward me. He wore the same colorless threadbare polo shirt that he wore at least two or three days each week. His oversized pair of khaki pants were held up by a frayed web belt.

I tossed a baseball back and forth in my glove and waited.

"Hey", said Bobby. "You play a lot with Philip."

"Yeah?"

"Don't you know?"

"Know what?"

"Man, you're supposed to be smart." He paused. "Philip's a negro."

"A what?"

"A ne-gro." He pushed his head back and studied my face. "You don't know, do you? He's black!"

Bobby acted exasperated at my ignorance. "Look at him. Look at you and me and everyone else in school. We're different. You're white. I'm white. I talked to the other guys about it. We don't play with black kids."

I looked across the playground at Philip. He laughed and played kickball with a bunch of other kids.

"Why?" I asked. "Are they bad?"

"My folks tell me we're not supposed to. We're different. We just don't do it."

Philip wasn't my best friend, but he was a friend of mine. We got the biggest sheets of coloring paper the school provided and colored in military battle scenes together with a huge box of Crayola crayons.

I peddled them around my neighborhood door to door and sold them for fifty cents apiece. We split the take and splurged on ice cream in the school cafeteria. "Philip's my friend, Bobby. We do stuff together all the time; nobody else says anything."

Bobby's eyes narrowed. "Well, if you don't stop, you'll be cut out of everything just like he is."

I looked across the playground again at Philip as he played with the other kids. I couldn't think of anything that Philip was "cut out of." Nor me.

"Look," said Bobby. He reached forward and gave me a tap on the shoulder. "I'm just trying to be a friend. You and I play hard against each other out here, but we're really on the same side."

"Bobby, we can't both be on the same side or that team wins every time."

"No, not that way," he said. His voice picked up volume. He looked around at kids on the playground and drew their attention to us. "Maybe you should play with him! My dad says they're stupid! And you're stupid, too! You better wise up or you're gonna regret it."

My right hand nestled the ball into the glove on my left hand. I relaxed my glove hand; my grip loosened inside the glove.

Bobby called me names; then he called Philip names. I didn't know what they were or what they meant back then, but I do now, and I'm not going to repeat them. Right then, Philip's skin color looked alabaster, compared to Bobby's character.

Bobby and I had never thrown down into a fight. I stared at him. He looked at me, waiting.

My baseball glove slid off my left hand and fell to the ground. My right fist smashed into Bobby's nose and splattered blood across his face. My left fist instantly came across in a powerful hook that I delivered from the ground up through my left leg and body. My knuckles connected solidly with his right jaw. Before I could stop myself, my right uppercut came up from the ground and smashed squarely into his chin. Bobby crumpled to the ground in a motionless heap.

I stood still for a moment and looked down at Bobby. My hands were balled into fists, my dirty fingernails cut into my palms. I felt the pounding of my heart inside my chest, observed the vivid definition and contrast between the white toes of my black low-cut Chuck Taylors and the brown dirt. Bobby twisted around in the playground dust at my feet.

He struggled to get back up, his face a contorted mess of blood, dirt and tears. He cried; the screams that spewed from his bloodied mouth angered me even more.

My overhand right smashed down onto the side of his head. I felt my second knuckle sink into the soft spot of his temple. When he hit the dust again, he laid still. I didn't know what to do, so I backed off.

It was only third grade, but I already had two years of boxing work. For my seventh birthday, my dad brought home a speed bag. He taught me every punching combination he knew. Except the one that slammed back and smashed the cigar in his mouth.

Later, we hung a 75-pound sandbag from a rafter beside it. Each night after I did my homework, I hammered out combinations in our basement. My mom's cupboard doors in the kitchen above swung open in time with the resonance. She wasn't a big boxing fan.

Bobby came around and shook his head. He writhed before me on the ground and struggled to get up. His eyes burned with hate. He hissed through blood and spit that he was going to kill me. He didn't know when; he didn't know how, but he was going to kill me.

That's when my right foot drop-kicked his face through God's goalposts of life. His head twisted hard and cords stuck out on his neck. He dropped flat in a light brown puff of the playground's dust and laid still. Blood trickled from a corner of his mouth and dripped into the dirt.

The girls on the playground shrieked and ran inside to tell the teacher. I looked around at the small ring of other boys. Bobby's friends' eyes and mouths gaped with horror. A second later, they turned and ran.

Diego Garcia was a friend from playing soccer. His father's black Cadillac Sedan de Ville displayed Diplomatic license plates from

Guatemala for his work at their Massachusetts Avenue Embassy. He muttered, *"El Peligro ..."* He and a couple of my other friends kept their heads down. They murmured about getting back to class, then wandered away toward the building together.

A few minutes later I sat in the principal's office. He knew me well. Due to the frequency of my visits over three years, we became friends. We watched more than one World Series game together on a rolling cart TV in his office.

Principal Holland pressed himself back into his puffy black leather chair. He looked down at me through the thick black frames of his glasses. He took a deep sigh, then said, "Young Nick ... Nick, I'm afraid you're going to have a long row to hoe."

* * *

That night my dad wore his striped military bathrobe when he led me into the sitting room of our Bethesda, Maryland home. This was our Christmas tree room, my parents' cocktail party room. Clad in his officer's military robe, he nonverbally communicated that tonight it was my Heap O' 'Splain' room. He carried his *Légion d'étrangère* coffee mug in one hand and his pipe in the other.

We lived in Maryland on the northwest side of D.C. because he headed up the Defense Intelligence Agency at Joint Base Anacostia. But he never lost his love for the French Foreign Legion.

Our fireplace was dark. So were the windows of our brick two-story home. My mom's classic black baby grand Steinway stood open and silent at one end of the room.

The mechanical pendulum of our Westminster chime mantle clock made the only sound in the room. Its heavy action matched the energy; I could feel every *tick*, anticipate every *tock*.

Lighting was limited to the soft spread that illuminated a middle eastern rug from a floor lamp beside my father's Eames reading chair. He sat down, extended one leg and pushed its ottoman a couple of feet in front of him. I took a seat and faced my dad.

"OK," he said. "Mr. Holland says you have a new nickname. Tell me about it." By the time my dad came to take me home from the principal's office, it seemed like everyone in the school tagged me with *El Peligro:* The dangerous one.

I told him about it, word for word, blow by blow.

"So why was it necessary to kick him in the face when he was down?"

"He said he'd kill me."

46

I watched the features in my father's face change and melt from the look of a concerned parent into the pained acquiescence of a chess master stunned in sudden stalemate by a novice.

He took a sip of coffee. He didn't disagree. He wanted to, but he couldn't. "Mm-Hmm."

"Plus," I said, "I hated his guts. He's a jerk. He's lucky I didn't snap his neck."

"That would not have been good," said my dad.

I waited.

He peered into his mug of coffee, decided against another sip. I studied the dark five o'clock stubble on his chin and jaw as his mind worked.

Later in life I observed how my mom adored him, how he loved her, how he was who he was in the service of his country. He saved many lives. That meant also taking some.

But when I was in third grade, this was the guy who played catch with me in the back yard, took me fishing, helped me with homework, came to my Little League games when he was home from overseas, cut my hair at home to save money – for the first and last time. My dad.

He set his coffee down and continued.

"Taking the life of another person is a dreadful, desperate last resort. Killing in war is one thing. Everybody's targeted for death. That's a far cry from second-grade playground fights."

"I'm in third grade, dad."

"OK, third-grade playground fights."

"Not to me, it isn't."

He drew in a deep breath and let it out. "So, let's say you get in another knockdown, drag-out fight with this kid. And you probably will. Only next time he'll have trained, and he'll come at you loaded for bear, probably carrying something bad you won't see."

"But let's say you fight, and you win. And let's say in the fight, this time you do somehow, for some reason, *accidentally* kill him."

He paused. "You take his life. You snuff him out. He's a corpse. He's in a coffin getting lowered down into the ground. He isn't there for Thanksgiving or Christmas. His father has lost his son, and his mother lost her baby boy. If he has a pet dog, his Master will never come home again. And there's another guy who's pretty pissed off at you. We refer to him as God, and you just broke His First Commandment."

The thought shocked me.

"All for a third-grade playground fight." He paused, sipped his coffee. "Know what will happen to you?"

"no."

"Son, you have to think ahead. You have to plan for the consequences. It isn't enough just to do something. You have to be prepared for what will likely follow as consequences of your action."

I was nine. I knew if a guy was an asshole to me, I punched him in the face. I sat and listened.

"You'll get thrown into juvenile jail. Your mother and I will have to appear before the police. We'll have to hire an attorney. It'll cost a lot of money."

"If you lose the case, you're young enough you'll go to Juvenile Detention. You'll be a Juvie. You'll grow up with future criminals with a high likelihood of becoming one yourself. You'll see drugs, tats, jails, low rent criminal minds. And no girls, if you know what I mean, and I think you do."

I didn't.

"And who knows where it goes from there. But it's never good. Do you want to spend your life in a smelly, sweaty juvenile prison with criminals? Or do you want to enjoy the life of freedom and fresh air you have now?"

"OK," I said. "I won't kill anybody." Then, "Dad?" The look on his face said he waited for my question. "You've killed people."

"Like I said. War is a different situation. And then there's self-defense. And learn that lesson. You *must* have a clear-cut and provable case for self-defense. Ironclad."

My face wore a serious expression, but I bit the inside of my cheek to hide the smile I felt inside. This could have been a horrific ass-whipping from my dad for beating the snot out of Bobby Clingingpeel. But it somehow turned into a father-son counseling session about the strategy of killing.

I watched my father inhale a deep breath. I used to watch football games on TV with him and hear ABC sportscaster Keith Jackson say, "Big Mo just changed jerseys."

Now the pipe came out. It was always serious when the pipe came out. He popped open the lid of a round black and white can of can of Borkum Riff. The rich aroma of fresh tobacco emanated into the room. I watched him reach inside, pinch a bit of the dark leafy contents, then push it down into the bowl of his simple black dropdown pipe.

He tilted his pipe sideways and lit it with his father's lighter from WWII, a worn steel-case Zippo with black crackle finish.

"Nick," he said, "when we enter this world, on a scale of zero to ten we are born as tens. We start our lives as perfect little human beings. When we're born, we only know two fears: fear of falling and fear of loud noises. All other fears are learned."

47

Dad also savored rich black coffee. He'd drink a cup of Yuban dark roast half an hour before he turned in and have no trouble with sleep. As he prepared to continue his unplanned home-school lesson, he sipped from his ceramic connection with the French Foreign Legion and blew out a smoke ring.

"But then people come along during our lives and try to convince us that we aren't perfect little human beings, perfect in our imperfections. They try to make us feel like we're less than ten. They teach us all kinds of psychological fears to worry about. Usually because they see themselves as less than ten and want to bring other people down to their level."

"Like who?" I asked. "Why would they do that?"

"People all around you. They do it because they don't feel good about themselves, so they try to bring other people down to their level instead of bringing themselves up. You'll learn to develop your internal crap detector to tell who's real from who's fake."

"Most people in our society believe they're just a little bit above average, and they live their entire lives that way. They get by, but that's all they're doing. Getting by, just making it through. Not achieving, not excelling, just laying low and doing enough not to get into trouble."

"These aren't bad people, Nick, they just choose to be average. They believe they should live mediocre lives because somebody else told them they should, and they believed them."

"Then there are people who are beyond brilliant. It seems ironic, but I've learned these are often the most miserable people you'll meet. "Too smart for their own good." Some are helpful and kind. These people are the happiest. Some are stupid. They don't mean to be harmful; they just don't know any better."

He raised his coffee mug and examined its artwork of a flaming grenade. He continued, "And then there are others – a small minority - and they're just flat evil."

I asked, "What happens with the evil people, dad?"

I watched another smoke ring puff forward from his mouth. "Usually not enough, it seems. But what's important to you is, never let yourself get set up against an evil person. Stupid people are harmless. They don't know enough to come back at you."

"But evil people are insane. They have little regard for consequences. They're crafty; they're conniving; they'll bait you in. They'll brainwash you to their way of thinking, then they'll destroy you. Whenever you confront evil, bring twice as much threat and power as you think you're going to need. Because you'll probably need more than that."

"And smash it at the first available opportunity. With maximum prejudice."

He looked across toward a framed 5"x7" photo on the fireplace mantle. My dad stood with our President of the United States, taken years before he ran for that office.

I followed his gaze. Their smiles were genuine. "Nick," he said, "Hey, Nick. Look at me."

I did. "Watch out for yourself 360 degrees on all sides. And above all, if you get in another altercation, make sure your case is stronger than Fort Knox."

"Is that why someone like Bobby wants to try to make me not be friends with Philip?" I asked. "Is Bobby evil?"

"No son, he's just stupid. But we can go into that later." He looked across the room and examined our large family painting, prominent on an easel in one corner. He said, "You're a lot like your brother..."

At that moment the front door flew open. My little sister ran in ahead of my mom, an A&W root beer cup in one hand.

Tracy bounded into the room, fresh from gymnastics practice in her team sweats. Somehow without spilling a drop, she placed herself between my father and me, stood face to face with him and said, "Guess what we got?"

Before he could redirect his thinking to reply, she levelled a guttural belch at him that would have sunk the Enterprise. "Root beer!" she said and ran off to join my mom in the kitchen.

"Is that why her middle name is, 'Trouble'?"

The thin smile that compressed his lips grew just a little more when he clenched his pipe between his teeth and said, "No comment." He dug out more tobacco and replenished the bowl.

I had tossed the dice and was winning; I was way ahead for the night. In my youthful exuberance, I rolled those bones again with, "That bitch is crazy!"

It was about two seconds before my dad unwrapped his fingers from the pistol grip handle of his coffee mug. It was another second before he rested his pipe in its ash tray and touched it into its precise balanced position.

A split second later his right hand cupped my left jaw in a Kodiak papa bear slap. It knocked me off the ottoman, onto the floor. "And you will respect your elders," he said as he stood and walked out of the room.

I called after him, "Dad!"

He stopped and asked with only a half turn, "What?"

"What's 'maximum prejudice?'"

"It isn't tea and sympathy," he said. "It means, take no prisoners."

*   *   *

The early November clouds threw their shadows between skyscrapers to the streets below. The autumn daylight spilled across fenders, melted over hoods, and made cars with curves look like a million bucks. The cab driver pulled off on the East River Esplanade and drove me as far as he could to its south end.

I spiffed him and carried my gear toward the secure steel door of my four story building. The cars parked in the neighboring pay-or-tow lot all looked familiar. *A Citroen? Who the hell drives a Citroen? Must be a friend of T's.*

The explosive sound of automatic gunfire thundered overhead from inside my building. A burst of five, a pause, a burst of three more, then three more. The deep tones of the big bore weapon reverberated my insides like the roar of a male lion. A Tommy Gun.

I checked our mailbox. When I turned the key, magazines, envelopes, boxes and flyers blew out and crashed to the ground. My boots disappeared beneath a mound of disheveled papers.

My hands were full of travel gear, so I resigned myself to defeat and set it all down. I bent over and gathered the explosion in a shingle factory at my feet. My sister Trouble hadn't opened the mailbox since I left. *Artists.*

Again, the automatic weapon resonated in the fillings of my teeth. I filled my arms and hands and turned to open our secure inner door. But it already hung open on one hinge.

The solid steel stormproof portal was three inches thick and gaped as if we aired out the house. I heard another single blast, but with a lighter, higher pitch than the other groupings.

I dropped everything, let it spill down the staircase as I sprinted up the steps. Without thinking, I filled my mitts with my resident lethal hardware. The sounds came from the third floor, Trouble's studio. I charged up to the door and listened. Nothing.

The handle twisted in my hand without a sound. I cracked the door open and looked inside. Another shot banged out. A 9 mm. It was answered by the thunderous roar of two .45 automatic shots - and the loud click of a firing pin with no cartridge.

I heard my sister grumble from behind her steel flat file storage cabinet. Three new bullet holes in its side gave it customized ventilation. The shooter heard the click, too. He sneered with that sick, overconfident laugh of another Eurotrash assassin.

Though I caught glimpses of movement, I couldn't make out the shooter behind a thick concrete interior support column. The gunman stepped out from his cover, cavalier with confidence. He stepped sideways for a better angle to shoot my vulnerable sister with her empty gun. I gripped my .45s, silently pressed the door open wider with my elbow.

I slipped my gun hand through the opening. He moved away from the column into my sight plane; one more step ...

Before I squeezed my trigger, he flew into a tornadic fit of convulsions. His chest exploded, both arms flailed wildly from his sides. His organs blew out his backside and left a mess for the maids. His legs and knees danced, then buckled and crashed down to the floor in a heap against a wall. Trouble's Thompson .45 blasted its full drum clip of 50 rounds into him until it clicked again.

I held my position. The room fell silent, but the strong smell of gunpowder filled the air. I spoke through my crack in the door, "Trouble?"

She answered back. "Nick? Nice timing."

She stepped out from behind her massive flat file cabinet. Her blonde hair touched the shoulders of a pair of black overalls on top of her burnt orange long-sleeved turtleneck. And boots, flat boots. A welder's face mask made of bulletproof Kevlar was cocked back onto the top of her head.

I watched my little sister slide the drum magazine off her submachine gun. She reached behind into her back pocket and produced a fully loaded straight stick 30-round magazine, slammed it home. Her chest heaved with deep breaths of anxiety; her blue eyes were wide with rage and battle lust.

This was my little sister who scored 191 on her IQ test at age 12. This was my delicate sibling whose 1600 SAT scores received an offer for a full scholarship at the School of the Museum of Fine Arts in Boston.

She chose instead to run rampant for four years throughout Hartsville, South Carolina among Coker U's massive student population of 1,000. But she stretched her artistic genius there like she could no place else.

Her Tommy Gun Art gained rapid global notoriety, which proved to be great for business. From 25 feet she could mash her trigger and draw a Native American Chief's profile in full feathered headdress on a sheet of half-inch plate steel. Her artist's signature was a T inside a circle, which she trademarked with the USPTO: (T) ®

I looked across the room at the bloody mess of the assassin. He wasn't recognizable after Trouble signed her name across his heart with her Chicago typewriter. I asked, "Where's Cody?"

48

"You've been gone awhile," said T. My little sister lowered the 11-pound wood and steel submachine gun to rest at her side. "He's been fine on his feline Zupreem diet, but with no raw meat for over a week, he wanted to play."

"Where is he? Is he OK?"

"Him? He's doing great. Can I have one of your smokes?"

I reached into my coat pocket, tossed her a half-full deck of Reds. "Two guys," she said. Trouble tore open the pack. She was trying to act with steady composure, but her trembling hands and fingers belied her anxiety. "Who the Hell they were and why they were trying to make me into Swiss cheese I'd like to know."

She shook a cigarette loose, got it to her mouth between quivering fingers, lit it and tossed the pack back to me.

Her black and white Shih Tzu ran across the studio floor to her side. She picked him up and nuzzled his face. "I know it isn't Winston's fault."

I popped open her studio's dorm fridge. The chilled glass bottle of a Champagne of Beers cooled my palm. Its cold sweat felt better to my hand than its frigid contents tasted across my lips. I handed it to her and clinked a couple of glass bottles when I grabbed mine.

She popped the cap off her Miller and knocked back half. She wiped her lips with the back of one hand, slammed the bottle on the steel cabinet. She was silent while the suds flowed over its top. "I just shot the greatest piece, a Texas *Come and Take It* flag on that 5 x 8 steel plate over there."

I looked across at the bulletproof indoor shooting range that served as her studio. A large sheet of half-inch plate steel hung in the space by steel chains. Trouble and her Thompson had etched into it the outline of an old cannon with the famous Texas slogan.

"Anyway, I took a snack break. Winston curled up with Cody to take a nap. When his ears perked up and he started barking, Cody did his cat thing and jumped up above. So, I picked up my paintbrush."

"Thanks for the narration, T, but where's my cat?"

She shrugged and blew out a cloud of smoke. She was regaining her poise. "I got my man; he got his. I told you; he hasn't had any raw meat for over a week. I don't think you'll interrogate what's left."

She was definitely my little sis; daughter of two of the nation's leading intelligence authorities. The cigarette and the beer served as a prescription for calm. Still, she was an artist, not an agent.

Somehow all the flying lead managed to miss shattering the framed picture on her coffee table. Signed by Mr. T, it was an 8" x 10" studio publicity shot inscribed, *To Ms. T: I Pity the Fool! Mr. T*

She said, "I don't like this, Nick. What the Hell is going on? I shoot pieces of iron. Not people. I'm an artist. You're the private eye. We've lived here for years and never had a break-in."

"My life is an art gallery, Nick. With pleasant, creative, artistic people. Harmless people. I need to go back there."

"Stop," I said. She reacted as if slapped, looked at me in disbelief. I said, "Sorry, but just, stop. I'll fill you in later. It's been a rough week."

"I follow the news," she said.

This time, the bottle I retrieved from the fridge delivered crisp cold relief.

"You saw the headlines. It goes deeper than that." I holstered my pistol and took a seat on a nearby shop stool. The scene in T's studio was grisly. "This isn't going to be easy to explain to the boys downtown."

* * *

Homicide Lieutenant Ralph "Happy" Moynihan proved me correct. We ran into each other often enough for me to know that his nickname was a sarcastic moniker hung on him by his peers. He was indeed "Happy" Moynihan, to a select few.

After he and his note-taking assistant climbed the two levels of stairs, he caught his breath. He stood about 6' 2" with a buzz cut and a Glock G20 Short Frame in 10 mm beneath his jacket. Between deep inhalations he said, "At least this time you didn't call me out at four a.m. To the end of Pier 54. In January. In the wind. And freezing rain."

I reminded him; "You made the morning papers for that one."

"What is it with you private types? You all think you're Dirty Harry? You could never be a cop. I'd run your ass out your first day."

"Lieutenant, that time I got a call to meet an informant and got jumped by five guys."

"Yeah," he said. "One of 'em lived."

"Sorry, I'll do better next time." The look he gave me said it was time to move along.

I related for him and his comical sidekick the exciting details from A to Z: I exited my cab, got the mail, ran upstairs, watched a guy get obliterated.

He stood with both hands in his pockets, twisted his torso around and studied the scene. He stopped when he saw the bloody heap of Eurotrash that soaked one wall of the room.

Happy looked at Trouble. "You didn't leave us much to work with. There were two of them?"

She said, "One tried to take hold of me. He was super-fast. I aimed Tommy here, but he flew around behind me and tried to strangle me." She stopped. She walked across to her counter, poured a cup of coffee. She opened a drawer and rummaged through its contents.

The lieutenant shot me a look of exasperation. "And!"

"Oh. That's when Cody came down from the rafters."

Happy looked up at the ceiling.

"Cody saw me struggling with that creep and - he's what, 150 pounds? He hit that guy flying from fifteen feet up. Fangs, claws, ripping, crunching, screaming – You won't have any trouble finding him. Just follow that red trail across the floor and up the stairs."

She sipped her coffee and continued. She indicated the human mass against the wall. "That one held off shooting. Afraid he might hit his boyfriend. But he twisted off when our guard dog jumped his sweetheart and started munching on him. He shot at Cody, then at me."

Trouble found the foil-wrapped chocolate she was looking for in the drawer. She unfoiled it, chased it with her black coffee. "The first shots missed my head by inches. Inches! Excuse me, but I lost my temper. I'm an artist. In my home. They tried to kill me. And my pets. I let him have it. All of it. And I was testing out a drum clip full of 50 hollow points."

Lt. unHappy took a seat at a barstool at T's kitchen island. "Oh, great," he said. "Now I've got to get animal control in here." His note-taker followed, a desk-bound bureaucrat who never skipped a beat in his scribbling. "And that's not a dog," he said.

"You know all our federal and county permits are in order. And the city."

"And that's another thing," he said. "I don't know how you got permits to have a mountain lion in your home in The City. God only knows how you pulled off a P.I. license."

I said, "Ralph, they broke into our home. They tried to kill T. And me too if I was here. Cody can't be held liable for protecting his master and his own life inside his own home. Against killers."

"It isn't that," he said. "It's procedure. Like any bullet wound treated by a doctor is required by law to be turned in to the police. Same thing with animal bites. I don't want to get the cat in trouble, but I've got to phone it in. Animal Control will just require him to be quarantined for two weeks to check for rabies."

"Ralph," I said. "I can guarantee you the second guy did not succumb to rabies."

Again, he assaulted me with the stern look of a Catholic school nun. "We need the body, Tarzan."

"You're welcome to go claim whatever you can come away with."

"Look, shamus, I saw all about your heroics in D.C. I think it's great. You'll probably get some People's Hero medal. But if I have to, I'll get animal control to come in here, shoot him with a dart and get that body out of there. Is that what you want?"

"I'm so glad I called," I said, with as little sincerity as possible.

Trouble cut in. "You two get a room," she said. "Better yet, I'm leaving you boys here. I'm going somewhere safe, like Bedford-Stuyvesant. Don't worry. I'm packing heat."

She pulled a down-filled ski jacket out of her antique armoire and stretched into it. I noticed the lieutenant when he noticed her. Though she was my full-blooded sister, I had to admit she was built like the proverbial brick shithouse.

The snug fit of her overalls and turtleneck accentuated the fact. Then, her oversized puffy coat obscured everything but her bright blue eyes and the perfect nose on her face.

The lieutenant said, "Don't leave town."

Trouble kissed me on the cheek as she passed by on her way out the door. "*Ciao!* Feed Winston."

Ralph's eyes followed her every move when she walked away. As she descended the stairs, he asked, "Hey, is she …?"

"Don't know. Don't care. Ask her yourself."

"No thanks. I like my health."

I excused myself from the cops and went to visit my cat. Lt. Moynihan called in for the M.E. and crime scene team.

In our building, Cody the cougar was the true penthouse resident. His domain was the fourth floor that featured wall-to-wall safety glass windows on four sides. We constructed a ramp entrance to his elevated loft lair that was easy for him to climb up and down.

From the dark inner space of his upper chambers, I could tell the big cat heard me approach across the wood laminate floor. Afternoon daylight streamed in through the safety glass windows. His warning came as a guttural, low growl, followed by a threatening hiss.

A mountain lion. Domesticated or not, it was still the largest cat in North America. With fangs. And claws. And a three to one strength ratio compared to humans.

Any human idiot, I'll take them head-on. But I'm not idiot enough to take on a wild dangerous animal with a fresh kill in his mouth. Even if he is my buddy who curls up against me back-to-back to sleep during thunderstorms and likes to watch football on the big screen.

49

I coaxed him as gently as I did the little girl in the pizza shop. "Hey, Cody buddy. I need to get that guy for fingerprints. I'll trade you a Porterhouse."

Eight feet above my head, I noticed a foot, a shoe. It dangled from the open entrance to Cody's elevated cat house. I climbed his ramp with as much stealth as possible. He repeated his resonant cautionary growl, finished with a violent spitting hiss and a paw smack on his floor.

The shoed foot, with its sock and ankle and shin attached, fell to the floor below with a splat. It was a start. I retrieved Cody's table scraps before he changed his mind.

When I looked back up, I saw an elbow, then a wrist and hand push forward toward the front edge of his elevated entrance. A moment later, they flopped down to the ground at my feet. What Cody just told me was, that was all I was getting, and to get lost.

I picked up the front and hindquarters and carried them inside T's studio. "You can get prints off these," I said as I handed them to the lieutenant. Or tried to. He stood with his hands in his pockets and glared at me.

I laid them on top of T's flat file cabinet for Moynihan's minions to deal with. "But that's all you're going to get. The rest of him is in the digestion phase."

* * *

The next morning, I rediscovered my routine at the dawn of a brand-new day.

Breakfast at the Metro Diner. It was the same morning meal I enjoyed at the White House; the same food prepared by the chef at the White Mansion. But it wasn't refined, and it wasn't served on fine China. The eggs weren't poached, the bacon was greasy. The coffee needed eggshells. I was home.

I sat in a sidewalk level booth with a ripped seat that was repaired with mismatched colored duct tape. A foot away outside the glass, the sound of Manhattan music: ubiquitous muted conversations among real people as they walked by on the street.

The jukebox played a song by Al Green, and I left my cash on the table with several bills. I hoofed it four blocks up Montgomery Street to East Broadway past apartment buildings and trees.

On Grand Street, the sign that hung on the building's brick wall since 1963 was lit day and night. Jack's Gym. I opened the street-level glass door and climbed the creaking, worn-out wooden steps.

Before-and-after photos of Jack's disciples lined the 27-step staircase. At the top I entered the sights and smells of the nation's oldest owner/operator gym. Weights that got dropped onto the floor and speed bags that pounded back and forth resonated below inside the street level 7-Eleven.

Jack, the joint's founder and sole employee for over 50 years, worked with a guy on a bench press across the room. I trudged across the worn and splintered hardwood floor to the men's lockers among paint that peeled off the walls. Ancient, pressed tin tiles hung down from the ceiling; dark fluorescent overhead light tubes needed to be replaced months ago.

Despite this, probably because of this, Jack's Gym was a national shrine. It was known throughout the industry that Jack forgot more about strength and health training than most of today's experts will ever know. For that reason, in every year's polls, the bodybuilder and muscle magazines named it, "Best Old School Gym."

During workouts, we opened the windows and ran massive shop fans because there was no air conditioning and little heat. I paused outside the curtained locker room at the standing drinking fountain that was retired from a Greyhound bus station. It too, dated back to 1963.

It felt good to work my muscles in a familiar exercise pattern. I took my time and let them find their way back into place. Tomorrow morning I'd spar a few rounds.

When I finished, the fragrant bouquet of a dried-out cigar told me Jack was back in his office. I walked in and sat down. I rocked back in a 50s postmodern western chair, green, with a bas relief bucking bronco stitched into the vinyl.

Jack looked at me through his oversized reading glasses. He grinned around the thick half-lit stogie in his mouth. "We've been following you in the news, my friend," he said. He looked up toward his door.

Rosinski ducked to fit his head through the entrance to Jack's musty office. The Polish giant lumbered across and took a seat in a worn brown leather chair by the window. The tiny conference room was now full.

"Jack?" he asked. His glance asked my approval to butt in. I nodded. "I'm going to buy gold today. You think? Coins? Bars?" Bishop Rosinski stood 6' 5" and weighed in around 350 pounds. He competed in powerlifting competitions and just couldn't quite break 900 pounds in his dead lift.

Jack ashed his cigar in the grapefruit juice can that served as his desktop ashtray. "Buy the cheapest coin per ounce of gold. Coins. It doesn't make any difference if it's Krugs or Eagles or Maple Leafs. It's all one ounce of gold. That's what you're buying and that's what you'll sell. So, get the cheapest cost per ounce with the lowest premium."

Rosinski's huge head of long wavy blond hair nodded his understanding.

"And don't keep it at your house!" said Jack. He looked at me for some reason and continued. "People get funny around gold. It doesn't matter who they are. If they know you have gold, and especially if times are bad and they know you're holding it, you won't be safe. It doesn't matter what kind of safe you have at home. It's there. It's accessible. How much are we talking about?"

Rosinski leaned inward and spoke in a low tone. His voice was deadened within the cramped, dusty old vestibule constructed from mobile home paneling and fake wood trim. "About forty grand?" he asked.

"Oh, hell. Put it in a safe deposit box! Hear me? Nobody knows where. Nobody. Put the key in your safe at home."

Rosinski nodded. He looked at me, stuck out his hand. I slowly met him in a palm-to-palm clasp. His hand felt like raw concrete covered with white talcum powder. It swallowed mine like a first baseman's mitt. "Good work down there," he said. "I've got kids."

"Thanks, Bish."

"Any time you need help – you got my number?"

We exchanged our info, then he went back to his weights. Jack leaned back in his chair. This was where he held court daily with SRO audiences in his office. He discussed workouts, exercises, and diets simultaneously with politics, economics, history and sports.

Jack brushed his massive case-hardened hand through his hair. He looked at me through clear blue eyes.

I said, "You've got to let me put up my 'Jack's Hall of Fame' photos. They'd look better than those old before and after shots hanging on the staircase. You've got movie stars, Mr. Universe winners, World's Strongest Man winners,

Olympians, WWE Hall of Famers; it'd be impressive as hell."

"You need to watch your ass," he said. His eyes didn't move. They weren't cold; they were steady, unblinking, unflinching. If we were old west gunfighters, the next move would have been mine.

"Love you too, Chief," I said.

"Listen to me," he said. He leaned forward on his desk and stretched his neck like a turtle to look out through his office door. There were only five guys in the gym. Bish and the others skipped rope or lifted weights at the opposite end of the gym.

"I like you alive," he said. "This thing you're in, you don't have any idea what you've stepped in the middle of."

I said, "That's funny, that's what somebody else told me." Then, beneath my breath, "*on the White House lawn.*"

50

Jack growled. "Don't screw with me, kid."

"Jack, I've been one step ahead of a bullet all my life. It goes with the territory."

"You were lucky. Your folks — both high-level secret squirrel types. They created you," he said. "You're a one-man A-Team, maybe more."

"Yay, me."

"You arrogant swizzle stick. These people aren't human. They kill kids to get that stuff out of their bodies and drink it."

"Adrenochrome?" I asked. "Shoot, I can buy that stuff on Amazon in powder form."

He leaned into his chairback. "They get it straight out of a living body. The more tormented and terrified the victim is, the more powerful they believe its effects are. Hell, they believe it makes them superhuman, a fountain of youth."

"I can't even talk about it. Terrible, horrible stuff. People who get in their face get taken out. And it always looks like suicide."

"At least in my case, you could tell the world differently."

"Not if they take out me and this building to get you." He leaned back in his chair and made a menacing sneer.

"Look, kid. If they want to take you out, they'll take you out. They'll blow your entire building down and kill 500 innocent people if they have to. They don't care!" Jack looked at the cigar stub in his fingers, pitched it into his desktop grapefruit can.

He rummaged around on his desk among the newspapers, books, cigar ashes and magazines. "They have unlimited resources," he said. "Money, manpower, guns. Untold power in the Washington D.C. swamp and worldwide. They took down the twin towers right here and got away with it. Killed thousands, created a war. Just to make a buck."

I said, "I know, Jack."

"No, you don't. That's just the beginning. These bastards are global. Hell, I got this German paper right here." He looked beneath his desk and between his legs, leaned down and made a rustling noise. He straightened up in his chair with a crumpled newspaper in his hands.

Jack found his reading glasses among the collateral damage inflicted upon his desk. He clipped the cheaters over his ears and popped open *The Wall Street Journal*. "But before that I got this one. More recent. June 7, 2023." He read out loud:

"Vast Instagram Pedophile Network Exposed, Group Uses 'Pizza Emojis' To Communicate" "Instagram, the popular social-media site owned by Meta Platforms, helps connect and promote a vast network of accounts openly devoted to the commission and purchase of underage-sex content, according to investigations by The Wall Street Journal and researchers at Stanford University and the University of Massachusetts Amherst ..."

419

"... Instagram doesn't merely host these activities. Its algorithms promote them. Instagram connects pedophiles and guides them to content sellers via recommendation systems that excel at linking those who share niche interests."

"That's your social media for you." He dropped the newspaper onto the floor and picked up another from beneath his desk. "OK. Here it is. Look here," he said. "Germans ..." He read out loud:

"GLOBAL DESK: Officials from the North-Rhine Westphalia cybercrime unit said on Monday it had uncovered the pedophile ring after a nine-month cybercrime investigation. 'I hadn't reckoned with the extent of child abuse on the Internet,' said state Justice Minister Peter Beisenbach. "They get instructions from other users on what sedatives one should give children in order to abuse them. A discussion ensues on which children can be abused ... I felt sick when I heard it, but it has also made us more determined to pursue this inquiry,' he said. "I fear it is going to be more than 30,000 suspects."

Jack flattened the paper on his desk. His blue eyes, enlarged through his reading glasses, peered out at me. "They're pulling in 30,000 perverts. From one community. I'd feel sick, too," he said.

"You take a German newspaper? When did you begin *spreching Deutch*, Jack?"

"I stay on top of my German marks and Swiss francs," he said. "This pedophile thing is global. I've got another paper here somewhere. From a couple years ago." His eyes swept the crowded room.

It would have been a large office, but there was only enough room for two guys to sit beside Jack's desk. The rest of the space was jammed with abandoned file cabinets, worn-out chairs, stacks of newspapers.

He found another cigar and brought it to life with a match, said, "Hell, right down there where you were, in Virginia. A couple years ago. You think you scored big at Halloween?"

"In one two-week period before Halloween, 99 kids went missing nationwide. Seventy-four of them were in Virginia. Seventy-four missing kids in one local area just before Halloween. And you know what the Hell they were doing to 'em. And people's pet dogs and cats, too. These people are sick."

Enter Nicolai. The powerful Russian came in and took Rosinski's vacated seat.

He started working out at Jack's a couple of years ago. His Batman looking tattoo of the GRU Spetsnaz on his right deltoid told me everything I needed to know. I saw no imminent need to trade chess strategies.

One evening, I pushed down triceps exercises on the lat pulldown machine. Nicolai finished a set of heavy deadlifts behind me. We bumped when we backed into each other and turned. For one millisecond our eyes locked.

The room stopped. Nobody moved. He was every inch as tall, every pound as heavy, and trained in every martial tactic as well as I was. He knew it. I knew it. He knew I didn't care. I read in his face that he felt the same way.

I said, "So, you working?"

He said, "Just back. Gone two weeks. You are decathlete? Yes?"

I nodded. "Awhile back."

He mimicked a discus windup. "Throwing events?"

And thus began one of the most unlikely and best friendships I ever developed. For some reason, Nicolai nurtured a passion to practice and compete in throwing events. I helped him with his shotput, discus and javelin. At his last competition, we had him put out over 18 meters and throw the spear 70.

Nicolai's cousin worked dispatch for the *Impervious* livery operation. This led to our hiring the Russians' valuable vehicular and security services. My friendship with him eased my rapport with Russian elite force drivers. Only a short time ago we who would have been vital enemies.

Thirty years ago, we'd kill each other with poisoned vodka drinks or icepicks. Now we buy each other drinks and laugh at our inept attempts to translate.

Jack stood up and walked to his office window, looked out through glass that hadn't been cleaned in decades. He said, "Did you look out your residential fortress windows when you got up this morning? The city that never sleeps. Everything you see happen in that world out there is planned. Scripted. There ain't no surprises to these monsters."

"They're all in positions of world power. Power is what they live for, and they won't give it up without taking you and everyone else down with them. They meet, they plan, they determine exactly what's going to happen in the next year, the next five years, the next decade."

"Economics, wars, elections, government coups, everything. And they gaslight the public with the media that's in on it with them. They're all part of this New World Order Globalist Great Reset crap together. And it's happening. It's creeping in. They're brainwashing the masses. It won't be long before we're all eating crickets."

He looked over at a silent Nicolai. "Just ask your throwing buddy here."

Nicolai shrugged. "C'mon," said Jack. "You worked security for those bastards."

"Birknerhaus Group, Da," he said.

I asked, "How do you know so much about all this, Jack?"

The only man left alive who I admired examined the cigar crushed between the fingers of his right hand. He dropped it into the grapefruit can. His full head of thick white hair had grown long, and Jack hadn't shaved in three days.

Quintessential Jack. Never saw a doctor in his life. Smoked cigars and pipes every afternoon. Completely clean chest x-rays. His age pushed 90, but when he spoke it was with the firm authority and smooth *savoir faire* of the most sophisticated world leader.

"Look at this crap," he said. He picked up the day's newspaper and smacked it with the back of his hand. "*The New York Times.* 'All the news that's fit to print,' so they say. So, here's your headline in *The New York Times* newspaper:"

He held the paper so he could use the window's daylight, "October 5, 2014: Pedophilia: A Disorder, Not a Crime." They go on to state that, "Pedophilia is a status and not an act." Not an act! What a bunch of crap."

"Then you got this article in *The Daily Caller* – July 18, 2018 – Here. It says, 'Pedophiles believe they should be part of the LGBT community.' They want to be referred to as, MAP – Minor Attracted Persons."

Jack paused to spit into his metal trash can. "All the news that's fit to print. What's fit to print about that?" He sat down in his creaking chair. "Like I said, kid. I ain't gonna tell you nothing. I like having you alive too much."

"It's the nature and name of my business, Jack. Take a look at this." I fished out the Armenian assassin's quarter and handed it to him across the desk. "I took it off a hired killer in D.C."

He turned it around in his fingers and examined it. He slid out his middle desk drawer. Out came the jeweler's loop. "This is some shady double naught spy stuff. From the 50s. The CIA used markers like this to confirm identities."

I said, "That symbol that's struck into the coin's center on George Washington. It's on their kiddy porn sites online. I also saw it in the pizza shop."

Jack leaned forward and rested his arms on his desk. He drilled me with both eyes, looked like he wanted to grab me by my shirt and pull me toward his face across the desk. Nicolai watched, nonplussed.

If Jack and I weren't friends, we would have been nose to nose when he said in a deep low voice, "You're outmatched, kid. Outgunned. Out moneyed. Stop now. Let yourself be a hero for a while. Take a vacation."

His last comment struck him. He relaxed and leaned back in his chair. "Take a long vacation."

Nicolai said, "Nick, Belize. Catching the bonefish."

He relaxed and leaned back in his chair, looked down and to his left. "Kid, I'm trying to wise you up. You weren't back in town what, a couple of hours before your home was attacked? You weren't there, and your sister had to fight them off alone? Imported professional hitmen?"

"How did you know about it?"

"Radio."

"Hadn't hit the news, yet."

He wrestled with a stubborn wooden drawer in his desk. He yanked it open, then pulled out a black police scanner with a thick, rubberized antenna. "Police band radio, numbnuts."

51

Jack's was an antique mahogany partner's desk. During the 1929 economic crash, desks were constructed so two "partners" who couldn't afford two desks, shared one. They sat one on each side and faced each other. Both sides featured the same drawers, with one long tunnel opening in the middle for both pairs of legs, opposite each other. If they were fat with cash, they lived large with two phones on top. If not, they shared one.

At any given time, on any given day, Jack led conversations in his office that ranged from hammering nails to global politics, often with standing room only groups.

His throne was a squeaky shop-worn green steel swivel chair. Whenever I talked with The Professor, I felt like I had a conversation with a partner. And damn if it didn't seem like he was right, every time.

The top right drawer on my side of his partner's desk had become my personal tobacco locker. I opened it and lifted out my emergency pack of Reds and my emergency red Bic lighter.

"Jack, this Thursday I go to the UN. A gal with the hots for me is addressing the General Assembly. She's the first ever female Secretary-General and chairs the Global Council on Missing Children. She invited me as her guest."

Jack grouched. "I know. You rescued a busload of kids. And you took down all those high-ranking baby-kissers. It's great. You're a hero. The media is naming you *Man of the Year*."

"You've probably got a TV crew of some kind waiting for you in your office right now to waste your time. Hell, I wouldn't be surprised if they don't hang some gaudy medal around your neck."

Jack's Gym provided a member amenity unrivaled throughout the city: chronically bad coffee. No matter what time I went in, it tasted like it was left on low heat for days. I poured some of the thick black liquid into a white Styrofoam cup.

Bish Rosinski finished a set of 250-pound lat pulldowns just outside Jack's office door. He looked in and winced when he saw my reaction to the resident molten tar.

Jack wrestled a balky wooden drawer back and forth. He reached in and pulled out a pouch of pipe tobacco. When he opened it, it the lush aroma took me back to my childhood home in Bethesda. He reclaimed his pipe from its resting place, packed it with tobacco.

His metal desk chair screeched when he leaned back and lit up. He drew in some smoke, released it from his lips in a slow stream. He asked, "Do you think you solved anything?"

"Solved anything? I don't know if I solved anything." I flicked the Bic and lit up to join my local Zen Master in smoke.

"I know I found a kid who was abducted minutes after I was the last one to see him. Play catch with him. I know the FBI botched the case on purpose. Director Moore was one of the biggest perverts – no wonder they couldn't locate the little guy and all the others."

"I know I crashed a Halloween sacrifice party thrown by elitist perverts. They're looking at life to infinity at Rikers Island right now. The other kids were on the evening's menu to be cooked into Little Boy Stew or Girl Meat. Those are the terms they use. And I stopped them. That's what I know."

I blew a stream of smoke out the side of my mouth to avoid hitting Jack in the face.

"Hero," I said. "Hero, my ass. Ask the little girl I watched fight for her life before they vivisected her and ate her organs while she was kept alive with drugs to watch. I wasn't much of a hero to her. So, if some group of pissed-off perverts wants to come after me, let them bring it. I've still got some killing to do."

Nicolai joined in. "Da! Killing them all. Letting God sorting them out."

I drew in a deep drag of smoke. "It'll just be more stiffs giving late night hours to the county morgue."

Some fresh brew would have tasted perfect right then. But even brave men feared to tread near Jack's war-zone Mr. Coffee. I looked down and studied the steaming dark syrup in my white cup.

The wizened nonagenarian scrutinized my face, then spoke. "I hope you're impressed with yourself."

I ran out of things to say. "How about if I fight fire with fire? I'll start eating their livers, like Jeremiah Johnson."

That cut the tension and Jack said through his hoarse, raspy laugh, "Hell, then they'd just want to recruit you."

The musty swayback bookshelves behind him struggled to hold binders and books, mostly unopened across dusty years. He spun around in his chair to face Chilton's guide for the 1974 Chevy Vega and searched among the other volumes.

Rosinski shot his giant mitt through the opened office door. Before my chin, he held a 7-Eleven coffee cup that sent steam up through the vent in the dark plastic lid. I snatched it, poured Jack's poison into a nearby rubber tree plant's pot. Before Jack returned, I replaced his tar with real coffee inside the gym's formal white Styrofoam.

Nicolai was nonplussed, observed out of his peripheral vision without reaction.

Jack said, half over his shoulder, "Who the hell do you think you are?"

A moment later the Lower East Side's supreme sensei spun back around in his chair. He cradled an overstuffed 6" three-ring binder, dropped it onto the clutter that covered his desk. A scratch-off lottery card perished beneath a half-eaten sandwich from the day before.

Before I could select a glib comeback from my mental list of glib comebacks, he asked a rhetorical question. "Are you bigger than the President of the United States? More protected and safer than say, JFK?"

"C'mon, Jack …"

He flipped the front cover of the binder open, blew some of the dust away from us.

Without looking up, he asked, "Coffee good?"

"Great!"

"You know my brother has his place in downtown Dallas. Sam's Gym. Sends me his stuff on JFK. I send him my stuff on 9-11. They pulled off murdering one of the most popular Presidents ever, in broad daylight, in front of massive crowds, then buried it forever. You're chicken feed, kid."

He turned the plastic-covered pages inside the notebook. "These are just a few things that we know for certain about JFK."

I savored the coffee's aroma. Thanks, Bish. Good rich coffee on a chilly autumn morning in New York.

I said, "Jack, I know about the assassination."

"You don't know anything, kid. Listen up. I can name each one of the six shooters in Dealey Plaza that day - and tell you where each one was when he fired. You've got confidential information? From the upper echelons of Special Operations? Great. Did they ever show you that?"

I exhaled, said, "No." I was getting so tired of getting psychologically beat up by my elders.

52

"Hell, it's all public information!" He half-turned in his chair and jerked at a book on the shelf. It was stuck to its adjacent books' covers. His JFK assassination library was a shelf-long brick of books, tapes, DVDs.

"It's all laid out right here," he said. He held up a red paperback book edited by James Fetzer, *Murder in Dealey Plaza*. He flipped through the notebook and pulled out an old newspaper article. "This is an interview with a guy Fetzer works with, Jim Sherwood. He names the names and backgrounds of all six shooters. Six. It's in this interview published Nov. 20, 2013 in *The Santa Barbara Independent*. The problem is nobody cares anymore."

I challenged my long-time friend and swami. "I do," I said. "What have you got?"

"Ha!" he said with a bark. "I'll bet you a donut you can't tell me how many shooters were in Dallas Dealey Plaza on November 22, 1963?"

"OK, two?"

"Six. Count 'em. Six. And Lee Harvey Oswald wasn't one of them. He was there, but he never fired a shot that entire day."

"First of all, that Zapruder film? Fake. He couldn't have filmed it. His secretary was standing directly in front of him, between his camera and the motorcade. There are all kinds of film alterations made that make a woman who was 5'2" look 7'0" tall. A man in the back of a pickup truck on Main Street is in some photos, but not the film. The Stemmons Freeway exit sign changes size and moves all over the place."

"Oswald was checked into the Dallas police station after being arrested at the Texas Theatre. The original Dallas police report stated he was immediately given paraffin tests on his hands and face. It reported that there was no gunpowder on his hands or face. Only traces of nitrates on one hand."

"There was no way he could have fired any gun, much less an old military rifle that day and been that clean. The Warren Commission deleted that, but the original police report on the paraffin test is in here. Also, witness testimony places him inside the Texas Theatre at the time of the shooting. Unless he's canonized as a Saint, nobody can explain how he was in two places at one time."

I shrugged. Jack said, "You owe me a donut. Krispy Kreme. None of that cheap grocery store stuff."

"You need to read this. Fascinating stuff from a bunch of different investigators in here. *Murder in Dealey Plaza.* He does an incredible job pulling things together from a number of different researchers and investigators." Jack looked down at a page in his book.

"The first shot came from the roof of the County Records Building. We know who fired it. The shot hit JFK 6" below the shoulder, to the right of his spine. He used a .30-06 through a custom-made silencer that was delivered to him a few weeks before the shooting."

"A CIA pilot named, Tosh Plumlee was there and smelled gunpowder down at the south end of the triple underpass after the shooting." And there's an image in a photograph taken by Frank

Cancellare that seems to show someone holding a rifle there. He shot through the windshield and hit JFK in the throat. There are photos of the windshield in here taken before LBJ and the FBI had that windshield replaced within 24 hours."

Jack was on a roll. I watched him as he read from his big binder of evidence.

"The third shooter was an anti-Castro CIA recruit from Cuba. His three shots came from the second floor of the Dal-Tex building. The CIA had a front there called Dallas Uranium and Oil. Think about that. In a clothing and textiles center; a uranium and oil business."

"He used a Mannlicher-Carcano, and he was unique, the only unsilenced shooter. Three shots — two missed. One of these shots is the bullet that sent concrete fragments up into the cheek of James Tague, who was standing downhill at a curb on Main Street near the south underpass. When the limo came to a full stop," he paused and looked at me over the top of his reading glasses. "The limo did come to a complete stop," he added. "The film and multiple witness testimonies prove it. You can watch it on that YouTube."

"The driver stopped the Presidential limousine immediately after the first shot was fired. You can see the brake lights come on in the film. When it should instantly have been pedal to the metal. Then two more shots hit JFK."

He looked up. "How'm I doin' so far?" he asked.

"Fascinating," I said.

"OK, so here's your grassy knoll shooter, shooter number four. I have his name in here, too. He was dressed as a Dallas Police Officer and was trained by the Marines. That's why he was photographed in a police uniform behind the fence. His wife reported that she overheard him talking with Jack Ruby and plotting the JFK assassination."

"His son had his diary. He explicitly stated that his father, dressed in his Dallas Police uniform fired a 7.65 Mauser rifle from behind the wooden fence on the grassy knoll. He said his dad ran off through the parking lot and later shot officer J.D. Tippit. The son gave his father's diary to the FBI. It's never been seen again."

"I don't think FBI Director Clinton Moore will be seen again any time soon, either" I said.

Jack flashed a brief, reluctant smile – he was having fun. "So, we know who Badge Man was, the guy who wore a police uniform that was photographed shooting a rifle from behind the wooden fence on the grassy knoll." He paused, turned a page. "That's four," he said. "Ready?"

I nodded.

"The next one's the big one," said Jack. "Numero Five-Oh is LBJ's personal contracted hitman. Down in Texas, Billy Sol Estes wrote a detailed letter via his attorney to the FBI. Estes told them that this guy murdered several people on behalf of LBJ. He named their names. He described how the hits went down. And then Billy Sol Estes said the guy also shot JFK."

"To confirm it, in 1998 an assassination investigator named Walt Brown claimed that a mystery handprint was taken from a box on the 6th floor 'sniper's den'." It matched LBJ's hitman. For a pardon and immunity from prosecution,

Estes promised to detail eight killings arranged by Johnson, including the Kennedy assassination."

"He reported that the guy not only persuaded Jack Ruby to recruit Lee Harvey Oswald, but that he had also fired a shot in Dallas that hit the president." He stopped, took off his glasses. Jack looked at me and said, "Believe it or not, that last part I'm reading is printed in the *New York Times.*"

"In 1984, Billy Sol Estes' lawyer, Douglas Caddy, wrote to Stephen S. Trott at the U.S. Department of Justice. In the letter, Caddy claimed that Estes, Lyndon B. Johnson, Malcolm Wallace and Cliff Carter were involved in the murders of Henry Marshall, George Krutilek, Harold Orr, Ike Rogers, Coleman Wade, LBJ's *sister* Josefa Johnson, John Kinser and John F. Kennedy."

"I have copies of those back and forth letters right here. In his letter, Caddy says: 'Mr. Estes is willing to testify that LBJ ordered these killings and that he transmitted his orders through Cliff Carter to Mac Wallace, who executed the murders.' Here's a copy of that letter, dated August 9, 1984."

He looked over his reading glasses at me. "But 'Not in our town,' right?"

I said, "Jack, this is incredible stuff. I want to talk about it in-depth one day. But I need to get going."

"Sit still." It wasn't a request. "You see? Nobody cares about the assassination of our American President because it wasn't on that Tic Toc thing last week. Besides, I'm not filibustering about the JFK inside job. That's sixty years ago. I'm showing you how bulletproof you aren't. Today."

"Can I see your book, Jack?" He handed over the red paperback book he referenced but kept reading from his big black vinyl binder.

"It's all in there. There's a minute-by-minute accounting for everyone involved that day in there. Names and everything." He looked inside his binder again. "Here's the last one, shooter numero six-oh."

"Hell, it wasn't even a Mannlicher-Carcano that was fired from the Book Depository. Dallas Sheriff's Deputy Roger Craig ran up there with another officer. They found and produced a 7.65 Argentine Mauser. Craig was later run off the road and made into a paraplegic, then was murdered by a rifle shot to his chest."

I said, "I find it hard to believe there were six shooters there. They have all those recordings, like from the motorcycle cop's radio he left open and all that stuff."

"All the shooters used silencers. Except for the Cuban, Tony. The one who fired three shots. In 1976 the House Select Committee on Assassinations concluded that there was a conspiracy because at least one shot came from behind the picket fence on the grassy knoll."

"A dozen witnesses saw a puff of smoke blow out from the wood fence at the top of the knoll and heard the shot. Plus, two different sets of acoustical scientists used sound signatures to identify the Grassy Knoll as a place for one of the shots. Here, listen to this:"

He read out loud: "A team of surveyors was hired once by Dallas, then again later by the Warren Commission. Both times they said they didn't see any way that a lone shooter on the sixth floor could have pulled it off."

"On their original detailed surveyor's map, there were notations that pointed out two narrow yellow lines on the south side curb of Elm Street, about 45 feet apart. What happened between those two marks? It was the kill zone where JFK was shot in the back, the throat and the head.

"About fifty feet before that, on the same south side of Elm Street, there's a surveyor's notation that says, 'Area of bullet shot on curb.' This is not the bullet that shattered the concrete curb in front of James Tague farther down Elm by the underpass. This is a totally different bullet strike from that. The team also marked a note where the alleged first shots struck the President: "This area hid behind tree for any shot from Depository as of this date May 64'."

"Hell, there was more lead flying around Dealey Plaza than at a skeet shoot."

53

Jack looked up from his binder. "That shows that the shots from the sixth floor of the book depository could not have hit their target. It was obfuscated by trees. This is the report made by a certified survey team. They were commissioned by the Warren Commission. But when the Commission published the surveyor's map, they deleted every one of these references from it."

"Let me read this to you. Here's a former senior instructor for the U.S. Marine Corps Sniper instructor School at Quantico, Virginia, Carlos Hathcock. He says, 'Let me tell you what we did at Quantico. We reconstructed the whole thing: the angle, the range, the moving target, the time limit, the obstacles, everything. I don't know how many times we tried it, but we couldn't duplicate what the Warren Commission said Oswald did. Now if I can't do it, how in the world could a guy who was a non-qualified on the range and later only qualified 'marksman' do it?'"

Jack launched into a mock conversation with himself, with one of them playing the dummy.

"Gee, I wonder why they would do that?"
"Who might have anything to gain from eliminating that evidence?"
"The people who did it would."
"But these people are the ones going after the bad guys."
"They're also the ones who covered up the evidence."
"So, gee, you mean that the ones going after the bad guys – might be the bad guys?"
"Nah. That's impossible."
"Yeah, and OJ is going to find Nicole's killer, too."

I stood up and stretched. Bishop began his 27-step creaking descent to the sounds and smells of the streets below. Jack got so wound up, it made me wonder why, with all this preponderance of new evidence, nobody cared anymore about the assassination of President John F. Kennedy.

Jack continued. "There was one bullet that hit the curb behind the limo and the first hash mark. Another shot hit the curb under the triple underpass and cut the right cheek of James Tague with concrete fragments. Dallas police officer

Buddy Walthers verified it in his report with photos."

"There was also a bullet groove in the grass in the median between Elm and Main Streets. There are pictures showing them when they rushed to it to clear it out. Then there's the hole in the limo windshield that LBJ and the FBI covered up. And that's all in the press. They sequestered the car and replaced that windshield and its frame within 24 hours. That was Kennedy's throat shot. Plus, two shots in his head, front and back."

He paused and waited. I looked out the window as I listened. Big city. I wondered where my sister was.

"Hang tight," he said. "We still have one more shooter." I parked my butt on the windowsill.

"This is a good one, he was also involved in Watergate. While the Air Force trained marksman fired away from the south end of the triple underpass, this guy shot from his position at the north end of the overpass. He confessed this to a New York City Gold Shield Detective when he got caught trying to kill Castro's mistress, Marita Lorenz."

Jack leaned back in his squeaky old office chair. "Hell, Oswald worked for the FBI in New Orleans in '63. And he and Ruby worked together for the FBI in Dallas."

He paused and flipped to another page. "Here's this waitress in Dallas, Mary Lawrence. Swore she saw both Ruby and a person identical to Oswald together after midnight. She worked the early morning shift at the B and B Restaurant on Lemmon Avenue November 22 and saw them both there together."

"I've got a copy of a letter right here stating that Jack Ruby worked for the FBI in Dallas. It's from J. Edgar Hoover to J. Lee Rankin of the President's Commission. It's written on FBI letterhead dated June 9, 1964. Here's a copy of it right here."

I peered down into my white Styrofoam cup, steaming with black coffee.

"Don't not look at me like that, kid. You're poking the hornet's nest of the Perverts That Be. But they're the same monsters and murderers that are the Powers That Be."

"You know about *Operation Northwoods* that Kennedy vetoed. Hell, the Joint Chiefs of Staff tried to set up a 9/11 false flag incident, just a few decades early. They wanted us to attack Cuba. They planned to create all manner of havoc around Miami and make it look like the Cubans did it so we would let the Joint Chiefs take over and launch a full military invasion of Cuba. Public information now. Sound familiar?"

He puffed some smoke and looked dead at me. "JFK wanted to completely dismantle the CIA. If they can kill an American President and get away with it because he won't play ball with them; if they think they can destroy an airliner filled with American citizen passengers as a false flag and get away with it; if they can destroy the World Trade Center to get the billions that they want, launch us into a war and walk away clean… Do you think they'll stop at anything to swat a bothersome gnat like you?"

"Come on, Jack. Give me some credit. I'm an Anopheles mosquito at least."

"Kid. The media covers it all up by gaslighting the public. They're in on the game, too. They stand in front of a burning riot scene and tell the world it's a peaceful demonstration. Those guys meet every year with American and European unelected global elitists and plan this stuff in advance. They get together every year on that Caribbean Island and if you're caught within a mile of their resort, you're arrested or shot. Right, Nicolai? You worked for them once."

My throwing event trainee nodded.

"Right now, they're trying to pull off what they call AGENDA 21. The U.S Government is already buying up land left and right or seizing it outright by eminent domain. Hell, China owns about 100,000 acres of U.S. farmland conveniently located adjacent to many military installations. It's happening across Europe. Farmers are clogging up their cities with tractor convoys in protest."

"Tell me about it."

"Then they're going to force everyone off the land and into what they call Smart Cities. "Smart" means total government control of your life. Smart Meters everywhere, Smart cameras everywhere, everyone under constant surveillance 24/7."

"Facial recognition video software. Digital IDs. Central Bank Digital Currency. Totalitarian control. The end of freedom. It will be like Jim Carrey's life in *The Truman Show*. But everybody in the nation will be Truman."

"Their mantra is out there: 'You will own nothing. And you will be happy.' Sure - and you can work until the day you die because you have no individual wealth, no equity."

"Do you know that the USA now has the highest retirement age in the world at 67? No, you don't. They snuck that one through Congress when nobody was looking. So, the average U.S. lifespan is 77. That means you've only got 10 years of retirement in the US. That's *less than* Russia, Saudi Arabia, China and North Korea."

"They want to link all machines, appliances and other devices to a smart CHIP or something that they'll embed under your skin, or in your brain. They'll make it so that if you don't have a CHIP, you won't be able to access any money, food, transportation, entry to anywhere through door locks. All under the central authority of one global government that places a social value rating on every human being."

"They're working on enslaving the entire planet. You think they're gonna let you slide because you create a nuisance in their sick lifestyles? This is driven by people with lust for world domination."

"This global domination crap has been tried many times before and failed. But this time ... this time ... they've figured it out. No wars. Just lies and technology all supported by the media."

"Remember that waitress in Dallas I told you about - Mary Lawrence? She got a phone call. A guy told her, 'If you don't want to die, you better get out of town.' I'm telling you the same thing. Take a vacation."

Jack's handshake grip felt like he could press his fingerprints into a lead pipe. I headed down the stairs and hit the pavement toward my office building.

* * *

Murgatroyd was beside himself with joy to see me. The moment I pushed through the office door he greeted me like the national media celebrity I wished I hadn't become.

"For Christ's sake! Nice of you to drop by. We've got to get a receptionist. Like yesterday. And technical help. I can do everything, but not all by myself all the time, every day. I mean, it's wonderful for you to be our poster boy front man and lead rainmaker for these new funds, but …"

"Murgatroyd," I said. I showed him both palms. "Murgatroyd, take a deep breath." Sure enough, as Jack predicted, a sound guy, video guy and an interviewer from a TV news channel sat in our coffee break area.

I took him by each arm and looked him straight in the eyes. "My friend, give me one minute. We're all good." His energy felt more intense than a wind-up dancing doll. He caught himself, took in a breath and calmed down.

"Give me one minute, Kemosabe," I said. I walked to the news team that sat around a table. A few moments later they packed their gear. I returned and said to Murgatroyd, "You and I are taking the day off. Today. Right now. Coney Island. The Waldorf. Fishing. Whatever. Fuck'em all."

Murgatroyd looked like he'd been hit in the back of the head with a shovel by Daffy Duck.

"I told the TV crew to come back tomorrow morning. I'll give them an exclusive and all the time they want."

"I – I don't know what to say," he said.

"That's OK. I do. That's why I run this outfit."

I smiled and waved while the news crew carried their gear out of the office. I turned to Murgatroyd. "Look, we're going to get everything you want. We'll get a gal Friday and an IT junkie flunky. As fast as you want to hire them. But you handle the interviews."

He laughed. "Can those be their titles?"

"Sure," I said. "Jane Doe, Gal Friday and her comical sidekick, Geek Gadget, IT Junkie Flunky. For what we pay them, they won't care if we spell their names right. And we'll treat them better than anyplace else in The City."

He took half a step back, looked at me up and down. "Wait," he said. "Have you been talking to God again or something?"

"I don't talk to God," I said. "I try to listen. Big difference."

Murgatroyd laughed. "So, now you're Son of Sam? Are you sure it's God you're hearing? It might be Cody the Cougar channeling. He might be telling you to bring home some pork chops."

I poured myself a tankerful from his overpriced "Made in Switzerland" automatic coffee machine. I said, "See? I'm holding it with both hands, so I don't fumble on the one-yard line."

"We can't both take the entire day off, Nick. Ten prime cases have come in. You've got to choose between them. We can't handle them all. And one deal is with the XL pipeline. Seems they need a bit of a hired gun."

"That's a trite storyline, Murgatroyd. Is it a remake of *Blazing Saddles*?"

"Don't shoot the messenger. Check out the XL file I put in your dropbox."

"All right, Pilgrim."

"Seriously, you own the joint. You can do what you want. I can't do that too, at the same time." He smiled. "My boss would never go for it."

I said, "That's only if you have a boss, Murgatroyd." He stopped, stunned. "How would you like to be a partner in the whole enchilada?"

"What do you mean?" he asked.

"Do I stutter? I'm offering you to be a full partner in the firm like they do with shysters."

"Oh. So, shamuses can do the same as shysters?"

"Shit yes."

His face showed his inner workings. It took time for Murgatroyd to follow the gears in his head. They turned and interlocked to process the thought of what he was being offered.

"It isn't all gravy," I said. "Currently, you get paid; well, I think. You can go home and leave everything here. I've got to deal with the accountants, IRS, State Comptroller, Secretary of State, bookkeepers, attorneys, cops, PI license bureau, plus this other F.L.O.T.U.S. stuff I'm doing now."

"I get the profits of the business, but I also absorb the losses. A partner takes a ride on the same pendulum I sit on. Fortunately, things look good for our stock futures."

"OK. I'm in," he said.

"Great. Congratulations. Now, for your first duty as a partner in the firm."

His face asked the question.

"Play hooky. Today. All day. With me. *Wolfe and Murgatroyd's Day Off.*"

My new business partner astutely surmised, "You banged your brains out down there, didn't you?"

54

Murgatroyd wanted to begin with late morning Bloody Marys at Bleeker and Bowery Streets. We met his request, but after I took us to my private member's underground shooting range. The capstone moment was the incredible steaks on 36th Street.

The next day was taken up with the cable TV news crew, as I promised. It was easy work for me; all I did was talk. They did all the sweating.

While I dealt with the TV crew, Murgatroyd spent a hectic day contacting professional references for leads. A hotshot IT junkie flunky was easy to find. That came down to deciding which one we believed matched our unorthodox, unpredictable workplace.

Gal Friday was a different matter, and those final interviews were mine. The first candidate was beautiful but stupid. Just flat, stupid. Then there was one who had great skills but the personality of a maddened mink. Another seemed OK but looked like death warmed over and I chose not to look at a frowning pallid corpse every morning over my coffee.

Throughout the day we juggled TV interviews and job interviews. Then the place started to come apart. The program producer talked to me about my TV appearance opportunities, and two telephone lines rang.

Murgatroyd stood in my office doorframe. His impatience showed like a cartoon rabbit that looked at his watch and tapped his toe.

A few minutes later, it got easier to talk with the cable crew. I noticed that the commotion in our outer office died. While the broadcasters wrapped up their gear and made polite conversation, I looked up and observed an angel who stood in my office doorframe.

Above black stiletto heels, she wore skin-tight black denim jeans that defined her lovely legs. Her figure was lithe, athletic, and her jet-black hair cascaded down below the shoulders of her pink silk blouse.

She looked at a clipboard she held in her hand and spoke in an alto voice, "Excuse me. I'm sorry to interrupt, sir. Mr. Fontenot has two candidates in his office. He would like you to meet with each one and then make the final decision for your new IT person."

"And there are four applicants in the front office area. They're waiting for an interview for Gal Friday. I took three phone messages. One sounded important. Mr. Penfield Collins for the XL Pipeline. He sounded kind of Ivy League, if you know what I mean."

"And I think I do," I said. "What's your name?"

"Donna, sir."

"You don't have to call me sir. My name is Nick."

"Yes, sir."

"Where do you live, Donna?"

"Brighton Beach."

"Donna?"

"Yes sir?"

"Can you type?"

She laughed. "Yes."

"You're hired. For your first official act would you please thank the other applicants for the job you have just filled and let them go?"

A wry smile played across her upper lip and told me more than any lengthy interview would. "Yes, sir," she said and turned on her stilettos to leave.

"And Donna," I said.

She turned back and let her face ask without words.

"Let Mr. Fontenot know I completed my hiring task for the day and will be there shortly to help him finish his."

She wanted to laugh but knew it was too early in her new position. She nodded with a smile and left. The TV team struck their gear and split four hours after we began.

We, or I should say, they, covered everything, details I would rather have forgotten. They were professional but I feared what kind of media spin they'd put on the whole thing.

Later that evening, fog rolled in and dimmed the city lights. The boat horns in the East River were lonesome calls from faceless voices. I shared a cigar and whiskey in our office's penthouse wet-bar lounge with my new business partner.

"I'm having you carried by our comrades at *Impervious* tomorrow," he said.

"Interesting," I said. "As a new partner, I would think you'd cut back on expenses."

"I would, but I have to protect our principal asset."

"All seriousness aside," I said, "If that fracas hadn't happened at home, I would have thought it was over."

Murgatroyd said, "You had an established ETA getting home, right?" I nodded. "And you had a pre-set appointment time at the Capitol with the Speaker, right?"

"And I'm invited at 11:00 tomorrow at the UN," I said.

"Give the man a cupie doll!"

"Why do I have the most difficulty when I'm not on a case? What's this guy's name tomorrow?"

"Valeriy. Valeriy Bubka. Another Spetsnaz."

"Oh, well. I've never had an issue with overkill."

*   *   *

The next morning was a beautiful, clear autumn day in New York without a cloud in the sky. I expanded my lungs to take in the cool sea air during my walk to breakfast and then to Jack's. The Metro's breakfast hit the spot.

Bill "Jet" Wilson gave me three grueling sparring rounds with 12-ounce gloves. Years before, Jet was 9–0 until he met an upcoming kid who'd just turned pro. Young Tyson got in a lucky left hook

"Andriy is being cheapsteak! Tightwad, penny pincher. We say, "*skryaga*."

I laughed. "Cheap*skate*."

Valeriy resumed driving. "Used Escalades. He is adding. Add-on armor."

"It saved our hides; I can tell you that."

"Valeriy is knowing this! This is why today - using Range Rover. Half million dollars! Original armored vehicle. No aftermarket. STANAG 4569. V8. VPAM 10. Stops IEDs, 7.62."

"It's, nice," I said. "I feel better now." *I didn't know what the hell STANAG 4569 was.*

He asked, "You are expecting Knight 15? Paramount Marauder? Beasts attract bullets. Valeriy is stealthy man. Looking like Range Rover. No see – no shoot. Unconspictable."

"Sold."

The easy route to drive to the UN Building from Manhattan's Lower East Side, is to stay north on

First Avenue all the way. But the morning was gorgeous.

The East River looked like a deep blue waterway instead of a 16-mile ditch that served as a final resting place for crooks in concrete overshoes. Sunlight glinted off its surface and reflected cheerful rippling reflections up onto the riverside buildings.

"Hey, Valeriy – take Delancey to the river - FDR Drive north. It'll be like a Sunday drive along the waterway this morning." The 10,000-pound vehicle rode as smooth as glass when we made the turns onto the north-south roadway that ran adjacent to the river.

"Your brother Andriy's a great guy. He endured some adversity down there."

"Loving brother," he said. "Still, cheapsteak."

The heavy SUV cruised north on the roadway with the heavy ride quality of a Rolls Royce. We passed beneath the Williamsburg Bridge and approached the running track and baseball fields alongside the water. It was a crisp autumn morning, and I took in the shimmering scenery of the Big Apple.

From East River Park I had an unobstructed view of the sparkling water and the BBQ buildings on the other side. I noticed a sleek white helicopter low above the water on our starboard side. It cruised along, then climbed and performed a couple of aerial maneuvers.

"Valeriy, do you know what kind of helicopter that is?"

He dropped his head and looked out the passenger window. "H160. Airbus designed by Peugeot. Andriy and me – seeing this at Dubai Air Show last summer."

It was fast and agile. I watched it sweep down close above the waves. Must be a security team for the UN meetings. "What were you doing at the Dubai Air Show?"

"Wife's brother. Having two of them. Not white. Gold."

We neared Stuyvesant Cove Park; the chopper turned. It flew low across the river in our direction then swept into a turn and paced itself parallel to our ride. I said, "Valeriy."

He was already on it. The big Range Rover lurched forward. He swerved across lanes in serpentine evasive maneuvers. The side door of the Airbus chopper slid back into its open position. Valeriy slammed on the brakes. Our massive tires screamed and smoked.

The front end of my five-ton taxi dived as we slid forward to a screeching halt that threw rocks and dirt and dust ahead of us. The bullets from a fully automatic 7.62 240 Bravo ripped through the car in front of us. Valeriy punched it as the flying eggbeater shot ahead and past.

We veered down a construction exit ramp off FDR Drive to the waterfront deck below. White dust clouds from concrete work kicked up behind us.

The whirlybird pulled a fast inside loop and swept down; it twisted and came straight at us. Its door was open; the gunner leaned out the side. He fired his lethal automatic rifle forward past its nose. More bullets pinged off our armor and smashed white blotches into our bulletproof windows.

A shot cracked the windshield. Valeriy maintained perfect control, but his stress release was understandable. "Bastard!"

I said, "What firepower do you have in here, Valeriy? I'm only packing pistols."

At the edge of Skyport Marina, he threw us into a 180-degree turnaround. Our wheel lugs stressed to their maximum limits. The Sentinel came out of its spin and roared forward.

We jumped back up along the FDR Drive Service Road. The Skyports Seaplane Base lay dead ahead. Valeriy wheeled us through the gates.

Ahead of us loomed parked cars and trucks among stacks of construction materials. Valeriy changed modes from an armored bodyguard to a formula one racer and swerved through them all.

Why, now of all times, did I appreciate the luscious aroma of this interior's leatherworks? This was life and death. I couldn't believe I sensed how rich the interior smelled. And that I realized it at all.

The Airbus shot past overhead and held low above the East River. It turned, then raced back and fired another volley. We roared inside the giant concrete structure. Valeriy plowed forward past parked cars. The chopper slowed and hovered outside.

I could feel the intensity in the eyes of the guys inside it as they tried to spot us beneath our concrete cover. We slowed to a crawl in the shadows under the cement ceiling. Valeriy introduced me to 100 Russian curses under his breath.

Our perspective looked out from dark to light. Though we spotted the helicopter, it couldn't find our dark SUV under the cover of the concrete structure and its shadows. The chopper diverted out over water and made a slow, sweeping sea-level look along the length of the Seaplane Base.

An immaculate blue and white Grumman G-111 Albatross gently rocked at its seaplane dock moorings. As the Airbus flew back out over the water, Valeriy crept our vehicle out from our garage shadows, as close as possible to the big plane. The Albatross became cover and blocked us temporarily from the sight plane of the chopper.

My mad Russian escort bolted out of his driver's door. He stormed to the back of the truck. I jumped out on my side and rushed back with him. "Nyet," he said. "Insurance not allowing passengers being in firefights."

I said, "Open up, comrade. This is my fight." I indicated the back door of the Range Rover. "Give me something. Anything. A slingshot with a hand grenade. I've had enough of this shit. If I have to, I'll go full Patton on them with my .45s."

He opened the rear door and revealed the vehicle's emergency ordnance. I looked down at a hard-shell olive drab storage and transportation container. It fit nicely in the SUV, about a foot wide and five feet long with four clasps along the front closure seam. On its top were written the magic words: "GM K42AI."

"A potato masher! Valeriy, you've got an old Brit potato masher!"

"Liberating it," he said with a shrug. "Moldova."

We each grabbed an end of the 50-pound hard case and swept it out and down to the ground. The latches snapped open and when we threw the lid back, the box revealed its odd-shaped lethal contents.

Inside the protective outer case was a protective inner case. And inside the protective inner case was a gift from God: A Blowpipe Missile.

The term preferred by the Brass was, "Blowpipe Man-Portable Air Defense Missile System." This was often shortened to simply, "potato masher" because of the awkward and unbalanced appearance of the missile and launcher.

An oversized cylinder at the front contained a missile. This tapered to a narrow cylinder at the back that contained the initial firing propellant.

Valeriy snatched the inner case and opened it. The missile and launcher rested inside. He lifted the

Blowpipe from its case. Then he snapped the horseshoe-shaped control unit into place behind the short, fat missile cylinder up front.

"You know these things can't hit the broad side of a barn," I said.

Valeriy didn't appreciate the comment. "Not needing barn! Only helicopter."

"I've fired one of these in combat." I took the contraption from him and checked its heft.

He stood aside. He wasn't happy, but he understood. "I missed," I added.

I said, "There's a plan here, comrade. Show them your ride. Let them know we're here."

He climbed into the Sentinel and pulled forward a few yards. He crept out from behind the Albatross as if he took a quick recon. Then he backed it behind the plane again.

The chopper was several hundred yards away above the East River. It turned and flew at us. It came in low, headed straight at the Albatross.

I positioned myself, took aim from my cover position behind the vintage twin-engine seaplane. I held steady on the bow of the attacking chopper through the Blowpipe's crosshairs.

The pilot flew straight in, confident of a kill. The 240 Bravo's barrel appeared out the side door. It aimed straight forward at us.

It was a light-colored target with a sleek aerodynamic body that attacked us head on. All I had was a bow shot. Down the throat. 1,000 to one chance. Hell, might as well make it 10,000. And that's if I used a new Stinger missile, not this battleax.

Just a little more, let him close the gap, get as big and close as possible, a little more, patience, hold, hold, squeeze ...

I fired.

The front end of the Blowpipe blew off and the missile launched its booster rocket. A couple of seconds after it blasted away, the sustainer rocket kicked in.

The missile guidance automatically switched to its manual Command Line-Of-Sight interface.

Control of the missile was in my hands and eyes, with a tiny thumb joystick.

My focus on the approaching pale specter of death was laser tight. The aim of my right thumb was steady as a rock. Bullets blasted past me. They ricocheted off the concrete and into the Sentinel.

By the time the pilot saw the approaching blowpipe missile, it was too late. We were too close. No time to react. I watched the dark plume that followed my trajectile and steered it straight into the Airbus.

The helicopter blew apart in a giant fireball that blazed in the morning sky above the river's Yankee blue waters. Its mid-air death throes seemed to linger, to defy gravity and hang, suspended in the air.

It finally gave in to Sir Isaac Newton and fell to its baptism in the waterway below. The saltwater extinguished its flames as it joined other failed killers at the bottom of New York's East River.

I lowered the Blowpipe's tube. "*Sayonara*, bitch." I dumped the apparatus of the assassins' nemesis into the water to join them in Davy Jones' locker.

56

Valeriy was stunned. "We wait now for *politsiya, da*?"

"Hell, no," I said. "Let's get out of here!"

Valeriy stared at me. A moment later he shrugged and broke out laughing. "Americans! Cowboys! Riding off into the high noon!"

Valeriy proved to be an expert stealth driver. He steered us through the Seaplane Base and discovered a sneaky way to exit. We slipped out and roared up onto 23rd Street, then headed north on First Avenue.

He continually checked his 360-degree cameras, plus his mirrors and windows. In the distance behind us, we heard a siren.

I said, "Add the potato masher to my tab."

"Fifty thousand, American."

"Thirty-five. And that's how much it cost, new."

"Forty. And that's how much it cost when it saved our lives."

"*Touché*," I said. "I don't know about you, but I don't know what happened back there ... Out of nowhere, some white chopper started strafing traffic on FDR. We scrambled away like everybody else and the next thing I knew I saw the helicopter explode in mid-air. How about you?"

"*Da*," he grunted. "Good enough."

"I don't care who was in that thing. I know where they came from."

"Surprise, kill, vanish," he said. "Where they are coming from?"

The United Nations Secretariat Building appeared ahead. Its 39-story glass and concrete curtain wall structure towered above everything on the Midtown side of the East River. From FDR Drive the lean silhouette of the world's first glass skyscraper appeared, followed by its green glass grid.

I thought the bullet-ridden body and windows of the Range Rover looked a bit ostentatious for an entrance at the UN at the height of its session. Valeriy dropped me off a couple of blocks from the big building in the Turtle Bay neighborhood. I hailed an Uber Black.

The UN General Assembly meets each year in regular session, from September to December. Security measures throughout the city get complex. Traffic comes to a near standstill.

Manhattan is only 22 square miles with over a million and a half people living and working in it. On top of its regular intense policing, throw in a meeting of 1,200 global dignitaries, and things are complicated.

My replacement black SUV maneuvered through the congestion and into the UN complex off First Avenue. I checked in with the ID office at 46th street to get my grounds pass. A minute later, we rolled up to the General Assembly Building's northern entrance between 45th and 46th streets.

I pushed some bills into the driver's hand for gas money and got out. The doors to the building opened into the north lobby. I walked across the expanse of gray and white checkered flooring and had to watch my step to navigate the maelstrom of human activity.

The UNGA is the biggest and most involved annual global security event. Incident command at the UN involves the U.S. Secret Service, FBI and FEMA. Plus, the UN's own Diplomatic Security Service employs 700 people under the U.S. State Department.

An inviting face smiled at me across the crowded expanse of the lobby from behind the first available security desk. Terema was an attractive woman with an engaging smile that caught my attention like a lighthouse beacon in a fog. She wore a long wraparound dress in the red, black and green colors of the Kenyan flag with their shield on the front.

I was running late; I needed to check in and get down to the Assembly room before I missed Ursula's speech. I approached Terema and completed our connection when I got straight to the point.

"*Hujambo. Wanawake warembo wenyenywele nyekundu.*"

Her blushing face only added to her attractiveness. She said, "*Hujambo.*"

"Sorry. I have a thing for redheads," I said. "Ursula Schicklgruber is speaking. She arranged a VIP Pass for me."

"You're with the Argentinian delegation?"

"More or less," I said. She examined my Triad with curiosity when I handed it to her and suggested she apply it to her security card reader. 60 seconds later I met the UN Chief of Protocol, a kind old guy with stooped posture.

He made it his personal duty to escort me through the four-story General Assembly Building. We entered the doors of the The General Assembly Hall and I stopped; I had to pause to take it all in.

The first thing I saw was – everything. I had been a lot of places; I had seen a lot of things. But this was impressive to the point of being overwhelming.

The huge room was lined on both sides by two levels of enclosed booths dedicated to translaters and media. The hall was packed to its 1,800 person capacity. All six allocated seats for every one of 193 delegatons was filled, plus every seat open to the public. Except one.

UN Chief of Protocol Franco Gato held one index finger to his lips to indicate silence. He pointed with his other one toward my vacant seat. Of course, it was all the way down front. Table One.

57

A very long, very empty aisle of green carpet between rows of seats filled with dignitaries led down to my empty blue chair at the table of the Argentine delegation. Situated at the far south end of the room, directly in front of the speaker, the seat was glaringly vacant.

1,200 delegates, 160 reporters, 300 members of the public and 100 advisers could not help but notice whoever arrived late. And at the front, on the rostrum that faced the SRO delegation, stood Ursula Schicklgruber.

She personified elegance beneath the sky-blue shallow dome with its lighting grid of floodlights. Ursula's position was center stage, in front of the wall of bright gold that displayed a huge centered golden UN logo.

The classic green marble background behind the black speaker's tribune podium pronounced her golden blonde hair. Her slender figure was defined by the soft fitted fabric of a classic black and white Chanel suit that had never seen a hanger.

It was 11:45 a.m. We stood in the rear and watched in silence as she spoke:

"This session of our General Assembly is vital to the welfare of the world. We are realigning geo-political norms, establishing continuity of governments and economies, disrupting the global financial system and fragmenting democratic societies."

Then, she saw me as I walked toward her down the center aisle.

She paused.

I trekked through the silence down the long green aisle. Row after row of dignitaries and leaders turned in my direction. Ursula let her pause linger.

I felt hundreds of eyes that stared at my back as I passed by beneath a heavy dome of silence. When I reached the halfway point to my vacant VIP seat down front she spoke again.

"I believe there is a seat here in front ..."

I slowed my pace. Then some more. I drew closer to my seat before the speaker's podium.

Ursula's hazel eyes were twin lasers that glared at me in a vain attempt to turn me to ashes. I turned to the seated delegations from Sweden, Zimbabwe, Chad, Germany, Canada, Brazil, Madagascar ... Stone faces, stone silence.

I turned to the gentle lady from Argentina. "Please," I said. "Continue."

I sat down beside her personal assistant, Birgitta and whispered in her ear. "Thanks for my passes. This is so much fun!" I think she growled.

"Of course," Ursula began, "our work here receives commendations from all manner of people."

I enjoyed my front row seat; I observed her eyes and almost laughed out loud. Her desperate attempts not to look in my direction, to focus her speaker's training outward to the greater audience, were embarassing. One of her hands trembled with anger as she concluded her speech.

"The future is not just happening. The future is built by us. By a powerful community such as we, assembled here. Isn't it great that we few people in this room can change the way of the entire world? And we will. Our time is now!"

I withheld my applause.

"Imagine – a world without war, because there is one global military force. Imagine – a world without crime, because there is one global police force. Imagine – a world under peaceful control, because there is one world government.

The New World Order is here. I invite you to enter it with me and we will walk together into our brilliant future!"

The delegates of the world broke into a crash of applause. Birgitta shot to her feet. The others at the Argentine table followed suit. Then a few more around us joined them and soon the entire General Assembly stood, clapping.

I stood - so I could reach into my jacket pocket. I fished out my lighter and a Marlboro Red.

Birgitta turned and looked at me in horror as I lit up. Ursula briskly exited the podium. A member of the French delegation approached me. He waved his arms in protest and exclaimed, "*Monsieur! Pas de fumer, si'il vous plait! Pas de fumer!*"

I flicked the butt to the floor. With a loud, "*Mon Dieu!*" he turned and departed. I turned and faced the crowded hall, pulled out another Red and lit up again.

It was too much for Birgitta. "Security will escort you out for that!"

I said, "No, they won't. How do I catch up with Ursula?"

Her voice was frozen with reluctance. "Come with me," she said. "The GA 200 room."

The meaning of this revelation was obviously lost on me.

"It's the office of the Secretary-General. She is meeting with the press in the lounge there."

I suppppose these offices were supposed to be swanky affairs. The place looked like someone went crazy at the local Ikea store. A bunch of european minimalist crap. Give me Jack's worn out office any day. It had a soul.

Both sliding partitian office doors of the Secretary General and of the General Assembly President stood open; press people and delegates scurried about. I flicked my butt, walked across to the lounge area.

Ursula looked radiant, a tall, erect woman of power surrounded by sycophants and press. Until she saw me. Her eyes narrowed.

"How nice of you to join us, *Herr Gefahr*. Unfortunate that you missed my speech."

I said, "I heard enough. You only have to step in bullshit to know it stinks, ma'am. Don't need to wade in it."

She grimaced and smiled at the same time. "I take it you do not approve."

"You misunderstand me. I approve all right. I agree with everything you said, exactly as you said it."

Her countenance softened; a smile grew within the classic lines of her face. I had to admit, her posture, demeanor and features combined into a beauty found in classic statues.

"But we both know that isn't the truth, don't we. Sure, world government and world military and world police sounds great. To about five people at the top of your pyramid scheme. The other side of that same coin is totalitarian control of the global population."

She said, "That's ridiculous." The bartender set an old fashioned glass in front of me, half full with bourbon and water on the rocks. "I took a liberty," she said.

I waved off the barkeep, said, "You can't name one country where this communist garbage the UN pushes has ever worked. And who leads this enormous global government? Captain Nemo? I thought world domination went out with Jules Verne, or your countrymen, Eva and Dolf."

She reacted instantly. Her face flushed red. She said, "That history is not true." Then, "This is not global domination!" The reactions of some nearby faces in the crowd registered with her. She smiled. "This is international cooperation."

I said, "Let me take a wild guess and predict how it'll go down. First, you lead with a one-world central bank digital currency. That way, you can shut off anyone from their finances if you don't like them."

"And how do you know you don't like them? Because the next thing you'll do is invoke a digital ID system. With your facial recognition programs you can identify anyone who disagrees with you. Then you can terminate their ability to access their own money, to travel, to buy anything."

"We saw it happen in Canada with Trudeau and the truckers. And it's how they live every day in communist China with their social credit scores. We're lucky your attempts at vaccination passports bit the dust."

She camouflaged her grimace with a sip of champagne. I added, "You might fool the rest of the world, but the USA will never allow a National Socialist Democratic Party, if you know what I mean, and I think you do."

Her face flashed with indignation. She said, "*Herr Gefahr* – you certainly are American. The greatest nation in the world, you call yourselves. Yet you have riots, burning, looting, corruption, homelessness, lawlessness. Your youth is illiterate. You have no border sovereignty. So what is the difference?"

"The difference is, illegal immigrants from 152 nations flock into America. I don't notice them surging across borders to get in anywhere else."

She grew uncomfortable with our conversation among eavesdroppers. "You're so serious. To those of us looking in from the outside, *Gefahr*, it looks like your so-called tyrants are the only ones having fun."

"Sure. 'Let them eat cake.' Until the people take them down like Mussolini or Nicolae Ceausescu."

She studied my face and smiled. "Or Richard Nixon. Dismount from your high horse, Mr.

American Cowboy. This is a happy occassion. You should enjoy that drink the bartender made for you and meet some of our friends. I want to discuss something with you later."

"I'm busy later. Let's talk about it now."

"As you wish." She handed her empty champagne flute to the guy behind the bar. When she received it back, refilled with bubbly, she gently moved us to one side. My drink remained behind, untouched.

58

Ursula said, "Tomorrow I fly to St. Thomas in the Virgin Islands."

"The Birknerhaus Group meeting?"

"Yes. And I want you to escort me; as a personal adjunct to my security team."

"Why would I want to do that?" I asked.

"First, I will double your standard fee. Second, I can't imagine you have an invitation to a gathering of more incredible people. You'll be exposed to the most powerful people in the world. Who knows who you will meet there."

"Why would you want me to do that?"

A sly smile returned to her lips. "Did I mention the perquisites?" She turned outward toward the gathering throng of admirers. She smiled and nodded toward no one in particular. I flinched. She had reached behind her and grabbed my crotch. Well, not my crotch, if you know what I mean, and I think you do.

The Birknerhaus Group meetings were the inner sanctum of the world's elites, by invitation-only. Attendees were heads of state, corporate giants, people with money, power, or both.

It was named after the Birknerhaus Hotel on St. Thomas, USVI. There, business and government held annual meetings that used to be secret. They planned the direction of the world every year since 1971. Security was such a force that nobody was allowed within a large fenced off perimeter.

Armed security patrol boats circled the island 24 hours a day during the meetings. No incoming boats, airplanes or helicopters were admitted during the sessions without approved identification. None. I learned a lot from my shotput, discus and javelin throwing sessons with Nicolai.

This was a once in a lifetime opportunity to get deep inside the workings of the New World Order. And I could do worse than personal bodyguard of the Secretary-General of the United Nations.

Plus, she was hot. Elegantly hot. Which means, really hot. The kind of hot that makes you want to give this elitist civilised lady the King Kong treatment in your jungle treehouse. Hot hot hot.

She was also a complete Looney Tune. And I had been with my fair share of crazies. "Nawp. Cain't dewit."

After a beat she turned into me and nuzzled her words into my ear with her lips. "I'm leaving here shortly. Come with me for Christmas in New York this afternoon. We'll have a chance to talk."

My left-shoulder angel whispered to me. He said, "The day is already shot. You survived. You aren't likely to get hit in a limo with her. It is the holiday season. It is New York. And she is hot."

"That, I can do," I said.

I marked time with ninety minutes of mind-numbing cocktail lounge chit chat amongst a bunch of foreign looking guys. If these were supposed to be world leaders, they seemed weak. When we approached her car together she waved off her Hans and Franz bodyguards I met at the embassy.

Ursula's driver held our door as we entered her white limo. When we rolled out onto the city's streets, the Eurotwins jumped into another car with diplomatic license plates and followed.

"Hans," she said into the driver's intercom. "Yankee Stadium." She pressed a button and raised the wall between driver and occupants.

Her long slender fingers caressed the back of my neck. Her other hand found my leg. She said, "That should give us some time alone."

I said, "Maybe you should give me some guidelines about being your bodyguard."

Her perfect Chiclet teeth bit my earlobe. I felt her hand caress my inner thigh. "That's what I'm doing," she said with a teasing laugh.

I felt the softest grazing of her lips as she whispered in my ear. "Wolfe, darling. You should let me help you."

"You're doing a pretty good job right now," I said.

"I chair the Global Council on Missing Children. I have many connections. I can help you very much." I felt her hand enlarge my evidence that I was a man. "We can help each other."

My breathing was getting tight. I said, "And how am I supposed to help you?"

She smiled; her eyelids dropped. Her fingers unbuckled my belt. One hand held my pants, the other slid my zipper from its north pole to its south pole.

Ursula knelt on the floor before me; her mouth and hands performing a symphony of ecstasy. Her silky golden tresses slid through the fingers of both my hands. As we rolled through Yorkville, she popped a pair of ice cubes into her mouth. When we dropped down off the Cross Bronx Expressway onto The Deegan, my body tensed, then relaxed, stressed, then let loose. She exhaled with a soft moan.

Oh yeah. The crazy ones are fun.

She looked up at me. Her hazel eyes were softened but still as penetrating as laser sights on a gun. She said, "Make me a drink, darling."

I found a bottle of bourbon in the limo bar, mixed it in two glasses with water and ice. I handed her one of the glasses, savored the husky flavor of mine and knocked it back. Cool, dry, wet; it was just what I needed: She did the same.

I said, "Let's talk about how this is going to work."

She continued to caress my leg. "That duty does not begin until St. Thomas." One of her long, slender fingers that had previously shimmied up my maypole reached for the intercom button. "Hans. I've changed my mind. Take us to The Palm Court at The Plaza."

I had no desire to sit around in The Palm Court. My life didn't include sipping tea with a bunch of ladies who lunch. Aristocratic French pastries with a fine China cup of extended pinky Oolong tea were as appealing to me as wearing a tutu.

I didn't drink tea, and the tiny fru-fru sandwiches were the size of my thumbnail. I'd rather have a local fresh donut with some black coffee. I looked out the limo's tinted windows.

So why was I there? Ursula Schicklgruber visited Electra that fateful evening when we met. She was accompanied by House Speaker John Evans, the pedophile monster with a host of new friends at Rikers Island. He was probably sizing up her world organization on missing kids. And she invited me to the Birknerhaus Group. There were too many connections that didn't quite connect.

Evans was right about one thing; she was one of the world's most beautiful women. Everything about her oozed aristocracy and a stern, Germanic style of grace. Plus, she was hot.

The uniformed doorman at the Plaza Hotel beat Hans to open our limo's back door. Ursula seemed very much at home. Her classic Chanel suit blended perfectly with the throng of ladies from New York's Upper East Side. I, in my tan leather trench coat and cowboy boots, was not.

And to top things off, I saw the last thing in the world I wanted to see directly in front of us.

59

We walked in the direction of some tables nestled among potted plants. Nearby indoor palm trees stretched high to the stained glass dome ceiling.

I paused at the circular bar, pulled a C-note from my wallet. A mixologist palmed one of my cards I had printed up for noisy barrooms wrapped inside the bill: "Top shelf bourbon, water, on the rocks." I showed him two fingers.

When I turned back to Ursula, I froze in my tracks. At the table adjacent to the one we approached, sat Little Nick and Electra.

I walked over and gave Electra a hug. She remained seated and looked past me at Ursula. Her return hug felt like a token gesture, but little Nick's face lit up. He rushed me. I leaned over and gave him a hug, too.

Ursula sat alone at our table. I indicated our seats. "We just walked in. You two should join us."

Electra's eyes and facial features responded with a look that informed me there was no way in Hell she was about to join us at our table. I said, "I'm surprised. Why didn't you tell me you were coming to New York?"

A waiter arrived beside Ursula with my pair of bourbons. Without looking over at us, she ordered some designer tea.

Electra said, "I underestimated how fast you work. We just flew in to our hotel on Madison Avenue for some Christmas shopping. I thought you would join us."

Ursula beckoned with a soft laugh. "I was hoping he would join me at our table."

I said, addressing both women, "Electra – Ursula - your friend, Ursula, is inviting me to attend this year's Birknerhaus Group meeting. You know – invitation only." I looked between the two of them, leaned into Electra's ear, "It's a job."

"Oh," said Electra. The yellow rose among the ferns in the Plaza Hotel stood and dropped her napkin onto the table.

She was dressed head to toe in light brown suede. Tight leather pants emanated upward from a pair of whiskey colored knee-high ostrich boots. They met at her waist with a matching bolero jacket beneath a gaucho hat. The contrast of her white ruffled blouse's silk beneath the tactile suede jacket begged the question of what was hidden underneath.

As she moved toward her son she asked, "Isn't that on St. Thomas, next to Little St. James Island?"

Ursula replied, "The Birknerhaus Hotel."

Electra said, "Yes, I used to vacation there with my grandmother."

I moved her a step further aside. "Hey," I whispered. "This means getting inside the Birknerhaus Group. I have a hunch. All those elites in one place at one time - got to be something there. Besides, I'm getting warned to take a vacation – if you know what I mean, and I think you do."

When Electra spoke, her native Texas accent became pronounced. "They've invited me to those things. A bunch of elitist Europeans and Ivy League types trying to tell everyone else how to live. Hell, I could buy any one of five of those nations that are there. My daddy wouldn't go, and I won't either."

Little Nick was engaged in a conversation with Ursula. Electra summoned her son with a quick gesture. She said, "Enjoy your vacation." As she walked away with Nick, I overheard him whisper to her, "That lady's weird."

The decor of The Palm Court featured its namesake tropical trees throughout the room. But as Electra walked out, they and I were covered with frost.

I sat. I drank. Ursula's tea was served with The Plaza's fine China. She leaned back in her chair and studied me. She said with a coy smile, "Mister American cowboy, I would like one of your American cigarettes."

My face belied my surprise. "Oh come now," she said. "There are many things about me which you

507

do not know." She extended her hand, gestured for me to hand her my deck of Reds.

I knocked one loose and handed it to her. She waited for me to light it for her, so I handed her my lighter. As she begrudingly lit up she asked, "Why do you persist - *mich zu argern, Herr Wolfe*?"

"You're so easy to annoy, I can't resist."

"And why is that, Mister Marlboro Man? I have only been inviting to you."

"Since the night I met you and John Evans I've been been blown up, caged, cattle prodded, played *Walking Dead* underground against ghouls and perverts, had my home invaded, my sister almost killed, a friend murdered, and got strafed by a chopper on FDR Drive in broad daylight on my way here – there - the UN – this morning."

Ursula was shocked. "You were! That is terrible! But you look – fine?"

"That's why I was late. I turned the chopper into a submarine."

Ursula said, "I am happy you are in good health, Mister Wolfe. You are forgetting. You also met Electra White the same evening."

I knocked back the second bourbon. "When do we leave?"

She said with no hesitation of pride, "Tomorrow. My private jet. 11:00 a.m. JFK."

"Of course," I muttered. "You green types get around in your limos and private jets."

"There," she said, feigning hurt feelings. "You see? I offer you double your fee, a limousine and private jet to the world's elite conference, as my personal escort, and you insult me."

"I'm sorry," I said. "I'm sorry the truth hurts." Then, "I've got to go." I rose to leave. Her Eurotwins could keep her company. I wasn't on the clock until midday tomorrow.

"Don't leave," she said. "Sit. Relax. I will finish my tea. Hans and I can deliver you wherever you're going." She sipped and looked at me over the rim of her cup. "We can get to know each other more," she said with a smile.

And into her tent, I went. Her passion came alive as soon as the limo's divider wall went up. I was in a Manhattan limousine with a distinguished lady. And I was confined in a cage with a she-wolf in heat. She huffed and puffed and blew my pants down.

*   *   *

The neighborhood where I would find Trouble was not frequented by limousines, much less, white ones with diplomatic plates. The sun dropped while we crossed the Williamsburg Bridge. It was dark, getting cooler. Hans stopped the car close to Myrtle Avenue in Bed-Stuy and opened the door for me.

Three thugs shuffled past and studied us like we were aliens. Hans' demeanor was nonplussed; the road map that was his face showed a lot of miles. One of the world's "most beautiful women" extended her hand to me. I shook it. "See you in the morning," I said.

I walked a block as the long white car rolled away. Several doorways were boarded up. I stopped at a nondescript, unlit door near the corner. Tape secured the broken pane of full length glass in its metal doorframe.

I didn't knock; there was no doorbell. I stood, waited. They would make me for good or bad through their night-vision security cameras.

The door scraped across concrete as it was pulled open from the inside by a guy who stood two inches taller than me. He grimaced through a thick head of wild red hair and full beard. His faded overalls stretched across at least 400 pounds of hired muscle that didn't care whether I was there or not.

I felt a slight trepedation based on my recent encounters with Behemoths of the Ring. *Come on, Michael. Lighten up here. I'm tired.*

"I'm not here to play games," I said. His blue eyes widened beneath his mop of red hair and he drew in a deep breath. That probably wasn't the best way to put it. "I'm here to see my sister."

His face registered disbelief. "Who."

"Trouble."

"Trouble's your sister? Why didn't you say so?" With that he held the door wide for me to pass beneath his arm. His frown turned up into a welcoming smile that lacked a front tooth.

Freddy's Gameroom was a dark, spartan hole in the wall full of smokers and druggies who wanted to gamble. A rambling hallway connected several chambers, offices in some business years ago. They were all the same: gambling video games lined the rooms on all four sides.

There were only two sources of dim light. Colored LED ropes stretched overhead along the ceiling lines. The faces of players were illuminated by energy that glowed from video game screens. Cheap, worn out office chairs provided seating in front of each machine.

I looked into a room of subdued blue light. Three women sat on different sides of what looked like an oversized coffee table. A broad, flat glass surface of a video game was inset into it.

Electronic images of flying fish and firebirds moved across the table's screen.

The players each rolled a ball to aim their shots. They fired multiple electronic weapons at the moving targets to rack up points. One of them focused intently on her game; she fired with smooth precision at her prey.

Beneath her blonde hair, put up under a red Phillies baseball cap, I recognized her perfect nose. She wore black stretch running pants and an oversized Miami-Dade South yellow and black sweatshirt.

Trouble looked up and saw me. She focused back on her game and kept playing.

"Hey," she said.

"How you doing?"

"Good."

"What's this game about?"

"You kill stuff."

"How do you win money?"

"You kill stuff."

I pulled up a vacant dusty black fabric office chair to sit by her. The back was worn out and I almost bailed out of it. I found a different chair in another room and tested it, then rolled it in.

"When you take a break from killing stuff I want to talk to you."

She killed some more stuff. A couple of minutes later, she took a break. "What's up?"

"How are you fixed for ammo?" I asked.

"Why? You got a job for me?"

"I have one for me. I'm headed out tomorrow to go to St. Thomas. The Birknerhaus Group annual meeting."

She looked at me with mock sincere congratulations. "Wow! Look at you. A couple weeks ago you were a dubious PI and now you're going to play Risk with the .0001% at Birknerhaus Group."

An electronic purple elephant gallumped across the screen. Its sight was too much for her self control. "Wait a second," she said. She manned her buttons and zapped it into oblivion. The screen said 450 points.

My sister turned back to me with a smile. "Does my artist's intuition pick up signals of Electra White? Or Yvonne Jackson? They're the only ones you lnow who could get you into the world's most elite party scene."

"Neither," I said. "Ursula Schicklgruber."

Trouble's body froze. She shook it off and sat still, for the moment disconnected from her game. And me. She collected her gambling proceeds, stood up to leave.

"What's up?" I asked.

"She's nuts."

"So I've heard. But I can't pass this up. Call it a hunch."

"She's your type," said my sister. "God knows you're a magnet for psychos. I wouldn't waste my ammo on her."

"The ammo isn't for her, knucklehead. I don't want anything to happen again at home while I'm gone. I'm going to ask Nicolai to house-sit. He gets along with Cody."

"Oh," she said. "I like Nicolai."

"Yeah, well don't like him too much. I don't have enough friends to lose any of them over romance."

"Don't worry," she said. "It won't be romance. Unlike your trip. To the Virgin Islands."

I said, "If you're leaving, let's go home together. I'll call a cab."

"Right," she said. "At this time of night? Here? No cab in the city will answer a call to this address. My friend Donna will take us. She lives around the corner."

T bought her ammo supplies from the gun shop where Donna worked and the two became friends. Donna's brown eyes flashed in the lights as she drove us across the East River back into the city. She was short, cute in her houserobe with her bobbed black hair and button nose.

I should have gone by the White Hotel. I should have seen Electra and little Nick. I was too damned tired to do anything. And I had to be at the airport in the morning.

I managed to call Nicolai while I tossed some clothes into a bag. It was going to take more than a phone call to smooth things over with Electra.

The sound of automatic gunfire startled me. I was still too high strung. The stacato thunder was my sister getting back to work in her studio.

60

In the span of twelve hours, my modes of transportation ranged from the absurd to the sublime to the weird. Donna's ride from Bedford-Stuyvesant to our homestead warehouse in the Lower East Side was a gunmetal gray hemi Dodge Charger with 797 horsepower. A miniature disco ball that dangled from her rear view mirror reflected bothersome lights throughout the interior. She wore yellow shooting glasses to drive at night.

The next morning I fed Cody, then Valeriy drove me to JFK airport in another Spetznaz Special SUV. Ursula, her bodyguards and Birgitta waited for me to board their luxurious Lear 60XR jet.

Our direct flight from JFK to St. Thomas USVI featured full bar service managed by a staff flight attendant. I enjoyed a spicy bloody mary and eyed the scenery. My date to the prom relaxed into her luxurious white leather seat in her khaki skirt, white blouse and navy blazer. Her piercing eyes were shielded behind a pair of Chanel sunglasses.

For some reason, it was the first time I noticed Ursula's legs. Nice legs. Too long, too nice to be locked up inside a frumpy female politician pant suit. Her navy Chanel pumps put her height at about 5' 9".

When we landed on the island at Cyril E. King International Airport the weird part of my transportation odyssey began. St. Thomas is the only U.S. state or possession with left side driving. This is fun because the cars are almost all U.S. left side drive cars. So, our black Lincoln Town Car had a left side driver, driving on the left side of the road.

About 42,000 people live among the narrow twisting roads of St. Thomas. That swells when the world's global elites arrive for their annual shindig. As we touched down Uursula said, "We prefer our affairs take place on islands, darling. So much easier to keep secure."

The airport did not have room for all the private jets. Some had to be shuttled to other nearby Virgin Islands airports until they were needed to depart.

Nicolai was right about the intense security. During the three days of Birknerhaus Group meetings no commercial traffic was allowed to the island. Temporary chain link fencing surrounded the hotel's grounds.

Its perimeter was locked down by local police and security contractors that patrolled the area 24/7. Trespassers were immediately arrested. My assigned protocol advisor, Birgitta made a point to educate me before the evening's cocktail reception in the grand ballroom.

For example, the prime directive was that all attendees agreed to conform to the Cadbury House Rule. This secretive protocol was manufactured by the Royal Institute of Covenants. (aka: "Cadbury House") The bottom line was a group of elitists came up with a set of behavioral rules that amounted to, "What happens at Birknerhaus, stays at Birknerhaus."

Only the attendee list was made public - what topics were discussed and who said what stayed inside the Birknerhaus Hotel. Everybody there knew everything that went on and openly discussed whatever was on their agenda. And nobody ratted about anything anybody said to the press or public.

She also explained that, although my presence was to offer Her Nibs my security and protection, I was to appear as a social escort. Official bodyguards had limited capacity inside this gathering of elites.

My room adjoined the Presidential Suite, Ursula's temporary home. The Eurotwins and I accompanied her to her penthouse. We swept it for security and bugs, checked the bottles and items in the Servi Bar, found nothing. I checked the windows. All locked. No ledges.

I figured to find her there, alone, in a few hours.

Adirin and Adrean, Ursula's Teutonic twin bodyguards, shared a room across the hall. Their night duty kept their eyes focused on her temporary domicile. I was designated as the official evening escort of the attractive first female Secretary-General of the UN.

Steaming hot showers released a magic rejuvenation in me. I worked the water temperature all the way up until I felt the travel-tightened muscles in my shoulders and back let loose. I slipped into my new charcoal suit and strapped on my full ordnance.

One of the angular blond Eurotwins opened the penthouse door when I knocked. Ursula emerged in her signature halo braid and a couture backless spaghetti dress of champagne colored dupioni silk. The heels she wore beneath it brought the top of her head to my eyes. A sparkling necklace of diamonds adorned her, clustered around a large emerald cut emerald.

Tradition dictated a lavish formal dinner for the attendees. And traditionally, it was sparsely attended. The dinner served as a formality for those who chose to attend. The more popular event was the cocktail reception in the ballroom just ahead of us.

Ursula kept her arm tucked through mine as we made our way through the lobby toward the large ornate dance hall. *En route*, we paused several times as she made small talk with well-heeled dignitaries. Who was I? "I'm afraid to introduce him to you, darling. You'll try to steal him away."

A short guy with a shaved chrome dome kissed her hand. He spoke to her in German. They shared a quick knowing look and agreed, in German, to meet again later.

Among the elite multitude, Ursula's movements were ethereal. The lady in floor length champagne silk floated across the room like gilded moonbeams. She was a shimmering physical presence within an aura that seemed to glow red around her sexy formal ensemble.

When we entered the grand ballroom of the hotel, I had to pause. The UN General Assembly was extraordinary, but this was astonishing. I felt a temporary state of sensory overload. The facial identification of so many high profile people in one place at one time strained my mind's image recognition software. *Tall cotton.*

Ursula's personal magnetism commanded attention the moment we entered. We descended seven malachite steps to the ballroom's floor, made of the same gleaming green stone. Every head before us turned to look.

I was black and white arm candy in my gray suit. Ursula introduced me to this prince, to that Prime Minister and to another American billionaire. My head was buzzing.

One demure lady stood beside Ursula and gave me an unabashed once-over. She asked, "And who would this be, darling?" Her suit was very high quality, and very bland, the kind of overpriced and subdued fashion worn by the super wealthy.

My alleged date pulled me away. She replied, "Nick is my escort - who is about to escort me to the champagne bar. Isn't that right, darling?"

I've never heard so many "darling"s or witnessed so many phony kisses on cheeks. Half of the ballroom population looked like they already had one foot in the grave.

Except a young raven haired woman with tan skin and a broad flashing white smile of orthodontic perfection. She held court among several superpowers. I caught a quick nonchalant wink from her, thirty feet away. So did Ursula.

My date turned us toward a waiter with glasses of champagne on a silver tray. "You will need to remain near me every minute, *Herr Gafahr*," she said.

"I've been wanting to ask you about that," I said.

"You're here to do a job, Mister Wolfe."

"Not that," I said. "I notice you often speak in German. Isn't Spanish is the official language of Argentina?"

"Then you must also notice I speak predominantly in English. There are several hundred thousand of my countrymen who speak German."

"Like at the Eden Hotel in La Falda?"

"What about the Eden Hotel?"

Jack had shown me the FBI files.

"I understand that the founders, Walter and Ida Eichhorn were a hoot! Didn't they have the first Mercedes in Argentina? Sponsored by a man named Juan Keller, I believe. Sounds like a charming group of Germans who settled there. Right after the war, I believe?"

Her fingers bit into my arm. "Our country is rife with wives tales," she said. "Like the big, bad wolf ... Some were told to me by my nanny when I was young. Your focus needs to be here, now – tonight – with me."

The dark haired beauty across the room caught me again out of the corner of her eye. She sat among a convivial setting of furniture in a large Cobra chair, surrounded by men who attended her in their expensive suits. I asked, "Who's the number over there entertaining the League of Nations?"

Distaste dripped from her lips when she replied. "Natalie Cocks. Inherited the Cocks Network broadcast empire. Look further. She talks with the heads of NBC, ABC, major newspaper publishers, editors. She was invited as a joke. She is ... small fry."

"I wouldn't mind battering her up," I said.

Ursula never lost a step, or her smile. She was indeed one of the most beautiful women in the world. Brilliant, multi-lingual, globally powerful, enchanting. Then she delivered a sharp subtle elbow jab into my ribs.

The lightning flash it delivered to my brain brought with it the images of women in my life: Teresa was *Texas Monthly*. Victoria was *Allure*. Electra was *Town and Country*. Ursula was *National Geographic*.

Trouble? Trouble was ... trouble.

And I saw trouble headed our way. A matriarch in the European Rothberg family, worth several trillions, approached Ursula. She cut her eyes regarding my presence. Ursula acquiesced. Her grip loosened and she said, "I need a moment with my friend, darling. But don't be long."

I turned and strolled across to meet the attractive Miss Cocks. Halfway there, I was interrupted by someone I would have bet my guns I would never have seen. Especially there.

61

Birgitta had given me the agenda of subjects for their meetings: Geopolitical Realignments, Disruption of the Global Financial System, Fragmentation of Democratic Societies, China, Russia. And the list went downhill from there.

The list of attendees was a Who's Who of global totalitarianism: several members of the World Economic Forum, the WHO, the CDC, CEOs of every major Wall Street investment firm, every tech giant you could name and some you couldn't, the CEO of every newspaper conglomerate, media empire and television network, military Chiefs of Staff, Intelligence group heads, movie stars and royalty.

The people I was about to meet were were disparate in their individual functions and nationalities. They shared one principle goal: a collective desire for control of the world's population.

The sound of a familiar voice among the gathering caught me by surprise. Her Irish brogue cut through the subdued din, "Saints preserve us if it isn't the man named, Wolfe."

It took a moment for me to process that voice. I turned and looked up at the tallest woman I've met. The Marvelous Margo had to stand 6' 6" in her bare feet, and she loomed before me in six inch heels. Her long red hair hung past her shoulders. It created a thick fluid frame around a face that looked like Mr. Ed with blue eyes.

I was only at this VIP event for an hour, but it was already refreshing to talk with someone I knew was down to earth. It was an unusual adjustment for me to look up to speak with her. "Margo? What are you doing here?"

She replied with a laugh. "I'll ask you the same thing."

"Fair enough," I said. "Chasing a hunch. I have a feeling Washington was just the beginning."

"Should I leave now?" she asked. "I suffer a grave distaste for violence."

"Officially, I'm here with Ursula Schicklgruber. Escort/bodyguard. But I'm wearing my x-ray glasses to see what's beneath all this. Your turn."

"AI. We need to get it under control, yesterday. I'm meeting with the tech giants. You'll know them when you see them." Someone across the way caught her eye. "Excuse me. I need to catch him."

I never thought I would actually meet Margo in person. But now I could pick her out of a crowd, anywhere. Twenty feet away a group of well heeled men laughed and nursed their cocktails. She strolled into their center and immediately owned their attention.

The alluring Natalie Cocks flirted with her eyes again through her throng of admirers. *She doesn't look small-fry to me.* She turned her attention back to her suitors.

I moved toward her, but bumped into a gentleman of the rotund persuasion. Mister five by five stood level with my chest; his waist measured about the same as his height. He spoke in the unmistakable accent attributed to Afrikaner in South Africa.

How did someone with money have so much dandruff?

"Excuse me," he said. "Sebastian Sterling." The oversized perfect diamond in his ring signified the source of his wealth.

"Capetown?" I asked.

"Very good. For generations," he said and raised his glass. "To grandfather Cedric. You look new here. Haven't I seen you in the news? You're that Pied Piper of Washington fellow, if I'm not mistaken. I didn't catch your name?"

I focused my vision on his pupils, then grinned. "Guilty as charged. Nick Wolfe."

Sebastian broke out in a laugh heartier than usually allowed in the British Empire. He regained his composure, laid one hand on my shoulder. "By God, you're what we need here. What will your role be during our meetings?"

I said, "I usually find a way to annoy just about everybody."

He laughed again, more subdued. "I want to abandon my meetings and join yours." He leaned toward me in confidence, checked for easedroppers. "Actually, I think this is all a bunch of nonsense. I come each year for the party. Best on the planet." He enjoyed his martini.

Two men and a woman approached him. The guy was a Silicon Valley tech owner, the woman ran the World Bank. They exchanged greetings and the diamond merchant introduced me. "My friend here, Nick Wolfe is the escort of Madame Secretary General."

He turned to me and said, "And I'm sure you recognize this chap."

The chap was Josh Hitt, tough guy actor. He was at the zenith of a career that sparkled with awards from every thespian award program. His mega-hit action movies created a following of millions of adoring fans.

I said, "I don't need a digital ID to make him out."

This caused nervous little laughs all around. Sebastian chimed in. "Didn't I tell you? I'm seriously considering canceling my meetings to attend his."

The techie asked, "Will you be involved in the digital ID discussions, Mister Wolfe?"

I endured his verbal treatise in support of totalitarian control, then drove my Constitutional freedom harpoon into its heart. "The people of Sri Lanka called. They want their country back. They went all in and followed the communist economic guidelines foisted on them by the International Economic Forum and World Health Organization. It wasn't long until the entire nation went broke, bankrupt."

I wanted to have a drink. A double. Or two. But not on the job. Dammit. My new wingman was another matter. Sebastian's vodka led his way through an evening of conversational entertainment at my side.

I was holding my own on the world stage, so I decided to press my luck. I asked our little group: "So what is this annual meeting of big shots about? You all really believe in this Great Reset and New World Order propoganda? 'You will own nothing, and you will be happy'? What kind of nonsense is that?"

"Well," said Mr. Tech, "It isn't that we're striving for some kind of one-world government. But we don't believe in the idea of fighting each other in wars, killing each other, destroying lives, creating refugees. Our thinking is that a single global community would be beneficial."

"How did that end for your predecessors? Alexander, Ghengis Khan, Napoleon, Hitler - Captain Nemo."

"Ah, but therein lies the weakness to your point. Those were lone individuals pursuing a manifest destiny. They worked from the inside, out. Our endeavor is comprised of a global group people from diverse backgrounds and nations. We are working from the outside, in."

"So you believe in the Mastermind Group concept," I said.

"Perhaps, in a manner of speaking," he said.

"That a combined effort by a roomful of megalomaniac totalitarians with a collective lust for control is superior to the mind of the single most narcissistic, vainglorious asshole in the bunch."

"I wouldn't put it quite that way," he said. With that, the clique of three departed. Before he joined them, Josh Hitt turned to me and, with a smiling Hollywood wink said, "Let's catch a drink this weekend."

I said, "I'll have my people call your people." He laughed and rejoined the other two.

Diamond Sebastian Sterling enjoyed himself and his martini. "Now I really do want to be in one of your meetings!"

One of the wait staff replaced his empty glass with its brimming twin. He said, "This promises to be be a wild weekend, indeed."

Natalie Cocks had kept an eye on our little group. I said, "If you'll excuse me, Sebastian, I'm needed."

Sebastian caught her glance and said, "Oh ho ho – Miss Cocks. That could go in any one of several directions."

I excused myself, shook hands before I turned away. I brushed past Margo and her group on my way to meet the mysterious brunette. Natalie Cocks extended her hand to me through a wall of suitors. "Darling," she said, "What kept you?"

62

I said, "You know our friend, Dimitri."

Natalie pulled me toward her through the admiring throng. "How is good old Dimitri these days?"

"He misses you."

"I'll have to do something about that."

Several men in her entourage drifted away. One with tan skin and salt and pepper hair remained, steadfast. He spoke with an Italian accent. "I don't believe I've had the pleasure, Mister ..."

"Nick Wolfe."

He said his name was Pietro Tyro. "And whom do you represent here, Mister Wolfe?"

"Our First Lady."

Pietro's eyes widened. He looked me up and down from head to toe. "Yvonne Jackson," he said.

"And company."

"Such as your President?"

"More or less. He's usually busy saving the world from communism."

He scoffed. "Your Presidency is always the same. A new man takes office. He preaches about his reforms and how he's going to clean things up. Then he is visited by the men who wear dark suits and carry black briefcases. They inform him how things will be done. It's the same with every one of your administrations."

Natalie Cocks' eyes performed the same task that Pietro's did. But where his eyes surveyed me, hers undressed me. Pietro made a move to wedge himself between us when my wingman flew in as if out of the sun.

Sebastian tapped him on the shoulder. "Excuse me, Pietro. Now that we have a chance to talk ..."

Natalie gave me an amused and sexy smile. She asked, "Who are you?"

"My friends call me, Nick." I handed her one of my .45 ACP business cards.

Natalie turned it over in her delicate fingers, examined it with curiosity. "I see you're with the bitch from below."

"Officially, I'm not where her body guard is."

"I'm not going to get anything at all out of you, am I?"

"Not tonight."

"I own fifty-five radio stations and the top-rated television network."

I pulled out my lighter. "I have my grandfather's Zippo." Out came my pack of Reds. "Cigarette?"

"You're joking."

When I lit up my smoke she saw my .45s beneath my suit. She gently licked her index finger. Then, as she kept her eyes engaged with mine, she reached inside my jacket and touched it with her fingertip. "Big gun," she said.

"Big bad Wolfe."

She tilted her head back with defiance. "Yes," she said. "I'll join you."

I chain-lit another cancer stick and handed it to her. She took a puff without inhaling, and coughed like she had TB. Other than the attention of 100 of the 120 present, nobody noticed.

"Not your brand?" I asked.

"I think you're a professional ass."

"I'll get you a fresh drink."

"Stay here. My drink is fine." She took a long sip that quenched her coughs. "If you're here with Beelezebub I take it you'll be drifting downstairs later."

"Why? Will you?"

"It sounds weird."

"Your first time here?"

"Yours too?"

"A diplomatic novice, at your service," I said. "Maybe one of us should check it out and tell the other one about it."

"Good," she said. "Call me in the morning."

"What is the weird thing downstairs that I'll call to tell you about?"

"The orgy, darling."

63

I said, "An orgy? Now you're the one who's joking. Half the people here are waiting for God."

"Darling, I may joke about financial collapse or thermonuclear war, but never about an orgy."

"It's a ten-to-one male/female ratio here. I don't like to stand in line."

"This is your first time, isn't it, darling. I have it from good sources that it's the party of the year down there. Sex, drugs and rock and roll. For real. It sounds delightfully sordid."

Pietro extricated himself from Sebastian. The Italian placed his hand on Natalie's arm. He said, "You wanted to speak with the Senator."

He indicated a man in a small group who could never have been anything but a U.S. Senator. Tall, lean, tan, full head of wavy black hair with distinguishing gray at this temples. Gray suit, white shirt, regimental stripe tie, Oxford brogue shoes.

Natalie kissed me on the cheek. "Sorry, darling. Keep that motor running. The Chairman of the Senate Committee on Appropriations is waiting." As they walked away, I caught a very quick, very slight look of adolescent one-upsmanship from her escort.

Before I returned to Ursula I managed to piss off three major newspaper editors and the CEO of the world's largest energy exploration company. It was green energy here, dissolution of sovereign boundaries there, and climate change everywhere.

Sebastian said, "Beware, sir. I hear the sound of feathers rustling,"

I watched the conversation between Ursula and Madame Rothberg come to a close. Ursula's eyes beckoned. I said, "Excuse me, Sebastian. Duty calls."

He said, "On the morrow." He indicated the lady from Argentina with a quick motion of his eyes. "A mercurial mistress, my friend."

Ursula was on her third glass of champagne. She said, "Finished chatting up the country girl?"

"I dance with the one who brung me, ma'am. I thought I'd set her up with your bodyguards, Hans and Franz."

Her compressed lips registered her displeasure. "This was a mistake. Bringing you here was introducing a ruffian to the opera. You might as well have worn overalls."

"The best part of the opera is when the fat lady sings."

"You persist in proving my point," she said. "I had thought I could help you with the children. I thought you and I could create something grand together. Something global. But you must gallivant around, flirting with every female - " She didn't finish.

The lines in her face tightened. Her knitted eyebrows framed her intense hazel eyes. She said, "I'm bored. I am returning to my room."

I said, "Let's go." I hoped I had time to slide back in later with the lovely Ms. Cocks.

"Not with you," she said. Adirin and Adrean appeared on the steps. Without another word or as much as a goodnight slap, Ursula turned and floated away across the malachite floor to her bodyguards.

First, I pulled a cocktail from the tray of a passing server. Then I surveyed the room for a vixen with dark hair whose tan skin teased the tight fabric of her little black dress. To no surprise, she was centered in a group with her Senator and several admirers.

As I stood, an abrupt invasion of internal pressure descended on me like a curtain fall. Sinuses, eyes, the crown of my head, pain, tension, a high pitch rang in my ears. I got myself to a window and surveyed the night sky. Clear as crystal with a million stars ver the Caribbean sea.

Still, I needed to leave and get to my room. I was weak inside, bent with internal agony. A storm was coming, and it was a big one.

My chest tightened, breathing became restricted. My hands were clammy. I faltered as I crossed the room.

Josh Hitt broke away from his little group and walked over. His face showed genuine concern as he approached. He said, "You look like you just walked through the ugly forest. Let's get you to a seat."

"I need to get to my room."

"All right, tell you what. Keep close behind me; I'll run lead blocker through the crowd."

We crossed the ballroom full of dignitaries and captains of industry in tandem. As we passed by Natalie *et al*, I didn't possess the stamina to engage in conversation. It was all I could do to fixate on the back of the actor as we moved through the crowd.

When we arrived at the top of the green steps he said, "You gonna be all right?"

"This happens to me when there's a big storm coming."

He looked out a floor to ceiling window. "It's clear as can be outside. You sure you're OK?"

"I'm good. Normally, I'd tell you to get your car inside."

He laughed and gave me another one of his practiced Hollywood winks with a smile. As soon as he turned away he was met by another group of celebrity seeking VIPs.

I waited for the elevator to the 13th floor. When it arrived, I waited as several people brushed past me on their way out. Before I stepped across the threshhold marked, "Otis" one of the hotel servers approached. "Excuse me. Are you Mister – Wolfe?"

He sensed that I didn't feel up to small talk.

"A lady asked me to bring this to you." He handed me a wallet sized paper envelope. Inside was a credit card sized room key. 303.

I looked at him through bleary eyes.

He said, "Ms. Cocks."

"Thanks." My fumbling fingers lifted my wallet out of my breast pocket. I almost dropped it but managed to spiff him a Franklin.

When I opened my room door, I walked straight to my shaving kit. The "Break in Case of Emergency" glass cigar tube contained my Rx for these spells: Valiums, Advil liquid gels and Jim Beam miniatures. Within half an hour I fell asleep, living better through chemistry.

* * *

A flash of lightning followed by a loud thunderclap woke me up. My clock said 4:12 a.m. Rain hammered against my window panes, driven by high winds of a tropical storm.

My discomfort was gone. I explored the mini bar and popped open a Coke. Whenever I resurfaced from my layman's prescription a cold, crisp cola hit the spot. Natalie Cocks' room key lay on top of the desk with my wallet.

How do you dress for an orgy? Or, does it matter? I looked at my suit, held up my black silk PJs, decided to go with my black Puma track suit.

I slipped into my pants when Murgatroyd's call rang on my satellite phone. To say he was doing deep research would sell him short. To say I wasn't ready for what he told me would be the understatement of the decade.

Murgatroyd had no concept what time it was. He and our new IT Junkie Flunky spent the past 24 hours taking deep dives into the dark web. My hunch turned out to be more than a hunch. And worse than I could have imagined.

That was one of the worst weather beat downs I've ever suffered. What was my assignment from above this time? I strapped on my guns.

The hotel was dead quiet in the night's early morning. My knuckles made gentle taps on the door of Natalie's seventh floor suite. They finished their third rap when it opened. Natalie stepped outside.

She wore a track suit as well, pink. It was plainly evident by her jiggles; she wore nothing underneath. She whispered, "Shhh!" and stepped with quick feet into the hallway. The room behind her was dark. She pulled the door shut.

Natalie ushered us forward a few steps before she spoke, a designer clutch in one hand. "Bad sex!" After a few more steps down the hallway, "I'm so glad you came. I was waiting at the door for you."

"I'm not sure what to say, but the word 'second' comes to mind."

"Oh – these old guys. They seem so debonair and cool, then they just peter out."

"Literally," I added. We reached the lobby. There is something haunting about a big place like a grand old hotel at four a.m. Empty and still, it's welcoming and eerie at the same time.

She said, "Hopefully he'll be gone by the time I return," then guided us toward a wide stairway at the far end of the ballroom.

64

We reached the staircase and toed our descent with light, silent steps. The wide black marble stairs receded down ahead of us for several flights. Before we reached bottom the sounds we heard confirmed Natalie's intelligence.

It was obvious somebody was having a good time. We pressed ahead and down. Our ears were met with the sounds of a crackling fire under techno electronica music. And then, laughter. I wondered what the Hell was going on. We reached the bottom of the stairwell and peered around the corner.

My face was inches away from a man who urinated on the wall. I jumped aside and barely stayed dry. Natalie's face registered her shock. We stood next to each other, stiffened as we surveyed the scene in the grove before us.

We had stumbled into a drunken boys night out party. A long table at the bottom of the steps stood filled with stacks of red robes. The boys wore red robes with their hoods down. And across the giant cavern, in the very front, a group of them burned something.

The masonry of the stairs turned into a massive stone floor across an auditorium-sized subterranean party barn. In front of us, half a hundred men drank beer out of cans, pissed on the walls and smashed with women one-third their age.

I couldn't fathom how this God-awful music was orgy-friendly. Then I observed the participants. The collective lust that gleamed from the eyes of naked old men made them oblivious to musical sounds. As they pursued their bewitching prey, to them it could just as well have been a Mariachi band.

Some of the old boys didn't wear anything at all. Couches, chairs, the big round ottoman in the middle of the room – all were occupied by naked geezers who relived younger days with stunning young women. And not a nine in the bunch.

Every table provided a bounty of drugs. A coffee table was stocked with blue ones. The mirrored end tables were covered with coke. A sectioned lazy susan serving dish provided both, plus pot and sugar cubes.

Natalie stood on her tiptoes. She whispered, "I was right! Imported hookers – with – Oh, my God!" She pointed at one pair of beasts locked together in lust, then swept the room with her index finger. She indicated several other trysts and started naming names. She opened her clutch and pulled out her phone.

In the middle of it all, my new wingman occupied the round hotel-sized ottoman. The fingers of one of his hands pinched his omnipresent martini glass. His other hand caressed the thigh of a stunning young woman.

I stopped Natalie from shooting her video. "Turn off your flash." She took a moment and adjusted her camera.

I slipped into a red robe, then called to Sebastian. "Sebastian! Come here." I handed a robe to Natalie.

He looked over with a smile. It took him a moment to extricate himself from the deep leather of the
oversized hassock and resituate his robe over his body. He assisted his naked ladyfriend to a stand then schlepped across to us, wearing her on his arm. "My friend! You came to join in our revelry."

Natalie shot a long slow pan that didn't include Sebastian Sterling. The scene was a sweeping collection of strained faces on international dignitaries during their full penetration lap dances.

Across the grotto, a robed congregation crowded around a large sculpture of an owl-like figure. The leader of the group placed a small stick figure on an altar before it, then set it on fire. The inebriated followers cheered and drank.

I figured it was time to take Natalie upstairs. This was pointless: a bunch of elitist frat boys played pyro games, guzzled beer, pissed on the walls and banged hookers.

I thirsted for a real drink instead of a can of beer. My eyes couldn't help but fixate on another naked ten who served libations behind an open bar on the left side of the room. The fully mirrored wall provided a 360 degree view of the exotic bartender. A defibrulator hung behind her.

Camouflaged, mirrored doors stood open on each end of the bar. I caught the fleeting sight of a dark robed figure as it entered the left one.

Natalie said, "I'm deciding. I don't know if this makes for a sitcom, or hard news."

"What about the Cadbury House Rules?"

"What are they going to do? Not invite me back?"

"Kill you."

Another figure slipped behind the bar and entered the left side door. I grew curious. My hands patted the locations of my artillery beneath my track suit.

The media mogul reached up and touched my nose with her index finger. As she slowly traced a line down my face, over my lips, past my chin and down my throat to my chest, she whispered, "Come on, Wolfe. Get in the spirit of things."

One more partygoer spirited behind the bar. He too, moved through the doorway.

None of the three came out.

I said, "Stay here, or get back to your room. I'm going to check this out."

"Like Hell," she said. "I need a drink. Take me to that bar."

She looped her fingers through the top of my pants and followed close behind me.

65

The bar didn't hold my interest; the doorway behind it did. But the smoking hot naked lady who mixed drinks behind it provided a pleasant distraction. She poured my bourbon, straight up, and handed Natalie a Cosmopolitan. I threw my drink down in a single toss.

The dark opening led us to a stairway down, bathed in red light that emanated from red, flaming torches. Our red robes turned gray in their light.

The distant echoing beats of a large drum reverberated inside our arched stairwell. Between the strikes of its thunderous mallets, I heard the screams of an infant child.

I said to Natalie, "Go back. Fun's over."

She looked at me with horror in her eyes at the sound of the screaming child. "What's that!"

"Look, you don't want to go where I'm headed."

"Like Hell," she said. "This makes great television."

I grabbed her by her top and drew her up to my face. I spoke through clenched jaws and teeth. "Look, lady. This isn't some fun Spring Break day at the beach. This can get deadly serious. Deadly fast. Go back upstairs. There's an orgy going on for Chris'sake. Find yourself a young stud."

Her eyes were wide, unblinking. She said in a timid voice, "I thought I did." She moped as she returned up the stairs.

I listened to the repeated deep beats of the big drum that echoed up to me from below. An infant screamed again. The drum beat louder.

I gripped the checkered walnut handles of my .45s. My back pressed against the stucco wall of the stairway. I toed down one step at a time, toward something I did not want to see.

When I reached bottom, I paused at a pair of tufted red leather doors. I filled my other hand with my hammerless .38 and pressed them open.

Before me a dozen hooded figures in black robes faced away with their backs to me. The one who led the ceremony, elevated on an altar, wore a hooded robe of gold. The same red symbol of angular magic that John Evans wore was embroidered on the back. They worshipped a huge bronze idol.

The burnished effigy was a bull's head on top of a man's body, with outstretched hands. A gas furnace inside the figure burned blue flames that created furious temperatures. They worshipped Morloch, Satan's favorite fallen angel; the ancient Canaanite god of child sacrifice.

And before them all, the idol cooked a little black haired girl in its hands. Alive.

The bronze heated to over 500 hundred degrees. While screaming for its life, the infant was placed on its outstretched hands by the gold robed leader.

I wanted to go berserk. I wanted to go out of control with a Gatling gun. I wanted to toss an incendiary grenade in their midst and fry the lot of them. But I didn't have an incendiary grenade, and I didn't have a Gatling gun.

The drum continued its deep, powerful, booming in its attempts to drown out the infant's terrifying screams. Above the drumbeats, the child's cries tore at my heart. And again, I was too damned late.

The room was lit by a hundred red candles. They burned within a reconstructed old German building of dark oak woodwork. An antique church had been imported, reconstructed in this cavern deep beneath the hotel. It's backlit stained glass windows mocked Christianity.

The ring of worshippers exulted and raised their arms. The gold robed figure did the same, then turned to face them.

The face framed within gold fabric was Ursula's.

She proclaimed to her disciples, "Morloch has spoken! The world is ours!"

Behind her and on the walls hung flags of the Third Reich. An enormous banner that hung between two massive red swastika banners bore the image of Adolph Hitler.

I screamed. Her eyes of fire looked at me and scorched the air. The dozen robed murderers turned and stared at me with angry eyes. She pointed at me and yelled, "Kill him!"

They rushed me as one. I blasted with my right hand. I blasted with my left. When my .38 emptied into the chest of Madame Rothberg's black robe I grabbed my derringer.

I ran out of ammo when the bald German with the monocle charged. I levelled the double barrelled 12-gauge at his head and snapped the trigger.

Click.

Misfire.

The blade in his hand glinted. A Nazi ceremonial dagger, it's sharp point could be deadly in close combat. But he was a lightweight.

I picked him up and body slammed him to the floor with adrenaline charged vehemence. The thick red flow from the back of his skull said he returned to the Fatherland. I tossed my robe aside.

During the Satanic free-for-all, a number of candles were shot and exploded into nearby drapes that picked up their flames. The ancient dry wood of the old church caught fire like a tinder box.

Blond, bony Adirin and Adrean appeared on both sides of Ursula with maddened eyes. Their faces strained with rage. She laughed and said, "*Herr Wolfe*. My bodyguards want to play with you."

They rushed me from both sides. I sidestepped and threw them into each other with a low level Aikido move. Their next approach was more cautious.

My front kick caught the closer one by surprise. My heel sunk deep into his solar plexus and I felt his ribs snap at the end of my foot. He doubled over in pain and clutched his chest.

Blood billowed from his mouth onto the floor. I snapped around with a spin kick to his head. He hit the deck with a splat like a slab of meat.

His twin jumped me. He wrapped his king crab arms around me and tied me up in a hammerlock. I stomped the bridge of his foot.

When he released my arm in his painful reaction, I sidestepped and slammed a backhanded karate chop into his nuts. Basic self defense. But my chop was delivered with a practiced force that broke three bricks.

He shrieked and squealed, then groaned and clutched his balls. He fell to the floor on his knees, his face purple with anguish. His chin offered an irresistable target; I place kicked it with enough leg to make a thirty yard three-pointer.

His face turned purple with anguish; his eyes bulged from agony. He gasped for breath. I put my foot on his throat and turned to Ursula.

She screamed, "Otto!"

From the flames behind her, a monster white robot bounded up to its position at her side. It stood eight feet tall, with a clear viewable top. Four arms stretched out from its sides, and they each demonstrated their ability to exercise a 360 degree reach.

It secured its footing, then performed a standing back flip.

She said with an evil smile, "Otto will draw and quarter you in his hands." She commanded the robot: "Otto! Destroy him!"

I aimed my double-barreled derringer at his head and pulled off its second side. It fired and belched smoke and flame. This time, a .70 caliber lead ball roared out of its barrel.

It bounced off the thing's dome-like head, made of fighter aircraft Lexan. The ricochet went straight at Ursula and smashed into her hip.

She hit the floor with a loud scream. Her commands pierced the fiery cavern. "Otto! Kill him! Destroy him!"

Ursula clutched her hip in agony as Otto stomped toward me. Her last Aryan bodyguard curled in a fetal position, with my foot still on his neck. He gripped my ankle with both hands and tried to trip me over.

I stomped my heel into his throat. He gasped and gurgled. Then I stomped his throat again, harder. He stopped gurgling.

I thought I could outmaneuver the mechanical beast that charged me. But I was wrong. It was much quicker than I was. Bigger, stronger, faster.

Before I could evade it, one of the thing's four arms had one of mine in its grasp. It lifted me off the ground, then grabbed my other arm. My struggles against its superhuman strength were futile.

It drew me to its torso and, with the leverage of four hydraulic arms, crushed me against it. My head felt like it was going to explode from the pressure. I felt myself going under.

I was three years old. My brother Michael brought me a helium balloon from the zoo. I let loose of the cord and watched my balloon disappear over the rooftop, then over the horizon and gone.

I was twelve. My brother and I read comic books. The full page ad for a martial art called, Yubiwaza. "Disable a 300 pound man with just one finger." We joked, "Ha Ha! Maybe if you stick your finger in his belly button and twist it, his legs fall off!"

An inky blackness invaded my vision. It seeped in from all sides. "*Yubiwaza.*"

Through the void I heard it again, "*Yubiwaza.*"

I recognized my brother's voice. With my fading remaining strength, I moved my right hand into position in front of me. My index finger felt around on the white bulletproof body.

It found a soft round rubber button the size of my finger tip. I pressed in as hard as I could, barely got it to click. The machine stopped dead in its tracks.

Ursula screamed, "Otto! Kill him!" But Otto was OTL.

It was a struggle, but I managed to free myself from the crushing grip of Otto's bestilled mechanical arms. One leg of my track suit ripped when I slid down to the floor.

Exhausted, with ribs crushed and one arm immobile at my side, I tried to stand. I couldn't. I leaned over on my knees to catch my breath.

A shrill, high-pitched cry pained my ears through the roaring flames. "We meet again!"

66

I lifted my head. The sight of the Cyclops in his black tights and pink girlwatchers was not what I wanted to see.

"Left for dead!" He laughed, that shrill insane killer's laugh that made me want to silence it by grabbing his throat with both hands. But I wasn't capable of grabbing a dishrag. His voice screeched, "Now you pay!"

He was joined at his side by another Cyclops – his twin – in matching tights and girlwatchers. There was only one distinguishing difference between the two. The second one had both ears.

Ursula was surrounded with twins.

Cyclops-2 spoke in the same grating shreik. "Mush, Wolfe!"

The impact of the whip felt like I got shot by a .22. It sliced through the fabric of my tracksuit. And it burned. Both Cyclops laughed, their piercing, squealing laugh.

They both had long ballistic nylon bullwhips, and they knew how to use them. I couldn't dodge; couldn't catch them with my hands; I couldn't move. Hell, I couldn't do anything.

I counted five lashes that sliced through my clothes and my skin. Seven. Ten. With every snapping lash, the twin monsters shrieked with laughter. Behind them, Ursula's screams combined her pain with her rage. The flames of the old church blazed.

It didn't hurt much, anymore. Maybe I could just lie there awhile.

Suddenly the two red leather doors at the stairs burst apart. Every living eye in the satanic church turned and looked.

Electra stepped through the smoking wreckage, a white Armalite AA-12 automatic shotgun in each hand. She stood tall in knee-high white ostrich western boots. A form fitting cat suit of white stretch fabric was tucked inside.

The AA-12 is a marvelous weapon: 20 rounds of fully automatic 12-gauge shotgun, engineered to be fired with no recoil. It can be held in one hand and shot from the hip. The girl from South Texas opened up and blasted and blazed from both sides of her tall, lithe body.

Electra strafed the Cyclops twins with her streetsweepers. The blood of the Cyclops splattered the room. By the time her guns emptied, the sunglass brothers were unrecognizable heaps of bloody flesh.

Around them, the timbers of the ancient wood building roared with flames.

Electra came to my side, helped me to my feet. "Let's get out of here!"

I was in no shape to bolt. She supported one of my arms and shoulders as I dragged myself forward. We barely made it through the red double door wreckage when half the ceiling smashed down to the floor. The flames roared high behind us. We had to move up several steps to escape the intense heat.

From below I heard violent, desperate screams. Ursula.

Through the flames I saw her. She was trapped beneath a burning timber that crashed down from the ceiling. Its flames engulfed her body. She couldn't move and had no escape. There was no way we could get to her. The last thing I saw of her was her golden blonde hair, burning.

I said, "*Sayonara*, bitch."

I used the stairway wall and Electra's shoulder for support. Together, we managed our way up the steps and got back to the bohemian level. Smoke from the fire below followed us and filled the owl statue's grove.

The party was over. The last stragglers grabbed what clothes they could and scrambled up the staircase from the orgy. We stopped for a moment so I could catch my breath.

The huge, once festive grotto smoldered and smelled of smoke, beer and urine.

We stood in its blackened center, alone. I said, "How did you find me?"

"Natalie Cocks. In the lobby."

I shook my head. "How did you get to the lobby? Here? St. Thomas?"

"I knew you'd get into trouble. They can't stop me from coming here. I could buy this place tomorrow."

"Bad investment," I said.

"Now," she said with a stern look in her eye, "are you going to marry me or what?"

There are a lot of ways to answer a question like that. But when the woman who asks it is charged with battle lust - and holds a smoking automatic shotgun in each hand - you've got to figure that "No" is not a wise choice of words.

"You're out of ammo right?"

* * *

The sunrise began with the mother of all confusing incident commands on the small island. Because it involved so many of the world's elites: police, fire, EMTs, bodyguards, security, intelligence agencies – they were so occupied with assigning who's who in the zoo, the hotel burned to the ground.

Against the morning sun's backdrop of flames and smoke, Josh Hitt strolled up to my side with a sweating, cold Red Stripe beer in each hand. "Looks like we can have that drink, after all."

Pockets of remaining globalists stood on the hotel grounds in their pajamas and robes. They held impromptu meetings about what to do next with their lives. Electra helped me as we slipped away.

Sebastian pulled up to us in a Birknerhaus resort golf cart. Still sleepy in his silk pajamas and night cap, he had somehow managed to mix a martini. He sipped from his oversized glass and said, "I knew I didn't want to miss your meetings."

I was surprised when he asked where he could deliver us and Electra said, "Take us down to the seaport."

We were above the Atlantic Ocean, halfway back to New York City in Electra's blue Grumman G-111 Albatross. She sat back in her pilot's seat at

10,000 feet, a sight more breathtaking than the endless blue horizon below.

She said, "We landed and docked in Manhattan that morning, an hour before you played patty cake with your Airbus helicopter. You're lucky you didn't get my plane shot up in your little fracas on the East River. I wouldn't have been able to fly down to save your ass from - that - thing."

"I'm the one who hit the robot's kill switch," I said.

"I meant her," she replied.

"Where did you learn to shoot like that?"

"Hell, we're fighting off cartels and rustlers all the time on the ranches. My daddy taught me to shoot varmints since I was knee high to a jackrabbit."

You can take the girl out of Texas ...

I said, "How did you know about my shootout with the chopper?"

Her lips made a puff. "Darling," she said. "I'm next door neighbors to John and Yvonne. I know everything."

Uh oh. "Everything?"

"Everything," she said. "How was the bar in her white limo?"

I've got nothing.

She asked, "Were you onto her the whole time? You must have been. Who would want to run around with that – thing."

"I thought she was your friend. I met her at your house."

"Evans brought her when Nicky was kidnapped. Because of her involvement with her Global Council on - "

I cut her off. "Missing Children. That was a front for their worldwide child trafficking operation. He brought her with him to spy on you and the FBI while they had Nick. Let me tell you what really happened."

* * *

I had never heard Murgatroyd speak in that manner. He was beside himself with exhasperation, couldn't get his words out. He said, "I mean, I'm good at this stuff. I can hack into any computer you want; I navigated the dark web with no problem. But I played Hell finding this. I almost wish I hadn't."

I was in my room when his call came in, choosing what to wear to an orgy. *Or does it matter?*

He said, "I started looking up background information on your ladyfriend from Argentina. I ran through all the current public information, but then it stopped."

"What do you mean, 'it stopped'?"

"She doesn't exist. No birth certificate. None. And no next of kin. It's like she dropped out of the sky. That's when I called in Norm, our new IT Junkie Flunky to help me work on it."

"And?"

"We looked deeper. A lot deeper. We've been steady gettin' it on this for the past 24 hours, straight. What we found out — I had to connect the dots, but you better sit down for this ..."

"In 1945 German U-Boat U-977 sailed out of Norway and docked in Montau Plata, Argentina on August 17. Hitler and Eva Braun escaped Germany with Martin Borman and a number of other high ranking Nazi officers by submarine. No 'conspiracy.' I'll show you the FBI files on it."

"Martin Borman took the name of Juan Keller. When their war started going downhill, he raided the Nazi treasury and moved most of their wealth to Argentina. Peron welcomed them all with open arms. The Hitlers lived in La Falda in Patagonia at the Eichhorn's Eden Hotel. It was reconstructed as a fortress, where they planned the Fourth Reich."

"On the island of Huemul in the Nahuel Huapi lake, they built a miniature Manhattan project. German Nazi nuclear physicist Ronald Richter and Juan Peron claimed to have produced nuclear fusion there in 1951."

"Murgatroyd – I like *Hogan's Heroes* as much as the next guy. But I'm getting dressed to go to an orgy."

"No, you're not," he said with insistance. "Not until you hear this. What famous Nazi doctor also escaped to South America?"

"A lot of them. Josef Mengele?"

"Give the man a cupie doll. He was in Argentina, then Paraguay and Brazil. He was known as the "angel of death" at Auschwitz-Birkenau. And he's infamous for his experimentation with twins."

"I've heard that."

"He didn't only experiment with twins."

"What else?"

"In vitro artificial insemination. Test tube babies. Your ladyfriend, Ursula Schicklgruber was the first success. She was born some time after 1972 in La Falda, Argentina. They gave her the name Schicklgruber from her German grandfather."

"Who's 'they'?"

"Her parents."

"What the Hell are you saying, Murgatroyd?"

"Adolph Hitler died in Argentina in 1972. Eva and Dolph had Mengele perform an in vitro experiment."

* * *

I stood up from my co-pilot's seat. Two of my ribs were broken and I could only take in half breaths before it felt like a knife plunged between them. I tried to stretch but didn't get far.

In my stooped posture, I moved toward the cabin door to move around and step into the back. My fingers had the shakes when I lifted my lighter and Reds from my pocket. After several attempts to thumb the wheel of Pony's Zippo, its flame appeared.

I inhaled a deep drag. The first puff is always the best. I turned my body back around so I could enjoy the lovely picture of Electra White at the pilot's controls of her seaplane, above the Atlantic Ocean on a beautiful sunny day. I said, "The bitch was Hitler's daughter."

Afterword

Dear Reader,

I know your time is valuable. I am both grateful and honored that you chose to spend some of that time reading my book. Writing Maximum Prejudice was a labor of love, and I hope you enjoyed Nick and his exploits.

If you have a moment, please consider leaving a review on Amazon. It helps other readers find – and decide if they'd like to read – books by Indie authors such as myself.

Nick will be back in a sequel that is currently in the works! If you'd like to be notified about future release dates, you can join my mailing list at www.HiredGun2.com. Thanks again for the support!

- Bob

www.ingramcontent.com/pod-product-compliance
Lightning Source LLC
LaVergne TN
LVHW021219080526
838199LV00084B/4257